LIGHT IN A DARK PLACE

Where Faith Confronts Depression

D. M. Harrington

ISBN 978-1-64416-619-2 (paperback)
ISBN 978-1-64416-622-2 (hardcover)
ISBN 978-1-64416-620-8 (digital)

Christian Faith Publishing, Inc.
832 Park Avenue
Meadville, PA 16335
www.christianfaithpublishing.com

Cover photo by Courtney Fromen Thomsen.

Editing by Elizabeth Jensen Maurer.

Printed in the United States of America

CONTENTS

I am bleeding on the inside. I might as well be bleeding on the outside...

I catch myself fantasizing about slitting my wrists. Now, don't freak out. I don't want to cut deep, just a surface wound, just enough to draw blood. But I want to do it on both arms, so that a nice, solid stream of blood runs down each forearm. Why do I want to do this? Because I want to see manifested the pain I feel on the inside. I want the world to see my insides like a badge, like a statement, "This is how bad it really is," so the pain can't be disputed or covered up.

The thought of bleeding is comforting—decisive, willful, effortless, free bleeding. There's something liberating about bleeding. Somehow, you get something out of yourself that's eating at you from the inside. And that's how I feel: eaten at. When you're constantly being eaten at, you consider taking irrational measures to cease the gnawing. That's what bleeding feels like it will do for me.

Bleeding also wipes you out. It can make you comatose. It stops the feeling. To do without a part of yourself is a better alternative than allowing some alien substance in. Both accomplish the same goal, but by bleeding, you don't run the risk of a consequential addiction. It's the easy choice for me.

So, why haven't I done it? I haven't done it because (1) it looks crazy, and it flat out scares everyone you know and love, and (2) how dare any of us mock suicide? The greater tragedy would be to actually do permanent damage in an attempt to make a statement. That risk frightens me. I believe many people have ended their lives without intending to. I am not so arrogant to believe I could try it and survive.

Chapter One

Faith and depression are presumed to be opposites. A person who has a healthy, vibrant spiritual life doesn't battle depression, and if they do, then they're failing on a spiritual level. Sound about right? I wish it were that simple. If it were, then my faith would have prevailed, and much of my suffering would have been avoided.

Mental illness warriors don't live on the same planet as everyone else. You see us living among you, but our journey is much darker, our monsters more familiar, and our hurdles more frequent. The treacherous terrain catches us so off guard that many Christians forsake simple faith as it's taught because it's just not powerful enough to battle what we're fighting. Many give up before faith becomes the weapon they need most to live full lives. We must gather every speck of light God offers in order to be victorious. Then, and only then, can we say that faith conquers depression.

I tried to win the war against depression using only my faith, and it didn't work. Faith is simple, and depression is complex. It wasn't a fair match. Until faith is tested, toughened, and fortified, it will fail. Until it's whittled down to something digestible that a depressed person can process, it's like trying to win a tennis match with a baseball bat. Faith doesn't serve our case well in its natural form. It must transform into the tool we need it to be.

I was born sixteen months behind my older sister. My sister was the prominent figure in my childhood. We shared a bedroom, each with our own twin bed positioned diagonally across the room from the other. After bedtime, we enjoyed each other's company and were mutually invested in staying up as late as possible without being discovered, but in the daylight, my sister resented our shared space, and me, when her friends or our older cousin were around. She initiated many one-sided conversations with our parents about how much she deserved her own bedroom. Even after they added five hundred square feet onto the house, separate bedrooms were not in our future.

At three years old, I became the middle child and lost all memory of ever being the family's most needy member. In elementary school, I sought my identity in comparison to the self-acclaimed star, who was my older sister and my sweeter, younger brother, who was the only son. Our mother had also been the oldest of three children, two girls and then a boy, the same role and order as my sister. My father was the baby in a family of two boys, just as my brother was the baby boy. I came to the conclusion that I didn't share the birth order of either of my parents, which meant that they could see themselves in my siblings but not in me. Despite my sister's persistent condescension and my growing identity issues, I was a happy child.

During middle school, our world turned upside down. When my sister hit puberty, frenzy, fury, and fighting broke out between her and our parents. It took a couple of years before they concluded that she was mentally ill and slowly learned just how much of her behavior was beyond her control. Her teens and early twenties were spent consulting out-of-town doctors and therapists. There were two middle-of-the-night emergency rescues from college, which led to hospitalizations, before an accurate diagnosis of obsessive-compulsive disorder and bipolar disorder produced the correct cocktail of medications that worked for her.

When the crisis descended, it became clear that the way to a healthy sense of self for me was to be the daughter my sister wasn't, even though her problems were no fault of her own. The first time I remember differentiating from my sister was when she failed her entrance exam into the sixth-grade enrichment program at school because obsessive-compulsive tendencies prevented her from finishing the test. My superior was crushed.

I wasn't the least bit happy about her failure, but if someone as grand as she could fail, then there was no pressure for me to pass. I passed.

When things became volatile at home, our parents concentrated on our sister, and my brother and I primarily invested in each other. There was no envy. She had extreme needs, and we were able-bodied.

After college, my life took one step forward and two steps back in every respect: in my career, finances, and relationships, and in the careers, finances, and relationships of my friends. I didn't handle it well. Reality hit me upside the head like a two-by-four. The blows took way too long for a healthy person to recover from, but I received only mild sympathy and zero suspicions from my family regarding my mental health. I had already displayed a steady track record of achievements and a vibrant personal faith testimony, so why would anyone think something was seriously wrong with me? The only thing I wanted more than sympathy was for my sister to be the only sick one in the family. Therefore, I suffered in various states of distress untreated for thirteen years. I tried to fight it on my own with only my faith but failed.

It's possible to be both a believer and a diagnosed depressive. That fact alone was enough to worsen my condition because the more I labored in obedience, the more elusive God became. As my depression worsened, I proposed to God many ways that He could help me. When He didn't respond as I expected, demanded, wanted, or needed, I slid lower and lower into the pit.

Over the years, I lost loved ones and was exposed to tragedy. My repository of traumatic thoughts and feelings grew until facing the variable situations of life recalled only pain all of the time. When I reached the bottom of the pit, there was no hiding it anymore. I tried everything to keep from reaching that point but landed on the verge of quitting, never leaving the house, remaining in bed, and letting everything collapse around me because there was no strength to face one more heartbreak.

The people closest to me took on the role of torchbearers. They loved me enough to pray and intercede for me. They convinced me that anguish was not a manipulation tool I could use to coerce a loving God to alter my circumstances. They encouraged me that there were outside resources worth pursuing, and they convinced me that an unfiltered look at God could radically change things.

I'm happy to report that medication dramatically reduced my natural responses to environmental stimuli, but there was no medication to resolve the questions that pummeled me in the dark. My weaknesses compelled me to dialogue with God because I was so troubled and alone. In the process, God destroyed the faith I thought I could rely on and rebuilt it into something entirely different, something useful.

This book chronicles the questions I took to Him in the dark.

This book is written to anyone who has ever felt that life wasn't worth living. Hopefully, you haven't reached that conclusion yet, but you may have wrestled with why you bother and aren't quite sure that the day isn't approaching when you can't keep doing it anymore.

This is a dark place. And this dark place is vast because a thousand roads lead here. It's nearly impossible to avoid. No one chooses the path to despair, but many find it. I desire to expose the aid we have at our disposal while we are here.

Please don't think too narrowly of the word "here." "Here" applies to being at rock bottom, but "here" also means life on earth in general. Genetic orientation toward depression isn't curable, and life is full of obstacles, but we can learn to cope well and conquer obstacles at our pace. We just need the right kind of insight. I will point you toward more light, which will aid your ascension out of the pit and make the depths where you find yourself lingering more bearable.

We come here from many walks of life. A few of them are:

- The clinically depressed
- The abused
- Victims of tragedy
- The severely guilt-ridden
- The recently widowed
- The depleted caregiver
- The incarcerated
- The addicted

This book is for the despairing, the desperate, and the destitute. Does that description bring someone to mind? Is that someone *you*?

You are the driver on your journey. If we don't secure this state of mind, the rest of our discussion will be nothing but noise. I'm not asking you to feel powerful or in control. I expect that you feel powerless and out of control. But I am asking you to accept that you own the vehicle in the driveway. It's not a lease, you're not making payments, and you haven't borrowed it. It won't be repo'd once you finish reading. You own the car. Can you entertain this imagination?

What I mean is that you are of sound mind. I suspect some people you know would disagree with me, but I'm telling you that you are of sound mind. You're reading this, and you have control over your thoughts enough to give your undivided attention to this conversation. You are capable of making decisions. You are making this one.

And you have a life to live, which means that you have a future. The future may look dismal, and that feels discouraging, but it is yours, and it is undetermined. It isn't doomed. It's just unknown.

Perhaps your future looks distant. I understand if it feels that way. This is one of the things we need to discuss.

Or maybe doctors have said that your future will be brief. This book is for you, too, because the most valuable things you ever possessed, even in good health, are still yours. No one knows the exact number of his days, so it is likely that many of us are in the same position that you're in; we just don't know it. We could benefit from taking our futures as seriously as you do.

On this journey, you own the car.

But you have lost the keys.

And it's out of gas.

And you have nowhere to go.

Yes, we have a lot to figure out. But we are together, and I have been through this before. My hope is to empower you to drive toward the horizon before we finish.

I begin by saying that I need you to imagine yourself as the driver of this journey because I am only a voice. I don't have the power to lift you. So if you can't place yourself in the driver's seat, then we won't get anywhere.

Now I will ask you to make a second commitment. I need you to agree with me that there is something out there worth pursuing. Yes, it's shapeless and aimless. That's for certain. Your pursuit is not mine; they're completely unique, so I don't know exactly what it is that we're going after. But I believe that it's good, it's better than the pit, and it is worth our effort. Can you agree with me on this? It starts by believing that there is light out there, and the more of it we can grasp, the better our lives will be.

Take a look at the world. See people thriving and being happy, loving and being loved, creating art and eating good food? See people competing in sports, traveling the world, enjoying music, and making friends? There are things worth living for.

I understand that beautiful things seem to be out of your reach, and none of them seem intended for you, but there is the possibility that life is good and valuable. There is! Do you want it? Do you want life to be better than you have found it to be so far?

I am going to ask you to embrace a lot of new ideas. Some will be a stretch for you. But without the will to find something to live for, I would have never made it into the light. You might be shackled by some philosophies that keep you in bondage. This will be confirmed if you find yourself disputing the light as it appears. I will let you in on a secret: the shackles aren't locked. You can choose to take them off if you want to leave the pit. And the pit is nowhere to live out your life.

One of the marvelous things about struggling is that if you endure, you will eventually prevail, and then you'll have something worth sharing. That's what's in this for me. Every time someone takes a step from darkness into light, an additional ray of sunlight shines on my personal journey. The light that you discover shines on me, too, and that makes my path brighter. So I thank you.

The Pit

The bottom of the pit is black and cold. Your thoughts echo off the rock walls and distant ceiling somewhere in the vast darkness. There's no way to measure how low you are. But you are sure of one thing: that you are alone—absolutely, utterly, and completely alone. There isn't as much as the breath of a companion to warm you.

The air is thick and stale. It has a heaviness that bombards your brain and invades your thoughts. You think you've tried everything to keep from reaching this place, and look where it has gotten you. The ground is a muddy quicksand, which robs you of any progress. Quicksand releases its grip the less you struggle, so apathy becomes your means of survival.

Surrendering has been the only way to keep from going under. I don't know how long you've been in this holding pattern. You may have just woken up and found yourself here, or perhaps the descent has been a slow, steady one. Either way, you are exhausted. At some prior point, the mental, emotional, and physical battles merged into one massive knot. There's no point trying to distinguish where one wound stops and another starts. There is no strength to do so, and there is no light.

May I strike a match?

The first flicker reveals that the mire that engulfs you is made up of questions, assumptions, and expectations. You've been so weak that you entertained every doubt and suggestion that found its way into the pit. Some of these questions have the power to shed light on your situation. They are crucial as to why you are here and why you haven't gotten out. You need answers to these questions.

Others exist only to taunt and trap you. There is no constructive use for those questions. Do some of the arguments in your mind exist only to fortify your anger or defend your despondency? If some of your thoughts function only to keep you acclimated to the dark, then they are either unnecessary or destructive. You never initiated those thoughts because they are of no potential good to you. They are suggestions from an outside enemy and will only multiply your hurt if you continue entertaining them.

You need to learn to distinguish the helpful from the harmful questions. Perhaps you aren't yet strong enough to defy the negative ones and cast them out, but you are strong enough to silence them for a short time to focus on the helpful ones. Each new ray of light will restore your strength so that you can eventually speak against the negative suggestions. For now, let's just engage one good question at a time.

Why Am I Unable to Help Myself?

Because God is all-powerful and the Creator of all things, He can snap His fingers and remove depression. But depression exists because He permits it; therefore, it is purposeful. He created us this way or allows this temporary affliction for a reason.

Becoming a Christian is like being on the receiving end of a cascading waterfall of passion, excitement, and anticipation that you are a vessel fit to be used by God. With God's power and purpose in motion, you are poised for greatness. Blessed with an abundance of enthusiasm and hope, we fail to remember that the engine we're revving is a human one and not a divine one. Out of undisciplined joy, we gun the gas pedal and turn what God intended to be a following journey into a sprinting journey.

Following doesn't come naturally, which is why God must command us to do it. Frustration with God's sovereign will is a telltale sign of a thriving personal will. Sovereign means supreme, and in the context of an all-knowing and holy God, sovereign also means infallible. His opinions and plan are flawless. He makes no mistakes. You may be unaware of how strong your personal will is, but the Lord will reveal it. Reliance on the Holy Spirit must be learned.

God allows us to burn out or fail in the paths we choose for ourselves to teach us that He never wants us running ahead of Him. Even a person with the best of intentions has a powerful self pressing the pedal. God desires for the Holy Spirit to replace that self. How can the Holy Spirit reign in a human heart without first exhausting the selfish, sinful nature?

Romans 8:20–21 says, "For the **creation was subjected to frustration**, not by its own choice, but **by the will of the one who subjected it**, **in hope** that the creation itself **will be liberated** from its bondage to decay and **brought into** the **glorious freedom** of the children of God" (NIV).

God desires to bestow freedom and glory on His children, but He ordained that His children must first choose Him as Lord. In order to persuade us toward reliance on Him, God designed us to face frustration when acting independently from Him. Therefore, in hope and out of love for us, God hastens our surrender by accelerating our frustrations.

We despise frustration. We do not choose it. But God chooses it for us. He subjects us to it that He might, in that subjection, partner our longing for relief with a ravenous hope of redemption. This plague of inherent yearning will not go unfulfilled. Its end guarantee is liberation! Liberation from bondage to death and decay, replaced with immense freedom and glory.

The scriptures surrounding the above passage read, "I consider that our present sufferings are not worth comparing with the **glory that will be revealed in us**. For the **creation waits in eager expectation for the children of God to be revealed**… We know that the whole creation has been **groaning as in the pains of childbirth** right up to the present time. Not only so, but **we ourselves**, who have the first fruits of the Spirit, **groan inwardly as we wait** eagerly **for our adoption** as sons, **the redemption of our bodies**" (Rom. 8:18–19, 22–23, NIV).

After a person accepts Jesus as Lord, their spirit is redeemed but their flesh is not. Outwardly, it may appear as if our decision to join ourselves to God hasn't changed anything, but it awakens a frustration with the world and within ourselves that was never previously a problem (unredeemed spirit within unredeemed flesh had no conflict). This fresh wrestling affirms that an internal war is still being waged against sin.

"He [God] hath made every thing beautiful in his time: also **he hath set the world in their heart, so that no man can find out the work that God maketh** from the beginning to the end" (Eccles. 3:11, KJV).

We grind through suppositions, trying to make sense of what God is doing and why, yet arrive no closer to clarity than before the attempt. God's work remains a mystery. Reaching this conclusion introduces the foundation on which God centers all of our success, and that foundation is *faith*. There is a flesh versus spirit battle woven into the fiber of every human being. In order for God to reign as Lord over a life, there can be no rival authority, not even that soul's self. The will of the Creator has always offended the will of the created. This pattern was visible in Eden. The best approach to address this instinctive objection is to defer to God's ordinances *willingly*.

It's possible for faith to replace self-preservation as our survival strategy. If God is in control, and my will is to surrender to His control, then why am I frustrated? If God knows His perfect will for my life, and it is His prerogative to see it accomplished, then I should not offend Him by wrestling beneath His grasp, which implies that my plan is greater than His.

The following passage from *The Christian's Secret to a Happy Life* by Hannah Whithall Smith is my favorite quote of all time. The moment I read it, the passage rang of truth and permanently seared my conscience. It was remarkable to me because there was a vast difference between this mindset and my own. It conveys the sense of trust I lacked, but needed, in order to be happy.

Smith writes:

> I do not understand how it is that the eyes of so many Christians have been blinded to this fact. But it really would seem as if God's own children were more afraid of His will than of anything else

> in life—His lovely, lovable will, which only means loving-kindnesses and tender mercies, and blessings unspeakable to their souls! I wish I could only show to everyone the unfathomable sweetness of the will of God. Heaven is a place of infinite bliss because His will is perfectly done there, and our lives share in this bliss just in proportion as His will is perfectly done in them. He loves us—loves us, I say—and the will of love is always blessing for its loved one. Some of us know what it is to love, and we know that could we only have our way, our beloved ones would be overwhelmed with blessings. All that is good and sweet and lovely in life would be poured out upon them from our lavish hands, had we but the power to carry out our will for them. And if this is the way of love with us, how much more must it be so with our God, who is love itself! Could we but for one moment get a glimpse into the mighty depths of His love, our hearts would spring out to meet His will and embrace it as our richest treasure; and we would abandon ourselves to it with an enthusiasm of gratitude and joy, that such a wondrous privilege could be ours.

We don't want to be afraid of God's will, but we are afraid. In the real world, we see one case of hardship after another, yet we're admonished to trust God. How can we trust God when the odds seem so slim that we will escape this life unscathed?

We want so badly for our loyalty to God to affect outcomes that we treat trust like a deposit that can be paid toward specific results. In *Radical*, David Platt writes, "We already have a fairly high view of our morality, so when we add superstitious prayer, a subsequent dose of church attendance, and obedience to some of the Bible, we feel pretty sure that we will be alright in the end."

This presumption drives us to pray relentlessly, as if we can will the outcomes we want into existence. However, wanting does not make it so, and our desires will drive us to madness if we let them carry us that far. When things don't work out all right in the end, and we find our backs against a wall, then what? Then, we're forced to reckon with God, to decide once and for all if He, *without conditions*, is trustworthy.

Trust isn't a commodity that we can use in negotiations with God; trust is the relationship's operating system. Trusting God supersedes all circumstances. Maewussia Osgood, a Marine widow at the age of twenty-four and a mother of three, said in hindsight of her husband's helicopter crash, "Giving thanks *in* all circumstances does not mean being thankful *for* all circumstances." A trusting heart accepts difficulties with understanding that God only allows what is necessary to accomplish His great and mighty plan—a plan that we will praise Him for when we finally see it revealed in full.

Trusting God despite our circumstances is more difficult than it sounds because it requires us to demote what is seen, felt, and experienced in order to promote what scripture teaches. It ultimately means forfeiting our earthly lives to unknown ends. Wasn't that the very thing we professed to have surrendered at the moment of our salvation? Later in life, a tug-of-war with God over what we aim to claim for ourselves reveals that our original surrender was only partial.

In *Approaching God*, Steve Brown says, "We have this spurious view that once our sin has been revealed and we have turned to Christ for salvation, then everything is settled. The truth is that nothing but salvation is settled."

The apostle Paul refers to working out our salvation with "fear and trembling" (Phil. 2:12). A heavy-handed work follows the gift of salvation like lumps are kneaded from dough or lactic acid is massaged from stiff muscles. When these crisis feelings arrive, it doesn't mean that things are going wrong; it means that things are being worked out.

On the path of genuine spiritual growth, darkness precedes light. Didn't Jesus spend three days in the tomb before He was raised? Darkness preceded light prior to the creation of the earth as well. Our experience is consistent with the Master's experience and is a reflection of the Master's process.

It confounds us to discover darkness after salvation. Our whimpers escalate to moans, and the pressure we feel intensifies to pain. Anyone who digs in his heels and demands reparations in this state will never conjure the inner fortitude to continue. Many get stuck here, locked in the mire, perpetuated by their rigidity, or worse, turn to sin for a remedy that does nothing but spin them in circles. This isn't the point of spiritual development where you want your journey to slow.

Yet others prevail against this spiritual darkness. How? They finish strong by listening to the Holy Spirit who speaks truth to them in the dark. He convinces them that the present confinement is only a tunnel. Inside a tunnel, one must confront its darkest point, where all perception of light has fled, before daylight breaks. When at the darkest point, although real and frightening, the conclusion that light no longer exists is flawed. It's only perception, not reality. So what is real? God is real and actively involved behind the scenes. The perception of a dead end is only tunnel vision.

Sit on that thought a bit before you decide the direction you will take. Do you want to turn back toward the direction you came from and the light you remember? You already know the extent of its rewards and its costs. Or will you continue forward into the unknown, believing in something better? This is only a tunnel. There is light ahead. Is the possibility of something better enough of an incentive for you to move forward with God? It could be a long tunnel. Can you handle that? Or it could be a short one. Perhaps tomorrow is the day your darkness will graduate to dawn. You could be very close to daybreak. But even if you discover that tomorrow is not that day, you will assuredly be one step closer to it than you were yesterday. That's the way tunnels work, so choose your direction carefully.

A friend asked me what types of thoughts go through my mind before I get out of the bed in the morning. What differentiates depression from a lack of motivation or laziness? I answered her this way:

A web of "I can't" is cast over everything I do. It isn't the same kind of "I can't" as when you can but just don't want to. It's the "I can't" a runner discovers at mile twenty of a marathon: acknowledgment of the present fact that "I can not."

A depressive's actions are never as simple as the next task at hand. Each act is only manageable if it can be accomplished in tandem with all the other responsibilities that must be performed before the body and mind can shut down to replenish. Burdens beyond today may factor into today's heaviness if they are prerequisites to tomorrow's success; therefore, today may be debilitated by tomorrow's Everest. There's constant rebalancing, always recalculating what can be compromised from among what's expected of you, what you'd like to do, and what you're capable of doing in order to complete a day. Successfully managing depression requires identifying the wiggle room around responsibilities, then prioritizing the obligations to accommodate the amount of physical strength, energy, and mental fortitude available. Internal resources are limited. The reduction of demands is the greatest reprieve.

A depressed person who perceives that the demands placed on him are fixed targets will be engulfed by the magnitude of the whole. If his internal reserves are insufficient to meet the lot of demands, the first step will be insurmountable. He cannot start what he knows he cannot finish. The strength, motivation, and composure necessary to perform the day's full scope of requirements is absent, and the person finds himself incapacitated.

Depression is a dark place. And it's fairly consistently dark no matter how well you cope with it, like the difference in degrees of darkness between being twenty-five feet under water versus fifty. Yet a slender sliver of light streaks through this dark place. It may be unsubstantial in size, but it casts a gentle ambiance over our world. The window of opportunity for us lies in our attitude toward that slender ray of light, the wiggle room that we are often too discouraged to notice. Many depressed people can't even see that it's there because we acclimate to the dark by closing our eyes. With eyes closed, depression becomes a shared experience, identical to one another's reality, more predictable, and less scary. We all know the uniform emptiness. If we could just muster the bravery to open our eyes, we would find a furtive flicker requesting our investigation. It hints that the discovery within it will be uniquely interesting to each one of us.

Prayer Journal

Lord, my thoughts tonight are very primitive. Because they are so abased, I almost didn't sit down to converse with you, as if nothing meaningful could possibly transpire between us when I am in such a superficial state of mind. Today, I have been saturated with thoughts of myself: house-hunting, fantasizing about my next conquest, and visualizing my wishes established in the world I know. I have thought a lot about you-know-who, too. I cannot help but wish.

Wish…

Lord, how do you feel about that statement—that I am wishing and not hoping? My choice to say "wish" instead of "hope" is to say that I lack faith that you have a will and a destiny for me in this matter. I have no sign from you otherwise. In the past, I've gone fishing for hopes. I've projected my will into the universe and tugged on your ear with my constant "give me, give me, give me." And through those circular behavior patterns, I manufactured hope—hope that failed to transpire into reality, time and time again. And so, I openly admit to you, and to myself, that I don't hope for you-know-who. Not this time. I only wish. I wish that you desire something to unfold, which suits my personal desires.

I am literally scared stiff to hope for *anything*.

Doesn't your Word say, "Hope deferred makes the heart sick" (Prov. 13:12, NKJV)?

Well, my heart is sick. It's not the kind of sick that's going to kill me like cancer. It's not sudden like a stroke, but it came on gradually like a virus and has symptoms that impact every aspect of my life, just as a virus produces a multitude of ailments: fever, aches, fatigue, coughing, vomiting. Like a virus, there is no prescription I can take for this sickness; no treatment plan exists. It cannot be cured by any quick fix. This sickness can only be cured naturally, and it will stay around as long as it wants to linger. Eventually, I'll build up immunity to being devastated by dashed hopes. Maybe immunity will come in the form of adopting wishing tendencies instead of hoping tendencies. I think about the difference between those options.

For example, I can wish to come into a large sum of money, to have a sustainable writing career, or to lose weight and have a super-fit body, but the truth is, if none of those wishes ever come true, then I'll be just fine without them. Wishes don't have roots; they have wings. If one wish passes its prime and overstays its welcome, then it just floats away into oblivion, and another beautiful dream takes its place. No harm done.

But hopes are different. Hopes have roots: roots that sink deep into the core of a person's soul and spread out to every corner of their being, down each arm to every fingertip. When hopes go sour, oh, what a painful process begins! The person grieves or stumbles or is confused or tempted or angry with every fiber of their being because the roots have consumed every inch of their insides. There isn't a space within a person left untouched by their hopes. To survive a failed hope is a lot like trying to overcome an immobilizing virus. You will survive, and you'll emerge eventually, but it might take a very long time, and you might be pretty darn worthless for the duration. Maybe immunity comes from never hoping anymore, only wishing.

So I repeat, "Hope deferred makes the heart sick." Amen to that. Maybe I'll just acquiesce to not hope anymore. I'll just sit here in my safe place and wish.

Why Won't God Fix Me?

Plague a starving child with a devastating wheat allergy and then surround him with bread: that's what the flesh can feel like to a Christian. We have a base human need for intimate physical and emotional connection, and yet we're required to exercise holiness first and foremost. It's a burden we accept but a struggle we never master.

Romans 12:1 says, "I beseech you therefore, brethren, by the mercies of God, that you **present your bodies <u>a living sacrifice</u>**, holy, acceptable unto God, **<u>which is your reasonable service</u>**" (NKJV).

Reasonable—what an understatement! There is nothing that's too much for the Lord to require of us, His blood-soaked, hell-spared children. We live in full knowledge of the truth: that death has purchased our lives, and we owe our Savior all, each breath, each thought, each moment of every day. We desire to surrender all these things, but to our disappointment, life is not constructed so that we cease to live human lives with human frailties after accepting Jesus as Lord.

Proverbs 13:12 acknowledges, "Hope deferred makes the heart sick, but when the desire comes, it is a tree of life" (NKJV). There is some consolation in the fact that the Word of God doesn't neglect our heart's condition as we wait on provision, but when years pass, even consolation fails to comfort. A person can take Tylenol for tuberculosis, and it may dull the misery for a moment, but the sickness doesn't lose its potency. When pain becomes pervasive, our hearts cry for more than consolation.

"For the Lord God is a sun and shield: the Lord will give grace and glory: **<u>no good thing will he withhold</u>** from them **that walk uprightly**" (Ps. 84:11, NKJV).

In light of this promise, I stretch so far trying to understand my life that I nearly injure myself. I seek out any error within me like an archaeologist dusts away centuries. My search extends back into biblical references for applicable examples.

I question, "When did God withhold, or seem to withhold, from the righteous?" Then Jesus in the garden of Gethsemane comes to mind. "And he went a little farther, and fell on his face, and prayed, saying, O my Father, if it be possible, **let this cup pass from me**: nevertheless **not as I will, but as thou wilt**" (Matt. 26:39, KJV).

Who has ever been more deserving of His request than Jesus in whom the Father was well pleased? How can God promise to not withhold any good thing from the upright and yet deny Jesus, the most upright of all? Could this be a contradiction to the promise?

Something must be missing from the equation. An accurate assessment obliges us to consider *all* of Jesus's prayers in light of this one. Jesus's desire to be protected from personal torment conflicted with His desire to save the world from eternal torment. Jesus took *both* these dueling requests to the Father. "These words spake Jesus, and lifted up his eyes to heaven, and said, 'Father, **the hour is come; glorify thy Son**, that thy Son also may glorify thee… **That they** [believers in Me] **all may be one; as thou, Father, art in me, and I in thee, that they also may be one in us**: that the world may believe that thou hast sent me'" (John 17:1, 21, KJV).

How can God answer one prayer if granting it will compromise a later prayer? Wouldn't that disqualify one of the requests from being "good"? Assessing the goodness of any request requires determining its consequences in advance. What if our today's prayer competes with tomorrow's prayer just as Jesus's did? A benevolent God must choose from among our rival desires and grant some requests at the expense of others.

"For **consider him** [Jesus] **that endured** such contradiction of sinners against himself, **lest ye be wearied and faint**

in your minds. Ye have not yet resisted unto blood, striving against sin" (Heb. 12:3–4, KJV).

Oh, how great a weariness descends on the Christian solider bound by flesh. I know that fainting feeling all too well, and sometimes, I'm amazed that I haven't tumbled head first into the fire. The fight has often been too much for me. Yet I am always delivered, nursed, and nurtured by God's tender mercies, only to be restored to face further barrenness and trial. Although the years accumulate under a keen sense of suffering, I have never resisted sin to the point of shedding blood. The knowledge that my Jesus accomplished this length on my behalf is a great help to me. It is the example I follow. But in the quiet, I still cry, "Lord, you hear my heart. Fix me; I am broken!"

Is that your heart's cry, too? Are you swimming in a sea of brokenness? Do you look to your Creator to repair what you deem damaged? May I share with you a love story that might help you see your brokenness through a lover's eyes?

Auguste Rodin, creator of *The Thinker* and *The Kiss*, is one of my favorite sculptors. His prized possession was an artistic remnant from ancient Greece, a pocket-sized statue about four inches tall that never ceased to inspire his work. It was reduced to only a torso; the head, arms, and legs had broken off, but none of these imperfections registered in Rodin's eyes. He studied it daily.

When I first saw a replica of this trinket, my eyes saw something less than art because of its gross inadequacy. My first thought was, "Who better to own this artifact than the great Rodin? If anyone can repair this piece of nothing and restore its glory, it will be one of the greatest sculptors who ever lived. Give it to Rodin. He can fix it." This was my original point of view until I read Rodin's opinion of his tiny treasure. Even his hands of greatness wouldn't move to repair a brokenness so beautiful.

Is it not possible that God doesn't fix us because He sees our brokenness something like this?

Rodin wrote:

> Observe this little torso of a woman; it is a little Venus. It is broken; it has no longer a head, arms, legs, yet I never weary of contemplating it; each day, each hour for me adds to this masterpiece because I only understand it better. What could it say to our indifferent glance? For me it has the ineffable voluptuousness of softly maturing flesh. The effect lies in no part and in every part. It is perfection. This little childish body, has it not all the charm of woman? It does not catch the light, the light catches it, glancing over it lightly; without any effect of roughness, any dark shadow. Here shadow can no longer be called shadow but only the decline of light. She does not become dark, she grows pale in imperceptible depressions, in delicious undulations. She is indivisible; she is whole or incomplete, but her unity is undisturbed. Everything is full of the calm, the lightness, the serenity of pure beauty in the perfect confidence of nature. When I look at this marble in the evening by candlelight, how the wonder deepens! If those who have been telling us for a hundred years that Greek art is cold studied it with care, could they for one hour maintain this absurdity? This sculpture, on the contrary, is of an extraordinary living complexity, which the flame reveals; the whole surface is nothing but depressions and reliefs; but united, melted together in the great harmonious force of the ensemble. I turn the little torso about under the caressing rays of the light. There is not a fault, not a weakness, not a dead spot; it is the very

> continuity of life, its intoxicating voluptuousness hidden in the bosom of the molecule.

"The meaning of 'he will give us all things' can be put thus: one day we shall see that nothing—literally nothing—which could have increased our eternal happiness has been denied us, and that nothing—literally nothing—that could have reduced that happiness has been left with us. What higher assurance do we want than that?" (Packer, *Knowing God*).

Who Am I in God's Eyes?

It's possible that God is eager to be generous toward us and yet resists our crying petitions at the same time. Yet, if He is, and if we must subsist within these limitations, then we're going to need a lot more from Him than the things we can dream up and add to our wish lists.

Most people with a genetic tendency toward depression don't struggle with the deadly sin of pride. We're more inclined to inflate our flaws than our value. I'm not saying that we don't give care to our physical appearances or that we lack ambition. I'm saying that depression teaches us not to steamroll others for our own gain. We know how it feels to hurt, and we wouldn't wish that on anyone. Instead, depressed people tend to entertain self-loathing thoughts, which are also inappropriate. Let's consider how both of these pertain to our condition.

Pride is probably the hardest stronghold for people to break because it deludes its target into believing that they can't be wrong or make mistakes. Prideful people refuse to admit a need for anything that doesn't come easily to them because their identity is rooted in their sense of power. They reject what they can't control and reorder their world around people and circumstances that they can control. The majority of prideful people manage to perpetually maintain an elevated sense of self, but some fall into depression when forced to admit that life is beyond their control. When this happens, depression can hit them harder than those who were born predisposed to it because they've fallen into it from a greater height. Pride can damn a person if they live their entire life denying their need for a Savior, but depression readies us to receive help.

What if, under healthier conditions, my pride would have ruined me? What if there was no other way for me to accept a savior other than the extreme brokenness into which I was born? If God slayed my pride through weakness, which prods me to call out to Him, then He has given me a gift. My neediness may be essential for my salvation.

What if, under painless circumstances, I wouldn't be the vessel that I am of sensitivity, of emotional awareness, of kindness, and caring? What if the person I have become is a tool useful to reach other struggling souls of the world? If God, out of His love for them, permitted my difficulties in order to meet their greater needs, then again, He has given me a gift. My neediness may be useful for others' salvation. In order to embrace concepts like these, we must understand who we are and who God is before the terms we have been dealt can come into focus.

Scripture tells us, "And the Lord God **formed man of the dust of the ground**, and **breathed into his nostrils** the breath of life; and **man became a living soul**" (Gen. 2:7, KJV).

At our lowest common denominator, we are dust. I suspect that deep down, we already know this. It's hard to dispute the devil when he whispers that we're worthless because he disguises his lies in truths. Yes, we're helpless, but no, we aren't worthless. How can a dust pile be worthless if it contains the very breath of God? Apart from God, we are as ineffective as dust, but surrendered to His Spirit, we possess limitless potential.

"As a father pities his children, so **the Lord pities those who fear him**. For He knows our frame; **He remembers that we are dust**" (Ps. 103:13–14, NKJV).

The Lord knows full well that the only good thing about us is what we permit *Him to do in us*. This is said not to discourage but to encourage, because God is just as invested as you are in prospering the outputs of your life. He created you. He brought you to life by breathing into you, to make something more than dust out of you. He understands our needy condition and is eager to help us prevail as long as we're respectful toward Him. He intervenes because dust is incapable.

God's Spirit and His Word beckon that I draw nearer to Him. The closer I get, His holiness shines on my wickedness, and the depth of my wretchedness is exposed. I am disgusted, but even then, His love assures me that I am accepted—wretchedness, flaws, and all. He loves me. None of what I am learning about myself surprises Him. It is I who must come to terms with what I am before He can help me to cope with it.

Facing my shortcomings reduces my prayers to the simple mantra, "Lord, have mercy on me." It requires very little thought to reach the conclusion that my primary need is for His mercy. I utter this statement to Him as often as possible. Years after this became my core prayer, I read that Eastern Orthodox Christians have practiced this utterance for ages referred to as the "Efche." Their Efche is more formal: "Lord Jesus, Son of God, have mercy on me, a sinner."

As the Lord gives me breath, I expel those breaths in this posture. Our relationship is founded on the agreement that He will have mercy on me, and I will rely on Him. Nothing in my world is more secure or stabilizing than this. I am exceedingly needy, and He is exceedingly able.

The degree of value one places on themself explains many of one's choices and behaviors. Because of our inherent sin nature, I haven't met one person who doesn't have a volume of reasons to loathe themself.

In addition to the wrongs we choose to commit, we loathe ourselves for things we can't control: our looks, race, gender, or sexual orientation. Just existing fosters resentment for those who deem their containers are flawed.

Let us not forget to add addictions to the list. Many of us have compulsions, which whip us around against our logic and will. They conquer us repeatedly, some daily, and we loathe every repeated offense. We stumble over strongholds, and will continue to fall unless a greater power intervenes on our behalves.

Finally, we despise some of our learned behaviors. Think about this. We started life out small, vulnerable, reliant on caregivers, and deeply attuned to our dependence on them. Survival instincts prompted us to copy the adults we were given as examples. And yet, those superiors were sinners just as we are. There isn't an exception among us who hasn't been taught or copied the flaws of parents or grandparents. We aspired to be like them long before we learned that they were susceptible to error. Innocence has no concept of wrong. It is innately trusting, only aware of leadership and the sense of security, which is enjoyed under dominant authority figures.

As soon as we perfectly replicate the sin we saw or heard modeled for us, an unforeseen presence rises within us: the voice of conviction. It requires only a small amount of developmental maturity and one subsequent sin to come face to face with our conscience. When it corrects us, we jump to conclusions about our value, but we don't apply the same admonishment to our models' value that we apply to our own. They remain on pedestals, and we continue to pursue their approval.

Self-loathing begins when we appoint sinners as our standards of excellence. We chase the admiration of flawed human beings all our lives, first from our parents and older siblings, then peers and romantic partners, colleagues, customers, and upper management. We crave validation from sources who are competing for their own. The demand for affirmation is too big for the supply, and emotional need becomes a cavern that can't be filled.

If we blame ourselves for having such needs, then self-loathing becomes self-sustaining. When we define our self-worth by the regard we can attain from even the best among fallen creatures, we remain chronically insecure. The humans we admire may be *an* authority on our value, if we insist on giving them that power, but they are not *the* authority. We must set our sights on Jesus as our standard and His grace as our safety net.

While an awareness of our flaws is useful to restrain pride, a pattern of self-loathing is more than destructive. It is sinful because it disputes what God says about our worth. Jesus's love dismantles condemnation. He testifies to our worth by having died for us.

I am as valuable as the blood of Jesus. I am worth having His attention at all times. How do I know this? Because He tells me that I already have it. Psalm 139 is where I go to remind myself. To aid the application of it, I converted the King James Version of the psalm into a personal version supplemented by related scriptures I have read, learned, and experienced. Here are twenty-four reasons why a spirit of self-loathing is not permissible for me.

Psalms, chapter 139, through my eyes:

1. You [God] invade my privacy and have me all figured out.
2. You know my every move. You know what I am thinking far in advance of me having the thought.
3. My journey is charted out in your mind. You are fully aware of all my actions.
4. You know every word I speak.
5. You have established a protective hedge around me within which I am intimately guarded, close enough to be touched.
6. Such knowledge is too wonderful for me. From these visions, I am coming to understand how thoroughly you know me, but I cannot fathom all you are trying to show me. There must be leagues more, which my mind cannot imagine.
7. You are *all*. Nothing escapes you. Nowhere escapes you. All is in you.
8. You are the overseer of heaven. You are the guardian of hell.

9. You reign over the skies and everything in them. You reign over the sea and everything in it.
10. You hold my hand firmly, leading the way, never letting go. Wherever I wake to find myself, your good and righteous touch is upon me.
11. With my mouth, I profess that I cannot escape the wickedness and evil around me, but despite it, you outshine the filth and mire that reaches up to my neck. You are brighter still.
12. Darkness is merely the absence of light. Where you are, God, the night is as good as the day, for you bring light with you and send darkness fleeing.
13. My soul was originally in your possession. My soul was portioned off from your breath. You took to covering my soul with flesh while I was in my mother's womb.
14. You are worthy of endless praise! I am merely a created thing and am humbly aware that you wonderfully intended my life. My soul affirms this truth, which convinces my mind and emotions.
15. You predestined my existence when you formed Adam from the dust of the ground. When you formed him, you formed me in him.
16. At that time of creation, you foresaw all I would do and all the ways I would sin. You loved all of me, not neglecting to document one moment of my life in your journal before it began. The record of me preceded the reality of me. All of my life is a continuous sequence of events aimed to one end. None of the seasons of my life can be separated.
17. You think of me, God, and then you think of me again. Your thoughts toward me are not angry, loathing, or disappointed, but can only be described in one word: precious. Not just one of those thoughts are precious, but all of them, the great quantity of them!

18. The grains of sand do not outnumber the times you have thought about me. Whether I am asleep or awake, the Holy Spirit in me is always united with you.
19. God, you have reserved a day for wrath and judgment. I should not pander with those who relish wrongdoing.
20. In the presence of those who refuse salvation, my ears and mind are filled with the vitriol that spews forth from their mouths. My ears hurt to hear you blasphemed.
21. An enemy of my God is an enemy of mine. I grieve the persecution of Christ and His church.
22. On the Day of Judgment, when my sins have been removed, and I have been washed in righteousness, the perfection you bestow on me will make me a worthy judge of unbelievers who rejected you.
23. Since we have not yet arrived at that day, use today to dissect my heart, my motives, my schemes, and my dreams. Pull down and uproot. Dig deep.
24. There is much about me I don't even know, which lingers in my subconscious. Reveal it. Show me my depravity so that I may strive against it, laboring instead toward eternal pursuits.

Indeed, this knowledge is too wonderful for me!

Who Is God in My Eyes?

The concept of "God" is so profound, so unlike us that He seems removed, judging from a distance. We shut and bolt the door on attempts to understand Him because His complexity intimidates us. However, God "became flesh and dwelt among us" (John 1:14). When Jesus descended from heaven, He erased the expanse between God and man. Because He lowered Himself to our creature status, it does not insult Him when we explore His humanity. Instead, He delights in it. Understanding Jesus's humility is the only means of securing a Christ-like standard for ourselves.

"Therefore, **in all things** He had to be **made like His brethren**, that He might be a **merciful and faithful High Priest** in things pertaining to God, **to make propitiation for the sins of the people**" (Heb. 2:17, NKJV).

Take a deep breath and digest the central truth of the above scripture: Jesus became like us in *all things*. What is the burden you feel is yours and yours alone? Are you isolated? Tempted? Desperate? Besieged with anxiety? Are you starving for love? For provisions? Are you misunderstood? Falsely accused? Are you at the end of yourself?

My friend, I have good news: Jesus bore your burden. Not figuratively, but literally. He experienced your feelings in His body because He purposed to grow in mercy and faithfulness toward you. Taking on flesh just like yours enabled Him to do that. He was more human than you or I in that He harnessed Himself to your deepest woes in addition to mine. He could not be merciful and faithful to you if He wasn't just like you in every way, and He could not be merciful and faithful to me if He wasn't just like me in every way. Your woes and mine are very different but individually severe. Jesus embraced them both. The word "all" excludes nothing. He was made like us in "all things."

Just as man (Adam) was created in God's image, Jesus in return took on man's image, establishing a two-way relationship between God and man. He made our union with God possible at the cost of surrendering to flesh-bound confinement which could feel pain and be tempted. Skin was not some costume Jesus temporarily wore, free from the emotional and mental entanglements of being human.

What Jesus experienced for us is beyond comprehension. Why God would want to endure internal anxiety, a culture of conflict, and ultimate martyrdom is beyond me. But the Bible reveals that Jesus willingly welcomed these constraints to fulfill the role of Savior. He was not born our Savior; He *became* our Savior.

"Although he [Jesus] was a son, **he learned obedience from what he suffered** and, **once made perfect**, **he became** the source of eternal salvation for all who obey him" (Heb. 5:8–9, NIV).

The scripture articulates that He "learned obedience." Why did Jesus need to "learn" obedience? Not for His own sake, but because we learn to obey, He matured the same way. He started out just as naive as we do. His learning was no more comfortable or natural, but He suffered so that He wouldn't sin. Yet we sin so that we won't suffer. Only the raw humanity of Jesus can show us how to defy our flesh.

The scripture states that He had to be "made perfect." Was Jesus not always perfect? Jesus was always holy, but He was not always our perfect sacrifice. Not until He spoke the words, "It is finished," (John 19:30) did He effectively secure our salvation. Jesus's progressive perfection was like a mother cow's milk: it's perfect for her calf, and there's no better nutrition for her baby, but only after the milk is pasteurized does it become perfect for man. A process is required to make natural perfection likewise perfect in function.

Jesus was always perfect in nature, as the definition of perfection goes, but He wasn't the perfect sacrifice for our sins that starry night when He came into this world and was placed in a manger. If He had always been our perfect sacrifice, then it would have been timely for Jesus to have been killed in the massacre of the innocents in Israel when King Herod slaughtered all the male children two years of age and younger (Matt. 2:13–21). Jesus was targeted, protected, and spared so that He should suffer. He "became" the source of our salvation. He wasn't born qualified to save us; He earned His qualification through suffering. Jesus paid an extremely high price.

"**Because he** himself **suffered** when he was tempted, **he is able to help** those **who are being tempted**" (Heb. 2:18, NIV).

We underestimate the temptations of Christ as if they were easy to bear because He was divine, but this wasn't the case. Notice here that scripture describes Jesus's temptations as suffering. He was in distress when He was tempted.

Matthew 3:16–17 reveals what happened to Jesus just prior to His temptations. "When He had been baptized, Jesus came up **immediately** from the water; and behold, the **heavens were opened** to Him, and He saw **the Spirit of God descending like a dove** and alighting upon Him. And suddenly **a voice** came from heaven, saying, "This is **my beloved Son**, in whom **I am well pleased**" (NKJV).

Amazing! Glorious! Jesus and John the Baptist stood alone in the Jordan River, the heavens opened, and the Spirit of God descended in the form of a dove and rested on Jesus's shoulder. A thunderous voice from heaven was heard aloud acknowledging Jesus's heritage and approving of Him.

How much joy Jesus must have experienced in that moment, only to be rewarded with forty exhausting days of immense temptation. "**Then** Jesus was **led** up **by the Spirit into the wilderness to be tempted** by the devil" (Matt. 4:1, NKJV).

Why so soon after being publicly acknowledged as God's Son and praised by His Father was Jesus tried? We have already discussed how surprised we are to find that spiritual darkness often follows conversion. Perhaps this sequence of events is just one more way that Jesus's life parallels ours. We receive the Holy Spirit into our hearts or have a mountaintop experience of rededication, only to find the devil waiting on our doorstep. When this about-face occurs, we wrongly interpret the arrival of temptation as a sin and blame ourselves for its appearance. The devil suggests that we have already sinned in order to weaken our resolve, yet Jesus didn't dismiss His prior victory when the devil tempted Him.

"And when He had fasted forty days and forty nights, afterward He was hungry. Now when **the tempter came to Him**, he said, '**<u>If you are the Son of God</u>**, command that these **stones become bread**'" (Matt. 4:2–3, NKJV).

Without food for forty days, what physical and mental fatigue He must have been under. The Word tells us that He was hungry. The devil's suggestion was logical: if you're in physical need, and you have the ability to get your needs met, then do it! Makes sense, right? It doesn't even sound like a temptation. "God helps those who help themselves" is frequently spoken, but this isn't necessarily true, nor is it biblical. Sometimes, God wants those who have the power to change their circumstances to refrain from taking action, especially when motivated by faithlessness, selfishness, or impulsivity. Jesus was in one of those situations. He had the power to change things, but He also had God's Word, which retracted that clearance.

"But He [Jesus] answered and said, '**It is written**, "Man shall **<u>not live</u> by bread alone**, but by **<u>every word</u>** that proceeds from the mouth of God"'" (Matt. 4:4, NKJV).

Are the words of God's mouth more vital than food, more valuable than meeting the needs of our physical bodies? Yes! Jesus also says so in Luke 12:4–5: "I tell you, my friends, **do not be afraid of those who kill the body** and after that can do no more. But I will show you whom you should fear: **Fear him who**, after the killing of the body, **has power to throw you into hell**. Yes, I tell you, **fear him**" (NIV).

Jesus preaches this message in one circumstance and upholds it in another. He is consistent in word and deed. When the going got tough, forty-days-of-starvation tough, Jesus resisted temptation. God's will meant the prolonging of His suffering.

"Then **the devil took him to the holy city** and had him **stand on** the highest point of **the temple**. '**If you are the Son of God**,' he said, '**throw yourself down**. **For it is written**: "He [God] will command his angels concerning you, and they will lift you up in their hands, so that you will not strike your foot against a stone"'" (Matt. 4:5–6, NIV).

The devil targeted Jesus where an insult to His divinity would hurt the most: on the temple in Jerusalem. If Jesus had a rightful place as Lord, it would be in the temple, so the devil took Jesus to His home turf and taunted Him atop His very home. Jesus had proven that His flesh was submitted to God's ordinances, but what about His spirit? Was this the bait Jesus would bite? Jesus responded to the first temptation by claiming that His refuge was in God's Word; therefore, the devil went so low as to incorporate scripture in the second temptation.

"Jesus answered him, '**It is also written**: "**Do not put the Lord** your God **to the test**"'" (Matt. 4:7, NIV). Jesus announced that He was at the Father's disposal, not the Father at the Son's disposal.

With this second temptation, we see two forms of authority: Jesus's authority over the angels and God the Father's authority over the Son. The relationship between Jesus and God the Father is crucial to our understanding of Jesus's humanity. All the power of heaven was granted to Jesus while on earth, but He never abused it. He never exercised it outside of God's will. God the Father surrendered all authority to Jesus because He could trust Jesus to honor Him first and foremost.

In a separate scene, Jesus explained: "**The reason my Father loves me** is that **I lay down my life**—only to take it up again. **No one takes it from me**, but **I lay it down of my own accord**. **I have authority to lay it down and authority to take it up again**. This command I received from my Father" (John 10:17–18, NIV).

Yes, the devil was right. Jesus had authority over creation; He could turn stones to bread. He would feed five thousand men, besides women and children, on five loaves of bread and two fish a short time later. And Jesus had authority over the angels; He could summon them to protect Him. But Jesus was on call as the Savior of men. To exert His power at the devil's command would destroy His mission to defeat the devil in man's skin. The temptations that the devil proposed were targeted at disproving Jesus's humanity. He wanted Jesus to appear too godly to be human in our eyes, but Jesus remained relatable. Jesus protected our view of His humanity by enduring each attack. The more accurately we see Jesus's humanity, the more powerful His help is to us.

Jesus's suffering was voluntary, not because He welcomed pain, but because He had the power to stop it at any time. In suffering without relief, He accomplished His mission as our Savior and became the model for mankind. There is something else to notice about the authority of Jesus: He is practiced at restraining it. He has the right to exert His Lordship over us today, too. He could strike us dead for our disobedience or force us into submission with a glance, but He has not done it globally, yet.

During our time on earth, we're given the freedom to choose whom we will serve. This doesn't mean that God ceases to be God any more than Jesus ceased to be God's Son when He refrained from displaying His power at the devil's suggestions. Surrendering to God's will now, for no other reason than honoring His Lordship, is expected of us. Jesus proved it is possible. Everything Jesus accomplished on earth was accomplished in the flesh of a man by the power of the Holy Spirit. What was required of Him is required of us by that same power.

"Again, **the devil took him** to a very high mountain and **showed him all the kingdoms** of the world and their splendor. '**All this I will give you**,' he said, '**if you will bow down and worship me**'" (Matt. 4:8–9, NIV).

Motivated by his own greed, the devil tried to tempt Jesus with greed. The third temptation reveals the devil's ultimate goal all along: that Jesus worship him. The devil forgot that Jesus was the Creator of all the kingdoms that the devil claimed to have possession over.

All the kingdoms of the world would not derail Jesus. He had spoken them into existence (John 1:1–3, 14). In triumph, Jesus shouted, "**Away from me, Satan! For it is written: 'Worship the Lord your God, and serve him only**.' Then the devil left him, and angels came and attended him" (Matt. 4:10–11, NIV).

The devil had crossed the line. Jesus was offended. He exercised His authority as God's Son but in rebuke of the devil, not under the lure of any temptation. He commanded Satan to leave His presence, and the devil relented, ultimately powerless under Jesus's command.

Jesus didn't falter when His flesh was tempted, nor did He falter when His spirit was tempted. Jesus rolled with the devil's punches and rose to deliver the final blow. In the end, the devil went running. Isn't it ironic that Jesus was immediately ministered to by the very angels He refused to summon at Satan's earlier suggestion? God the Father sent relief as soon as Jesus resisted temptation and ordered the devil away. Relief follows endurance.

The devil's arrows will be direct and malicious when pointed at us, too. He'll hit us where it hurts the most when we're in a weakened condition, but we aren't ignorant of this. Jesus has shown us how to handle the devil. We are armed with "every word that proceeds from the mouth of God," just as

Jesus was. And we know that the Word of God sends the devil running.

Depression Has Layers

When a threat arises, emotional memories from the past involuntarily resurface and attach to present circumstances. The emotional onslaught is often disproportionate to the reality of the moment. It's like feeling your finger has been cut off and looking down to see your finger perfectly intact. You accept the fact that your finger hasn't been cut off, but what do you do with the sensation that it has? For depressives, we must weather extreme emotional responses that contradict our conscious objections.

I'll share an example of how depression twists reality.

I once housed a stranger's dog for several months while her owner was between apartment leases. The dog was eleven years old and had never been spayed. After keeping Karmen for two weeks, I volunteered to take her to the vet for a wellness checkup. Although she was an easy houseguest, I had not bonded with Karmen or seen her as anything other than someone else's dog. The vet conducted his examination and discovered a mammary tumor. My eyes filled with tears. To explain my reaction, I muttered, "I didn't realize I had gotten so attached to you." I mentioned that she had been urinating blood, which I assumed was her female cycle since she hadn't been spayed, but the doctor said it could be one of three things: a urinary tract infection, bladder stones, or bladder cancer. The doctor took blood and urine samples, and I left the doctor's office with a broken heart but a happy, senior girl wagging her fluffy, black tail.

Depressive people gather information in waves and retain that information in layers. Any uncomfortable angle of a situation can knock one or more of the layers loose. Only when every layer is balanced and still do we experience normalcy and calm.

The discovery of Karmen's mammary tumor triggered an emotional flashback to my first dog being diagnosed with cancer. It didn't matter that Karmen wasn't Macy. It didn't matter that she wasn't my dog, or that Karmen's tumor might be benign and her fate more favorable than Macy's. My brain heard Macy's diagnosis all over again. The portal to the past opened, and I was forced into that familiar pain. This was the first layer.

The second layer was that Karmen had an owner who loved her dearly. How was Laura going to feel when I delivered this devastating news? Empathy and mentalization are my secondary senses. I can't shut them off any more than I can shut off my sense of hearing. This means I see and feel the world from other people's perspectives. As I witness others navigating their personal lives, I embody the emotions that I expect others are having, and I think through the thoughts that I expect they are thinking. This quality can be positive, in that I experience joy at seeing other people happy, and I innately know how to comfort others in their time of need, but it also sends me into a downward spiral when I hear someone I know has undergone tragedy. I process it as if it happened to me. Even global tragedies can emotionally cripple me. I have been known to experience specific global events as personal loss. I began to process the emotions I expected Laura to feel.

Layer three was the financial crisis. There was no financial burden for me personally; I had the money and was glad to use it to meet Karmen's need, but Laura had many financial stresses. Laura was not a taker and had trouble asking for help with Karmen at all, but when her apartment complex required a pet deposit that she couldn't afford, desperate times called for desperate measures, and Karmen came to stay with me. I knew that the indebtedness of allowing a stranger to meet this financial burden was one Laura would carry heavily, because she deeply wanted to meet Karmen's needs herself.

Layer four: poor Karmen. If it was a urinary tract infection or bladder stones, how miserable did she feel? And the tumor—did it hurt? How long had Karmen felt this way? I imagined the pain she would face the next week after surgery, "Poor baby, you are going to hurt so much, and you aren't going to understand." I looked into her trusting eyes, and it made me so sad. I hurt just thinking about the forthcoming pain I would inflict on her.

Layer five: what's the worst that could happen? A high-risk situation brings with it an emotional foretaste of the potential catastrophic outcomes. Depressives become trapped in emotional non-realities. What if Karmen's mammary tumor was malignant? What if she had bladder cancer? She could already be dying. What if she didn't survive the anesthesia? I wanted to do a good deed for Laura but could end up killing her dog. Although I could logically entertain these possibilities as not-yet or not-likely realities, the worst-case scenario played out in my mind, and the related emotions forced their way in.

Do you see the layers tilting? After a few sentences spoken by a doctor, five layers of emotion began their pendulum sway. For a person who deals with depression, the cause of collapse can be quite unspectacular. Emotional instability also induces a physical reaction, which long outlasts the mental deliberations. Any shock, threat, or spike in anxiety sends crisis-reaction chemicals surging through my body. I must wade through every one of these layers before the chemical surge begins to wane. Nervous discomfort, sadness, or a sense of impending doom pulses in my body for days, often a week, long after I have reached mental resolution over a situation. Because the chemical surge lasts so long, my body continues signaling to my mind that permanent damage has occurred, and normal will never return.

Depression snaps at you on the inside like a viper, every day, sometimes multiple times a day. Anything can tip the first domino of the cascade. Once triggered, settling all the moving parts (mental, emotional, and physical) before another chain reaction begins is emergency work. A full-blown depressive episode can arise when traumatic scenarios piggyback faster than they can be righted. When this occurs, panic takes over, the flight instinct kicks in, and you must retreat to your safe place. Shutting down is your only sanctuary. This is the reprieve your mind and body need to reduce the doom back to practicality. Either our bodies try to do this naturally through inordinate amounts of sleep, or we resort to sleep to escape how horrible it feels to be awake.

Just as autistic individuals are bombarded with heightened sensory stimuli that they can't escape, depressives are bombarded with emotional and mental stimuli that ratchets their internal intensity to threatening levels. The increased heart rate, involuntary twitching, and inability to concentrate on the present contradict the depressive's acknowledgement of reality. Even while battling all this, we must shower, dress, get the kids to school, go to work, clean the house, pay the bills, and navigate real life. Responsibility and emotional maintenance rival one another for top priority.

Note: I'll share Karmen's results in a later chapter.

Where Do I Start?

God loves me and has everything under control.

I am needy and reliant on His strength.

Beyond His mercy, the next thing I need most from Him is forgiveness. I identify myself by my failures, and I hate them. I can't rewrite the past, but my wounds can be healed.

In the *Voyage of the Dawn Treader* by C. S. Lewis, a boy named Eustace is turned into a dragon because of his greed. He explains to his cousin Edmund how Aslan, a lion who represents God, rectifies his unfortunate condition:

> "I knew it was a well because you could see the water bubbling up from the bottom of it: but it was a lot bigger than most wells—like a very big, round bath with marble steps going down into it. The water was as clear as anything and I thought if I could get in there and bathe, it would ease the pain in my leg. But the lion told me I must undress first. Mind you, I don't know if he said any words out loud or not.
>
> "I was just going to say that I couldn't undress because I hadn't any clothes on when I suddenly thought that dragons are snaky sort of things and snakes can cast their skins. Oh, of course, thought I, that's what the lion means. So I started scratching myself and my scales began coming off all over the place. And then I scratched a little deeper and, instead of just scales coming off here and there, my whole skin started peeling off beautifully, like it does after an illness, or as if I was a banana. In a minute or two, I just stepped out of it. I could see it lying

there beside me, looking rather nasty. It was a most lovely feeling. So I started to go down into the well for my bathe.

"But just as I was going to put my foot into the water, I looked down and saw that it was all hard and rough and wrinkled and scaly just as it had been before. Oh, that's all right, said I, it only means I had another smaller suit on underneath the first one, and I'll have to get out of it too. So I scratched and tore again and this under skin peeled off beautifully and out I stepped and left it lying beside the other one and went down to the well for my bathe.

"Well, exactly the same thing happened again. And I thought to myself, oh dear, however many skins have I got to take off? For I was longing to bathe my leg. So I scratched away for the third time and got off a third skin, just like the two others, and stepped out of it. But as soon as I looked at myself in the water, I knew it had been no good.

"Then the lion said—but I don't know if it spoke—You will have to let me undress you. I was afraid of his claws, I can tell you, but I was pretty nearly desperate now. So I just lay flat down on my back and let him do it.

"The very first tear he made was so deep that I thought it had gone right into my heart. And when he began pulling the skin off, it hurt worse than anything I've ever felt. The only thing that made me able to bear it was just the pleasure of feeling the stuff peel off. You know—if you've ever picked the scab off a sore place. It hurts like billy-oh, but it is such fun to see it coming away."

"I know exactly what you mean," said Edmund.

> "Well, he peeled the beastly stuff right off—just as I thought I'd done it myself the other three times, only they hadn't hurt—and there it was lying on the grass: only ever so much thicker, and darker, and more knobbly looking than the others had been. And there was I as smooth and soft as a peeled switch and smaller than I had been. Then he caught hold of me—I didn't like that much for I was very tender underneath now that I'd no skin on—and threw me into the water. It smarted like anything but only for a moment. After that, it became perfectly delicious and as soon as I started swimming and splashing I found that all the pain had gone from my arm. And then I saw why. I'd turned into a boy again."

Our mistakes may not turn us into dragons on the outside, but on the inside, we are damaged and disfigured. Eustace doesn't say what his layers were comprised of, but they could have been formed from selfishness, anger, jealousy, or guilt. We can't discard the trappings of our sin, either, because we made them a part of us when we invited sin in. Sin took up residence much too deep to be easily cast off. Only God can uproot it.

One philosophy that causes many Christians to stumble is the misconception that being true to yourself is a virtue. The motive behind the message is to laud authenticity at all cost, but it does more harm than good because our unbridled natures have destructive tendencies and should not be granted permission to do as they please. Our sinful natures delight in falling prey to temptation because temptation ushers in excitement and the rush of living life on a high.

Anything that draws your attention away from that which you would prefer to attend to is working against you, be it as harmless as a daily Starbucks fix or as conniving as pornography addiction. I'm not saying that every craving we have is a sin, but

I'm trying to describe how easily damaging urges camouflage themselves as natural and, therefore, claim immunity from reprimand under the banner of "being true to yourself." Without inviting God to scrutinize all our inclinations for latent harms, we'll never develop discernment and self-discipline where it really matters.

There's a distinction between what's good and, therefore, good for our minds, bodies, and emotions, versus what's bad and, therefore, bad for our minds, bodies, and emotions. The distinction seems almost too subjective to guide decision-making, until God takes responsibility to define it. "But I say, walk by the Spirit, and you **<u>will not carry out</u> the desire of the flesh**. For the **flesh sets its desire <u>against the Spirit</u>, and the Spirit <u>against the flesh</u>**; for these are **in opposition** to one another, so that **<u>you may not do</u> the things that you please**" (Gal. 5:16–17, NASB).

Where does it say the desires of the flesh die when you become a Christian? On the contrary, it introduces a rift between your true self (your flesh) and that which is contrary to your true self, the Spirit. Have you noticed that "Spirit" is often capitalized in scripture? That's because the person of God, who enters the premises of your heart, is referred to as the Holy Spirit. When He enters, He objects to what your true self tells you to perform and aids you in carrying out actions contrary to your nature.

Flesh, which is thriving, is at the root of our distress, but the holiness of God is powerful enough to triumph over the things we assume we must have in order to survive or are too weak to resist. Like Aslan's claws, the Holy Spirit shreds the strongholds of the flesh to release, and then soothe, the soul. He isn't intimidated by our darkness, and He's eager to free us from all that works against us, even some natural parts of ourselves. Although mysterious, an encounter with the Holy Spirit is radical and nothing short of transformative. Our contribution to the transformation is the willingness to be changed.

In *The Spiritual Man*, Watchman Nee says, "The flesh is most defiled (2 Pet. 2:10–22); God accordingly does not attempt to change it. There is no method of deliverance other than to put it to death. Even the precious blood of Jesus cannot cleanse the flesh. We find in the Bible how His blood washes our sin but never washes our flesh. It must be crucified (Gal. 5:24). The Holy Spirit cannot reform the flesh... His abiding in the believer is not for the purpose of improving but for warring against the flesh (Gal. 5:17)... Indeed, we should never attempt to repair the flesh in order to make it cooperate with the Spirit of God. The flesh is ordained to death. Only by consigning the flesh to the cross may we be liberated from being enslaved permanently by it."

"There is therefore now **no condemnation** to them which are **in Christ Jesus**, **who walk** not after the flesh, but **after the Spirit**" (Rom. 8:1, KJV).

No condemnation means no consequence. It means freedom from penalty. Primal (non-spiritual) living, called "walking after the flesh," is a two-dimensional experience like watching a movie. But "walking after the Spirit" is like taking that first step outside of the theater into a three-dimensional world where sight is now closer and with many more angles, hearing is from all directions, and touch is right at your fingertips.

You can't hear or feel the wind blowing indoors, but outside, you're sure it exists because you can feel it and hear it, and that's enough. The kingdom of God is experienced by those who hear and feel the presence of God. Like a leaf turning in the wind, we see the hand of God in our lives by the things He moves in our midst. We don't need our eyes to see the kingdom of God; we have a different sense of sight, one that incorporates hearing and feeling, as well.

"Jesus answered, 'I tell you the truth, **no one can enter the kingdom of God** unless he is **born of water and the Spirit**. Flesh gives birth to flesh, but the Spirit gives birth to spirit. You should not be surprised at my saying, "**You must be born**

again." The wind blows wherever it pleases. You hear its sound, but you cannot tell where it comes from or where it is going. So it is with everyone born of the Spirit'" (John 3:5–8, NIV).

"Flesh gives birth to flesh," and yet you must also be born of the Spirit to enter the kingdom of God. To grasp this, let's consider the flesh part first.

What is an infant's birth experience?

Blinding light! Sight! Sound! Temperature change. Human touch. The love and adoration of its parents. A first bath to wipe away all the natural filth. Caregivers assess the baby's needs using thermometers, stethoscopes, heat lamps, and scales. Food helps it grow, and medicine helps it survive. All of its needs are met without asking. The child is given a name. A birth certificate is issued, dating and time-stamping the record of life, beginning the clock on the journey of a lifetime.

These are also things a new Christian experiences when they are "born again." We see with depth for the first time. We perceive the voice of God within ourselves for the first time. This is called conviction. Grace washes over us, and all we ever did wrong is removed as in a first bath. We receive a new name and a new identity, "child of God." A date and a time document the true beginning of life; nothing before that moment matters. Being "born again" is much like being born of water in all these respects, but unlike your flesh birth, your spiritual birth occurs only by choice. It is accomplished at your request that the Holy Spirit of God come to live inside you.

Revelation 3:20 says, "Behold, **I stand at the door, and knock**: if **any** man **hear my voice**, and **open the door**, **I will come in to him**, and will sup with him, and he with me" (KJV).

When the Holy Spirit enters a person's heart, He wars against the things we are too weak to defeat on our own. A conflict of conscience arises, and the Holy Spirit grants the self-control necessary to overcome sinful appetites. It can be very uncomfortable when the flesh and the Spirit battle for rights to you, but it's evidence of spiritual health and the only path to victory. It reveals that the Holy Spirit is alive within you, working to prevail over your true self, which previously operated undeterred.

Living honestly and authentically is admirable, but it takes much more than being true to yourself to be your *best* self. Limiting your personal mission statement to being true to yourself cuts you off miles short of where God wants to take you.

Jesus didn't die so that I could live out my life being true to myself. He died for me so that His death would replace my death, first eternally, then practically as I become His hands and feet on earth. So where does that leave my true self?

It leaves my true self dead.

Being born again opens the door to an eternal life, at the expense of a superficial earthly life. Jim Elliot, a missionary who was killed in Ecuador in 1956, wrote in his journal before departing for the mission field, "He is no fool who gives what he cannot keep to gain that which he cannot lose."

We are all losing our lives from the moment we're born, and we will only gain eternal life by giving up control of them to God. Those who are born again discover that the Christian life is a marathon and a free ride, a life sentence and a pardon, a funeral and a honeymoon all wrapped into one. These may sound like hard terms. Perhaps, but the only other option is the marathon without the free ride, the life sentence without the pardon, and the funeral without the honeymoon. Resurrection is the trade we are offered. Will you lay your life down as Jesus did?

God's Word identifies the ultimate goal of the Christian life; "**For you died**, and **<u>your life is hidden with Christ in God</u>**" (Col. 3:3, NKJV). It's only while wrestling against this that we find ourselves undone by the obstacles we face.

A life hidden with Christ in God depends on perceiving ourselves as dead. We allow the Holy Spirit to put to death the attitudes, actions, and words that come instinctively to us.

We forsake all defenses of our sin; the dead don't need defense attorneys. Confession and repentance become our steady diet. Nothing should be done out of strife or vanity, but humility is always appropriate, regardless of injustice or inconvenience.

Let's break it down: (1) a life, (2) hidden, (3) with Christ, (4) in God.

A life. You are an independent, indivisible, unit of life. You have many choices and opportunities. You are a valuable entity standing alone.

Hidden. You are not the captain of your own universe. An authentic Christian life is a hidden life. Think of it as a buried life, one that is deep and wholly surrendered.

With Christ. Your salvation does not exist in private. There's someone keeping you company in hiding. You are accompanied by the very person who ventured into death ahead of you, displaying all bravery and sacrifice of self, the Lord Jesus Christ. He is your constant companion who never leaves you nor forsakes you. If you can comprehend how Christ's life on earth operated under the oversight of heaven and the Father's authority, then you can envision the governance that applies to your life, as well.

In God. All things reside within God's sovereign control. Nothing that touches your life is external to Him; all things are *internal* to Him. Nothing is beside Him, nothing is in cooperative partnership with Him, but everything is *in Him*—swallowed whole.

Striving for a life hidden with Christ in God is the goal a disciple never stops pursuing. The hidden life is accomplished only in moments; therefore, strive to reduce the lags between moments so that your life may be as full of victory as possible.

In *Band of Brothers*, a World War II miniseries based on the true story of a company of American paratroopers, Lieutenant Ronald Speirs, a fearless veteran, has strong words for Private Albert Blithe, who is just beginning his military journey:

Blithe: Lieutenant, sir, when I landed on D-Day, I found myself in the ditch all by myself. I fell asleep. I think it was those airsickness pills they gave us. When I woke up, I didn't really try to find my unit to fight. I just kind of stayed put.

Speirs: What's your name, trooper?

Blithe: Blithe, sir. Albert Blithe.

Speirs: You know why you hid in that ditch, Blithe?

Blithe: I was scared.

Speirs: We're all scared. You hid in that ditch because you think there's still hope. But, Blithe, the only hope you have is to accept the fact that you are already dead. And the sooner you accept that, the sooner you'll be able to function as a soldier is supposed to...

Both Blithe and Speirs survived WWII and had military careers that exceeded twenty years.

Speirs's advice applies to Christian soldiers, as well. We hide in the ditch of depression because we hope there's still a chance that we'll get our way, but the sooner we accept that the blood of Jesus has purchased the full claim on our lives, and we no longer have rights, the sooner we can make our way out of the pit. It is our will that tethers us to the bottom. Accepting God's will is never a partial acceptance. It's all or nothing. Halfway up the slick walls of a ditch only leads back to the bottom.

A puppy is intent on chewing his master's fingers, but the pup must let go of them to experience the ultimate satisfaction of being petted. He must relent before the master loses patience, or the master will withdraw his hand, and the pup will find no fingers remain to be chewed or to stroke. The master will have His way.

Go ahead, release your rotting vision. Lift up your eyes. See the tiny ray of light peeking through the crack in the rock ceiling? Step toward it. Let it fall on you. One sliver of God is better than two handfuls of our best efforts.

Tired of Caring

Do you ever get tired of caring? Maybe "tired of caring" isn't the right phrase. Maybe it's "tired *from* caring," where you find yourself emotionally numb for good portions of a day, and you start to willfully ignore the things that push the threshold of your emotional stability. Maybe this condition gets worse with age or is genetically oriented. Or maybe it's a defense mechanism against depression. You elect to just not care. I find myself not caring more and more with each passing day.

I have grown so reclusive that I'm on the precipice of agoraphobia. I would much rather spend time entertaining myself or sleeping instead of putting forth the emotional investment of time, energy, and anticipation directed toward some unpredictable social encounter, which is likely to fail to meet my expectations or my needs. Where do people get the stamina to care so much about social activities? I'm not a hermit, and I'm not at all intimidated by people. Social events just take so much out of me. As extroverts gain energy by being around people, and introverts lose energy by being around people, depressives experience social engagement like introverts but on an exaggerated scale. The recovery after an event lasts far longer than the social activity itself. Usually, being home in my comfy, unpresentable attire with the unconditional affection of my dogs is more appealing. That doesn't cost me anything.

If I'm going to expend energy, let me go jogging or do something creative, like baking or writing. If you want me to be around people, send me to the prison to teach Sunday school, or show me someone in need whom I can help. I need to produce something in order to make my effort worthwhile. There's no enjoyment for me in wasting time around other people. Let me waste time at home watching a movie or in the bed or in the bathtub. Then, I'll at least restore my reserves for the next responsibility at hand.

I have known this cold truth about myself for quite some time. It's only when you sense a deepening of this introversion that things start to get scary. When the people in your life branch off into realms you can't reach with a phone conversation or confessions of honesty, you sense the distance growing. When you pour your heart out to your friends or even fight with family about something that affects you profoundly, and the circumstances don't change, then the people who used to be worth your emotional investment start to drift into the category of things that just aren't worth getting worked up over. Disappointment is the worst. In order to avoid it, you have to cease to care. My fear is that, pretty soon, I'll be so numb that I care about very little.

What Have I Lost?

We've discussed how perceiving ourselves as dead gives free reign to the Holy Spirit, but how does one carry out this prerogative? The hidden life is best expressed through a mindset of voluntary slavery.

"Don't you know that when you **offer yourselves** to someone to obey him as slaves, **you are slaves of the one whom you obey**—whether you are **slaves to sin**, which leads **to death**, **or to obedience**, which leads **to righteousness**" (Rom. 6:16, NIV)?

In *Knowing God*, J. I. Packer clarifies, "Whether being a servant is a matter for shame or for pride depends on whose servant one is." To be a slave of the Savior is an honor.

A steep ransom has been paid for the souls of men. As He hung on the cross, Jesus proposed a new slave-master relationship. In layman's terms, His message was, "*Here I am, willingly accepting this torture and death in aim to pour out my blood for your life. I will not see my beloved sanctioned to hell for their misdeeds. I will give all of myself to prevent it. I lay down the payment here on the dusty ground below the cross in drops of red. May I purchase you?*"

"Act as **free men**, and do not use your freedom as a covering for evil, but use it as **bondslaves of God**" (1 Pet. 2:16, NASB).

If I desire to see myself as God's slave, what does that look like? Slaves don't stake claims or have rights. There's no reservation of body, property, time, money, decisions, or reputation from their master's ownership. We're called to agree to these terms before the God who created us, loves us, and died for us.

How can we deny this arrangement if we have accepted that the ransom for our sin has been paid?

The world we live in teeters between popular opinions so frequently that it's easier to be on the wrong side than on the right. I am not saying that one side is right and the other is wrong, but our culture claims that the definitions of right and wrong are now subjective, so I won't be surprised if that which is praised today is despised tomorrow. Convictions and sensitivities, which were once the instruments of progress, have now become weapons. It's no longer acceptable to possess both. We are forced to choose between them.

Independent of a divine authority, human rights *are* preeminent in our society. As a child of the fall, my logic agrees with this. But if there is a God, and if I have sworn my loyalty to Him, then my freedom to negotiate my human rights is gone. As a child of the cross, I have lost my rights to human rights. The day that I encountered a holy God and asked Him to cover my sins with His blood, the pardon was granted in exchange for my absolute surrender. I cannot expend anything according to my natural instincts and remain obedient to the divine authority whose pardon determines my eternal destination.

In the daily devotional, *My Utmost for His Highest*, Oswald Chambers wrote, "Any fool can insist on his rights, and any devil will see that he gets them; but the Sermon on the Mount means that the only right the saint will insist on is the right to give up his rights" (the May 24 entry).

My rights are gone because I surrender them continually.

Chambers continues, "Jesus never insists on having authority; He never says—Thou shalt. He leaves us perfectly free—so free that we can spit in His face, as men did; so free that we can put Him to death, as men did; and He will never say a word. But when His life has been created in me by His Redemption, I instantly recognize His right to absolute authority over me. It is a moral domination" (the July 19 entry).

I am morally dominated. Would it be more gratifying to shirk discipline, dismiss conviction, and indulge in every human right the American way promotes? Of course, it would. I am still woefully human and easily tempted. The catcalls of pleasure never remain quiet for long. But to renounce Jesus's authority would cost me so much more than a lifetime of forsaken pleasures.

Finally, Chambers says, "According to the Bible, sin in its final analysis is not a defect but defiance, a defiance that means death to the life of God in us. Sin is seen not only in selfishness, but in what men call unselfishness. It is possible to have such sympathy with our fellow men as to be guilty of red-handed rebellion against God" (the May 22 entry).

Every day, something tugs on my sympathies: wrongs I want to right, harms I want to heal, and I seek out opportunities to respond in tangible ways. I wish I had more opportunities to make others' lives better—all lives, any lives—but the internal divide persists. I must restrain myself from certain forms of sympathy when God's Word forbids me to do as I would like.

There's a difference between being respectable and being righteous. Respect is cultural. Righteousness is biblical. I can respect someone who executes unrighteous behaviors, such as Robin Hood, for example. I respect him for assuming responsibility to meet the needs of the poor, even at the expense of the rich. I agree with his sympathies, but that doesn't make his actions righteous. Jesus would never have met needs the way Robin Hood went about it. I can agree with both of them, but I can't pledge my allegiance to both of them without being a hypocrite. I must choose one and turn from the other. Stealing from the rich to give to the poor, because I am compassionate toward their unmet needs, would be red-handed rebellion against God. And consoling a lover with sex when we aren't married, because love should be generous, would be red-handed rebellion against

God. It pains me not to exercise certain forms of sympathy, although I am gravely sympathetic!

Being wrong because of what I've done, or being right for why I've done it, isn't determined by my opinion as the doer but rests on the opinion of the judge. Only He has rewards or punishments to dole out. My obedience to the judge doesn't make me a judge, it only spares me from the forewarned consequences of disobedience. I've lost my rights, remember? This includes my right to judge.

When my wants and my will are at odds, and neutrality isn't an option, it's my duty to uphold the hierarchy of allegiance God has ordained. It's as simple and as grueling as that. In general, we are to be conservative with our behaviors but liberal with our feelings. Jesus modeled the ideal blend of both. We are to reach out, understand, learn, love, provide for, and welcome everyone from every lifestyle and background. My father once said, "If Jesus were walking the earth today, liberals would be shocked how conservative He is, and conservatives would be shocked how liberal He is." Jesus overflows with both convictions and sensitivities. The Christ-like among us will, too.

Jeremiah 10:23 says, "I know, O Lord, that **a man's life is not his own**; it is **not for man to direct his steps**" (NIV).

Dr. Adrian Rogers, pastor of Bellevue Baptist Church in Memphis, Tennessee, said, "Salvation is the last independent decision you will make." Accepting Jesus's blood as your ticket to eternal life means you have no remaining rights to this earth-based one, which is actually a good thing. Letting go opens your hands to receive.

If you're on the fringe of victory but just can't reach your breakthrough, then I would wager to guess that you aren't seeing yourself as dead or as a slave. You're laboring too hard to claim, gain, and guard things that no longer belong to you. Security, peace, and self-control are found in the One who embodies all three. We must hide in Him for His help to rain down upon us.

The Little Girl in Me

See there, that little girl, kneeling by the creek? She has one hand in the ice-cold water reaching for a scampering crawfish just beyond her grasp. Although she dips her hand in the water, part of her doesn't really want to catch the crawfish because she's afraid of its pinchers, but a voice inside her says, "Act fast, or it'll get away, and you'll never know if its pinchers are worth your fear." And so, she dips her hand in again, a little more aggressively this time, and grabs the crawfish in her hand accepting any pain attached to this new experience.

See there, the glory of the catch on her face? She's smiling now, and the crawfish is wiggling uselessly between her fingers because its legs can't touch the ground. But she won't hurt it. She'll take good care of it. She'll even let it pinch her just so the crawfish will gain some compensation for being caught. Soon the pinches will be a form of communication between the two of them. And so she plays for a little while before returning the crawfish to its habitat so it can be free.

With an unspoken goodbye, she releases her new friend into the rapidly moving current where it belongs, and the little girl accepts that their momentary friendship is all that she will ever know.

Oh, little girl, you'll always be that little girl, constantly friendly with your unfriendly surroundings. You'll never stop befriending creatures unlike yourself. You'll always welcome momentary pain to enjoy the fleeting treasure while it lasts. Some of the creatures will mildly pinch you. Some will sting beyond your expectation. Some will scurry away and ignore your hello. Some will allow your approach but only because they're already wounded and limping. And with each one, there is the novelty of the catch but also the sad awareness of the inevitable release.

Over and over and over again, little girl, you'll retrace these steps—notice, approach, contact, be pinched, release—notice, approach, contact, be pinched, release—and you'll always consider the contact worth the pain of the pinch. But is the contact worth the pain of the release? For the release lasts much longer than the pinch.

With each new encounter, this question weighs more heavily on the little girl.

And the little girl replies, "No, I suppose the contact isn't worth the pain of the release. But one day, when I find the one that doesn't pinch or bite or sting or scurry from my reach, it will want to be found as much as I want to find it, and that one will be worth all the releases."

Can Faith Be Defined?

To help wrap our minds around the concept of faith, I'll ask you to visualize an extreme mountain biker. Can you see him standing on an elevated base platform, anxiously awaiting his turn? He rocks his bike back and forth between his legs as he watches the rider ahead him. His heart rate increases. He waits for the signal, "You're *on*!" And then he takes off! He pounds his feet against the pedals, balances his body weight above the bike, and furiously pedals harder and harder with each stride, straining to project power through his legs to build up as much momentum as possible. He barrels ahead, aiming straight for the vertically arching ramp. Fearlessly, he assaults the ramp and then *lift off!* He's in the air, spinning and flipping, twisting the bike and his body in positions gravity never intended. He quickly gains control of the bike again, positions it perfectly beneath himself, and lands upright to the awe and applause of the crowd. A deep sigh of relief is heard. He's safe on the ground and circles back around to line up for another turn.

Hebrews 11:1 defines faith: "Now faith is the **substance** of **things hoped for**, the **evidence** of **things not seen**" (KJV).

Scripture says that faith resides where hope is not yet realized and the soon-to-be has not yet been revealed. It's a precursor of things to come. In our example above, the biker commits himself to the stunt before he completes it. He knows that success rests on the momentum that he puts into it. The accelerating momentum is evidence that something big is coming. Faith is that momentum, and it's owned by the one who exercises it.

Noah built the ark at God's command. Neighbors witnessed him building and thought his actions were illogical. Then the flood came, and every living thing on the earth was destroyed, save that which was sheltered in the ark (Gen. 6–8).

Simeon testified that God would spare him from death until he lived to see the coming Messiah. People watched him enter the temple and faithfully pray this request. There he met the infant Jesus and praised God for granting his petition (Luke 2:25–32).

David discarded the armor and sword King Saul gave him before his encounter with the giant, Goliath. He was unprotected by a coat of mail but protected by the mighty power of God (1 Sam. 17:37–51). Then Goliath fell to the ground from the impact of a single slingshot.

Where faith exists, it is visible. It's the evidence you can see in the actions of those who trust God. God's people *actively* apply His Word and trust His character to execute lifestyles consistent with those beliefs. If faith is the momentum behind an extreme bicycle stunt, then the Word of God is the ramp. Just as there's no successful stunt without vigorous contact with the ramp, God's Word must be applied firmly to produce the faith that yields flight.

We can't rely on things that are seen with our eyes to build expectations about things that are yet to come. Hebrews 11:3 says that by the Word of God, the world was framed. By that same Word, the future world will also be framed. Faith has accomplished impossible feats throughout history, and faith will accomplish impossible feats again.

"[The saints] **who through faith** subdued kingdoms, wrought righteousness, obtained promises, stopped the mouths of lions, quenched the violence of fire, escaped the edge of the sword, out of weakness were made strong, became valiant in battle, turned to flight the armies of the aliens" (Heb. 11:33–34, NKJV).

Through His Word, we learn about God's nature, commands, patterns, promises, and reactions. We learn what is acceptable and unacceptable in His sight. We discover the parameters within which He displays His will through miraculous signs and wonders. We seek wisdom to critique our passions so that our pursuits remain upright. Discovering that His ways are higher than our ways and His thoughts higher than our thoughts, we learn not to get ahead of Him or to presume what God's will is. Even Jesus prayed the concession over His personal prayers, "Not as I will, but as you [heavenly Father] will" (Matt. 26:39, NKJV).

The Word of God is the road ramp for a lifetime. The application of it will keep you busy. Faith is the confidence to push off that instruction and act on it. Just like the biker uses his own legs to pump the pedals, you carry out your faith by an act of your will until faith reaches an elevated state and proves itself through visible evidence. Faith precedes sight.

"But **without faith** it is **impossible to please him** [God]: for he that comes to God **must believe that he is**, and that **he is a rewarder** of them **that diligently seek him**" (Heb. 11:6, KJV).

It isn't God's aim to go unfound, but to be found. It isn't His goal for you to go unrewarded, but to be rewarded. The cycle isn't complete, and the reward isn't rich, without hot pursuit. From the heights of heaven to the depths of hell, He pursued us. If this means anything to us, then we will reciprocate by diligently seeking Him.

God *is*. And He is a *rewarder*.

To please God, you *must* believe that *He is*: that He exists, and that His Word is perfect and is intended for you. You must believe that the Bible is a sure foundation. You must act on what you say you believe. You must push off the ramp.

To please God, you *must* believe that *He rewards*. Without presumption as to the specifics, you must believe that God will reward your faith. No stunt is ever accomplished without foresight and commitment. If the ramp (God's Word) is reliable, and the momentum (your confidence) is steadfast, then the stunt is as good as complete. You must label God a "Rewarder" and never doubt that He is. If doubt arises, then just remind yourself of every Bible story you ever read to silence those insecurities.

"In the same way, **faith by itself**, if it is **not accompanied by action**, **is dead**. But someone will say, 'You have faith; I have deeds.' Show me your faith without deeds, and **I will show you my faith by what I do**" (James 2:17–18, NIV).

Only when the biker pushes off the ramp does his faith take effect. If he sits still and doesn't pedal, he'll never experience the rush of flying. If he only speaks about his ability to perform the stunt but never performs it, then how substantial was his belief? It was just as worthless as having no belief at all. However, when he decides to thrust himself forward on faith, he discovers that the impossible is possible.

How Much Faith Is Enough?

The atmosphere of faith orbits around a core of free will. A person's freedom of choice is like helium inside a balloon: if the helium wants the balloon to expand, it will; if it doesn't, it won't. The difference between faith that prevails and faith that fails depends on what is propelling it.

"But Jesus said to him, '**No one**, having put his hand to the plow, **and looking back**, **is fit** **for the kingdom of God**'" (Luke 9:62, NKJV).

Those are some strong words. I need to make sure I understand why this policy stands. I read this verse in context, and it seems like a bit of a stretch for an analogy. Jesus and His listener were not discussing farming, so why did He use the "hand to the plow" illustration?

Turning back, after placing a hand to the plow, means that, by purposeful decision, a person initiates a forward motion, with a mission in mind, in anticipation of a reward, under self-propelled strength, and then reconsiders.

Perhaps the farmer rethinks the direction he's headed.

Maybe the strain of the labor is too much.

Or the investment required to reap a harvest takes too long.

It doesn't matter what causes his head to turn back in the direction where he started. Whatever wins his focus proves his allegiance, for both the plowing and the looking back are self-initiated actions. No one is in the field whipping him forward or pulling him backward. He makes the choice, and the choice testifies to his sincerity. His sincerity, or lack thereof, makes him "fit" or "unfit" for the kingdom of God.

My grandmother used to say, "People do what they want to do," when one of her grandchildren would explain why they hadn't come to visit sooner. Her comment always aroused an eye-roll from me beneath the avalanche of guilt, but I have grown to appreciate the truth in her claim. People *do* make time to do what they *want* to do. If the farmer wants to plow, he moves forward in his mission. If he doesn't want to plow, he looks back. The looking back reveals the content of his heart.

Let's imagine for a moment that your faith is a visible mass. How bulky is it? How tall? How wide? Is it deep or shallow? Is it firm or flimsy? What are its boundaries, if we were to measure it? Is it immovable, larger than a mountain? Or is it thimble-sized?

How would you begin to take such a measurement? After all, faith is invisible. It's the fuel that stokes attitudes and behaviors. You can't see it with the naked eye, but you see the results of its indwelling. Just as you would not know a woman was pregnant unless her belly expanded, and a child was delivered, faith is the productive force at work transforming the one inhabited, as well as producing fruit from the inhabitation.

Hebrews 10:38–39 says, "Now **the just shall live by faith**: but **if any man draw back, my soul shall have no pleasure in him**. But **we are not of them who draw back** unto perdition; but of them that believe to the saving of the soul" (KJV).

Even though faith is intangible, it has limits, which will be measured either by earthly constraints or heavenly realities. If man reaches a stopping point where he will progress no further in his faith, then he has allowed earth to limit him. On the other hand, if conditions on earth hold no power over a man's trust in God, then he will reach heaven where his faith is manifested into precious metals and jewels (1 Cor. 3:11-14). This manifestation becomes part of his heavenly reward. But if his faith falls short this side of heaven, what remains to be manifested inside the pearly gates?

In the previous chapter, we laid the foundation that pleasing God requires active belief. If we please God by having faith, then we displease Him by rejecting faith. He no longer takes pleasure in us when we're in that condition. I envision that the man spoken of in Hebrews, chapter 10, reaches a point where his faith expires. He faces a situation where his trust in God shrinks in comparison to his obstacle. At that moment, his faith can be measured in proportion to the size of his fear, greed, or lust, which looms larger. As he recoils from walking after the Spirit, a figurative marker is planted around his faith like a tombstone. Like Nebuchadnezzar, this man will be weighed in the balances and found lacking (Dan. 5:27).

Can earthly affronts stifle your faith? Or can you say that your faith has no limits, come hell or high water, come feast or famine, come sickness or health, come life or death? I ask myself these questions.

I remember a crossroad where I put my faith on pause for a while. I came to understand that:

Faith assumes the worth of that which you forsake to uphold it.

Grief can put the brakes on faith. I'm speaking of faith-shattering grief, not biblical grieving with hope, but the kind of grief that tempts you to question the goodness of God. When you mourn to that extreme, the object of your mourning temporarily assumes a greater value than your faith. The loved one or the lost career or the botched opportunity takes the spotlight. But Jesus says, "Follow me, and let the dead bury their own dead" (Matt. 8:22, NIV), which means don't stop following Jesus to mourn the past. Don't turn back from trusting the Living God to wave farewell to the outgoing tide. Advance in your faith anyway. Realize that grief has assumed a place where faith should reign. While in the natural state of mourning, a decision to meditate on God's goodness, which exceeds our understanding, will gradually lift the heaviness. Then the love of God will resume the place that loss once inhabited. Faith can break free of the limits grief places around it. You can move forward in faith again.

Relationships can also limit faith. When you compromise holiness in your relationships, the person at the root of the indecision is on a throne where God belongs. You have capped your faith. Your faith is now measurable beneath your attachment to that person. Forfeiting the relationship, or at minimum forfeiting the sinful behavior within the relationship, erases that ceiling. Then faith can expand into uncharted territory, encompassing friendships and romances where it never has before. God's grace can descend into your relationships and usher them toward eternal bonds.

The need or want of money can certainly limit faith, as well. If you decide to pursue or preserve money over using your possessions to be the hands and feet of Jesus, then you concede to measure your faith in earthly terms. This isn't a limit you want to maintain. Motivated by the selflessness that faith demands, force money into a subservient role. Through deliberate acts of sacrifice, money and faith can reverse roles. Remember, faith assumes the worth of that which you forsake to uphold it.

Have you permitted earthly matters to limit your faith? Does your faith back down when temptation rises? If you hesitate in your faith, recognize that you're standing on a boundary that your choices preserve. As long as the barrier is in place, your faith will be measured by it. Pray for wisdom to discern if anything is binding your faith. If so, then cross that line. Return your faith to a position where it cannot be measured on earth, but only in heaven where faith becomes sight.

Knowledge of My Ignorance

Do you go in circles like I do, reliving the same life lesson again and again, year after year, challenge after challenge, and disappointment after disappointment? It keeps coming back to this: will I ever accept the knowledge of my ignorance?

As a child, I would go outside with a spray bottle of water in one hand and a mason jar filled with two inches of rubbing alcohol in the other, along with a pair of tweezers. My family had a shrub with prickly leaves, which attracted wasps each spring when it bloomed. I would spray the wasps with water to wet their wings, then pluck them off the shrub with tweezers and douse them in the alcohol until I killed thirty or so before losing interest and moving on to another conquest. I have always been quite proud of my fearlessness when it comes to insects. And it is with sadness that I now confess the unfamiliar fear of getting stung—by life. Why am I so afraid of things I can't control? And knowing they're beyond my control, why can't I just let go?

I can't figure out why I can't surrender to what I *know* to be true. God's ways are not my ways (Isa. 55:8), and God's ways are past finding out (Rom. 11:33). I can quote these truths more easily than the United States Pledge of Allegiance, but I can't master surrendering to the knowledge of my ignorance. I *know* I am naive. I *know* my perspective is shortsighted. I *know* my days are fleeting and my home is in heaven. I *know* God always does right by me even when I can't perceive it. I *know* all these things, but my heart remains chronically and tragically human. I struggle to have faith in the unseen. Let's just call it what it is: I struggle in my faith. My knowing opposes my becoming.

And so, life lessons repeat over and over again. When I chase good things, I draw back empty-handed, like one of those crane machines that clutches a stuffed toy among the heap only to lose it just as the claw moves toward the drop slot. The fact that the toy appears securely in its clutches baits me to try again and again. I convince myself that next time, I'll finally receive the prize. But all to no avail. The truth is, the seemingly perfect fit can't hold because the reward is much too heavy for the claw. It's simple physics. And yet I keep trying to defy it until I'm broke, figuratively and literally.

It's the same with the knowledge of my ignorance. I will never figure out what God has yet to reveal. I can sweat and strain and concoct new ways to tilt and angle my grip, but I can never keep what God doesn't intend for me. Similarly, I'm not at risk of losing anything God intends for me to have.

How can I know so much and rest so little?

Without touching a Bible, my heart convicts me of the scripture that says, "It is hard for you to kick against the goads." It comes from Acts 26:14 (NIV) and refers to an ox that kicks, refusing to cooperate, when it's firmly harnessed to a plow. These words were spoken by the resurrected Jesus to an unsaved, unbelieving Saul before his conversion into the boldest gospel preacher ever. The statement translates to, "It's useless for you to fight against my will."

How long must the Lord repeatedly say the same thing to me?

With this acknowledgment, my thoughts wander to the man who beseeched the Lord to help him when he was seized with doubt.

Mark 9:22–24 (NIV) reads: "But **if you can do anything**, take pity on us and help us. '**If you can?**' said Jesus. '**Everything is possible for him who believes**.' Immediately, the boy's father exclaimed, '**I do believe; help me overcome my unbelief!**'"

I understand that God will remedy my unbelief if I cling to Him. God will create in me a new heart, just like He did for David when he cried out, "**Create in me a clean heart**, O God; and renew a right spirit within me" (Ps. 51:10, KJV). David became known as a "man after God's own heart" (Acts 13:22). That description is not to David's credit, but to God's, for God was responsible for creating the clean heart within David, which he came to be known by.

Out of necessity, this will be my prayer for as long as it takes: "Create in me a clean heart, O God."

Am I Helping or Hurting My Cause?

Early in our spiritual lives, we learn to bring our burdens to the Lord in prayer. He welcomes fellowship with us and is eager to reveal Himself at work in our world. The routine is simple: we have a need, we pray, we release the burden to God, and then trust Him to exercise power over the situation. He tells us to, "Be still, and know that I am God" (Ps. 46:10, NIV). If we allow Him room to move, then He does. This is typically a failsafe strategy to getting divine help with our difficulties. This strategy works ninety-nine percent of the time, because we're right to rely on the power of God for our daily sustenance. We're right to perceive ourselves as dust and our success as creditable to God's movement in us, but God will refuse to get involved if a subtle sin is sabotaging the scenario.

This happened to me. I had a desire; I cried, prayed, sought the Lord, and attempted to leave my burden in His hands many times. Nothing happened: no change of circumstance, no change of heart. Why wouldn't the cycle end? Was He ignoring me? Was I asking for something frivolous that was a waste of His time? Did He care about my emotional state at all, or was He planning to come through for me in the end, using the delay to bolster the success story?

My recurrent prayer was, "God, please heal my heart. Conform my heart to your will. Don't let me pine for something you don't will for me. Help me where I can't help myself." I would say, "Amen," and then run to the object of my affection as quickly as I could get there.

When a desire creates so much pain in you that receiving it could never compensate for the distress you go through while living without it, you eventually reach a point where you're willing to hear God's honest opinion on the matter. Several years into the same prayer, I continued my plea, "Lord, help me! I really want you to heal my heart! I don't want this unrequited desire to continue to wreck me!" It was as if God finally said,

"**Prove it.**"

The begging had gone on for years, but the first time I meant it, He responded. God revealed that He wouldn't lift a finger until I cooperated in action with the words I expressed in prayer. I hadn't really wanted Him to intervene if it wasn't going to get me the result I wanted.

Pray all you want, but if your actions are sabotaging your prayers, then your prayers will be as ineffective as mine were. He made it clear: I must show Him with my actions that I wanted Him to take away the heartache. When I executed everything in my control to stay away from the focus of my desire, God intervened, the desire died, and peace arrived.

Romans 7:18 reads, "For I know that **in me** (that is, **in my flesh**) **nothing good dwells**; for **to will is present with me**, but **how to perform** what is good **I do not find**" (NKJV).

This verse explains that even though we have the desire to be good and to do good, we can't carry out that good will independent of God's involvement. What value is an internal good when the external bad contradicts it? The internal good is overpowered by a sin nature, which is actively in control. Struggling is the best any of us can do without God's help. There are many victories only God can perform in us.

Trying to transform your own heart is like telling a small boy he is to develop a cure for cancer, so he locks himself in his room surrounded by science books in an attempt to develop a cure, refusing food, rest, and daylight so he can fully invest himself in the work, when what he really needs to be doing is eating, resting, and exercising so he can grow up and *then* develop a cure for cancer. Without allowing God to do His part of growing the child, the boy will never accomplish the goal, regardless of how good his intentions are. We must surrender, or no good work will get done at all.

The next time you feel like God is ignoring your prayers, ask yourself, "Have I done *everything* in my power to *prove* to God that I want His help? Are my actions in any way contradicting my prayers?" Your actions are the sacrifice God expects to see when you seek His help. God won't fight the enemy on your behalf when you're loading the enemy's guns. Take responsibility for your actions so that they testify to the sincerity of your prayers. God requires surrender. Then He prospers change.

Why Wait on God?

I spent a season of my life burdened for the salvation of one particular friend. Very few of our peers took spiritual matters as seriously as I did, so I felt that his eternal destiny was my responsibility. If I didn't reach him, who would? I exhausted every idea I had, trying to persuade him to accept Jesus as his Savior: direct evangelism, invitations to church events, letters, and phone calls. He listened to me, because I had earned his trust, but none of my attempts persuaded him. The following year, our friendship grew strained by distance and the infrequency of our communication. I felt as if I was losing him. My prayers reached a fevered pitch. I cried, "Lord, *please*, *please* tell me what else I can do! I don't know what else to do, and he isn't saved yet." My anxiety skyrocketed, and my ears yearned for suggestions, yet God replied with a statement I did not expect to hear. He said,

"**You are a stepping stone and not the bridge**."

This was the first time I ever heard God speak to me in my internal prayers. The message arrived as an absolute. Peace washed over me, instantly removing the burden I carried. If God loved my friend enough to put me in his life to do all that I had done, then God would love him enough to send someone else to complete the work. There was no risk in letting go, because God took responsibility for his salvation. I ceased all my labors except praying. A couple years later, I crossed paths with this friend, two hours away from our hometown, and he informed me that he had given his heart to Jesus.

Through this experience, I learned that burden-bearing is God's job and not mine, but relaxing under God's sovereign hand on a consistent basis was not as simple. The stronghold within me was multilayered, constructed of impatience, doubt, willfulness, and fear, each of which had to be dealt with individually.

I've never been good at waiting. As a matter of fact, the concept is contrary to every fiber of my being. We're only given a limited amount of time to spend in this life, and I have an overzealous aptitude to make the most of it.

My mother described a vision she had of the way the Lord protects each of her three children distinctly according to their needs. She saw my sister encircled by angels protecting her from 360 degrees. She saw my brother with an angel standing behind his shoulder whispering, "Turn to the right," or "Turn to the left." And me, well, she saw one huge angel with arms outstretched standing ahead of me blocking my path. She saw me run full force and slam into him only to be knocked on my rear, pick myself up, and repeat the process again. This is exactly how I operate. God always has to stop me from outrunning Him.

Ecclesiastes 3:1 states, "To everything there is a season, **a time to every purpose** under the heaven" (NKJV).

I desire purpose in my life, yet I've never respected the timing required to accomplish those purposes. However, the Word of God insists that *every* purpose has an appointment. Where there is no purpose, there is no appointment. Where there is purpose, there is an appointed time for it. I need to gain proper appreciation for the appointment in order for the purpose to prevail. To rush the timing jeopardizes the purpose. My shortcoming, at the core, is a lack of patience.

There is a quality about God's plan that I've always had a hard time accepting: His process may not sync up with my approach. I've always wanted to dive into serving Him rather than wait on any leading whatsoever. I'm a person who looks at her resources and sees that I have corn kernels in hand. It doesn't matter where I am or what God wants to do with those kernels. So what if I happen to be somewhere where conditions aren't favorable for growing corn? I won't wait. I will plant corn kernels in a rice field, and then I will fret because the corn doesn't grow.

James 1:4 reads, "But **<u>let</u> patience have her <u>perfect</u> work**, that ye may be **perfect** and **entire**, **wanting nothing**" (KJV).

The bottom line is:

Patience is critical for perfect works to come to pass.

Do I want to be perfect? Yes! Do I want to be full and complete? Yes! Do I want to lack nothing? Yes! Then I must allow patience to do her thing. I must not resist. I must not run ahead. I must hunger more to become a watcher of God's will rather than a manufacturer of it.

Smith begins *The Christian's Secret of a Happy Life* by distinguishing between God's work and man's work. She says we must enforce an active passivity on ourselves: "The clay is put into the potter's hands and then lies passive there, submitting itself to all the turnings and overturnings of the potter's hands upon it. The clay is not expected to do the potter's work, but only to yield itself up to His working. We put ourselves into the hands of the Lord, for Him to work in us all the good pleasure of His will, and then, by a continual exercise of faith, keep ourselves there."

It's my responsibility to confine myself to a permanent position of supplication and surrender. I must become *actively passive.* We are always commanded to do what comes least naturally to our flesh, so that the Spirit may prevail. This is the thing most unnatural to me.

Second Corinthians 12:12 says, "**Truly the <u>signs of an apostle</u>** were wrought among you **<u>in all patience</u>**, in **signs**, and **wonders**, and mighty **deeds**" (KJV).

Hmmm, "*Truly* the signs of an apostle" are visible through "all patience"? How is that for a non-negotiable definition of apostleship? I certainly applaud the signs, wonders, and mighty deeds definition of a true apostle. *Right on!* Yet there is also an "all patience" clause, which I find much harder to accept. By that standard, I fall short of being a true apostle.

And so, I come to the conclusion that I must hone my perception of divine appointments by praying for God to help me recognize them. To invite the perfection that patience produces, I must praise and appreciate patience as often as I can remember to do so in my prayers. Intentional thoughts and words often perpetuate change. I can use mine to prosper the goal of receiving opportunities rather than forcing them. These simple acts are not too much for me to practice so that I may evolve into a true apostle. After all, I am a stepping stone and not the bridge.

Lord, sharpen my mindset to watch you instead of living as if your role is to watch me. You are working where I can't see. You are moving where I can't go. You are carrying what I can't possibly lift. I am to participate where I am called to obey, but first, I need to learn to watch for you.

If I Don't Do It, Who Will?

In the search for significance, have you counted up your good deeds? How many jewels have you earned for your heavenly crown thus far? Do you think you have merited God's approval? There's so much pressure from the world to do enough and be enough that we assume the same terms apply to how God sees and values us, but nothing could be further from the truth. The Bible tells us to be workers of the Word and not only hearers, and God interprets our love for Him by our obedience to His commands. Yet we add to the simple instructions we are given. We heap undue responsibility on ourselves and strain beneath burdens God never intended us to carry. Your worry is important to Him, because you are important to Him. He is already involved in the situation you're worried about. He just wants you to *join* Him there, not try to handle it without Him.

He doesn't give us orders because we're the only ones who can get the job done, and if we fail, then His plan fails. When God calls us to love our neighbor as ourselves, to make disciples of all nations, and to give our second item of clothing to a brother in need, it's not because we alone possess the resources to meet a need that He Himself cannot satisfy. God's will doesn't revolve around *you* or no one. It revolves around *God* and anyone.

"The **God who <u>made the world</u>** and **<u>everything</u> in it** is the Lord of heaven and earth and does not live in temples built by human hands. And **he is not served by human hands**, **as if he needed anything**. Rather, **<u>he himself gives all</u>** men **life** and **breath** and **<u>everything</u> else**"… "For in him we live and move and have our being" (Acts 17:24–25, 28; NIV).

God needs nothing. He provides everything.

The Lord spent years teaching me that I can't out-will His will, and I can't force His hand to make the sequences of life progress any faster. Once, when I wanted to go on a foreign mission trip, He convicted me to pray for doors to open and to resist forcing it to happen. Months passed and no doors opened, despite my daily petitions. Temptation rose to impose my will where God had not opened doors. I fought hard to restrain myself from taking matters into my own hands, but that didn't prevent me from throwing a temper tantrum before God.

"God, why won't you put me to work?" I prayed, "I have this desire, this vacation time, and this money which is going unused! I've developed these skills, and they are profiting no one. I am fruitless when my hands are tied from action. I am waiting on you to open doors, but you are *underutilizing* me!"

When God had tolerated my temper tantrum long enough, He responded,

"Would you sit around counting someone else's money?"

With those words came the image of me reaching across a coffee table, digging into a friend's purse, and taking a peek at her checkbook balance when she left the room. *Oh, the horror!* I would *never* do that!

God showed me that my complaint of Him underutilizing me was a similar offense, for not one thing that I had thrown up to Him was rightfully mine. I own nothing. He owns all. I must perceive the resources He entrusts to my stewardship as His.

Who has laid a gift at God's feet, which was not first distributed out of God's own pocket? The wise men who visited baby Jesus brought gifts of gold, frankincense, and myrrh to Bethlehem, and yet those gifts were first deposited in the earth and inside trees by the Creator Himself. Everything originates in God.

Hebrews 11:3 tells us, "By faith we understand that **the worlds were framed <u>by the word of God</u>**, so that the **things**

which are seen <u>were not made</u> of things which are visible" (NKJV).

I pause to take inventory of the "things which are seen" around me: this table, my computer, that coffee shop sign, napkins, upholstered lounge chairs. What is the substance of each of these items? Are they not made from wood, metal, animal products, and chemicals derived from natural resources? Were they not designed by engineers with working brains that turn to dust within a hundred years' time? If God hadn't breathed His breath into men, who became engineers, then they would have been as brainless as claymation characters. God is the source of all finite things. There is nothing new under the sun (Eccles. 1:9).

How can you or I bring God something He didn't first envision, suggest to our minds, and place in our hands? Nor can we attribute credit to ourselves when spiritual fruit is produced from our labors. Man is the vehicle God uses to carry out many of His purposes, but a vehicle without a driver is no more than an immobile, deteriorating heap of metal.

"He is not served by human hands, as if he needed anything" (v. 25 above).

God is all-sufficient. The service of mans' hands isn't essential to accomplish the purposes of God. He could have spoken Noah's ark into creation instead of moving through Noah's hands to cut down trees and nail wooden boards together. In building the ark through manual labor over many years, Noah displayed obedience for all generations to witness. Noah's faith became legendary. God blessed Noah by involving Him in His plan to destroy and replenish the earth. Noah didn't bless God by surviving.

Our holy God demands that we make everything we have available to Him: our time, decisions, loyalty, priorities, and money. He wills to exert ownership over everything we have, not because He needs it, but because He owns it. God has every resource at His disposal to accomplish His purposes. As tools in the hands of God, should we fail Him at any time, then God will simply call upon another tool.

Before our good works graduate into a sense of personal pride, let's remember who we are before the Almighty. Elihu exhorts Job, in chapter 35, that we are fragments so small that nothing we do advantages or disadvantages God.

"Look up at the heavens and see; gaze at the clouds so high above you. **If you sin**, **how does that affect him** [God]? If your sins are many, **what does that do to him**? If you are righteous, **what do you give to him**, or **what does he receive from your hand**? Your wickedness affects only a man like yourself, and your righteousness only the sons of men [other people]" (Job 35:5–8, NIV).

"If your sins are many, what does that do to him?" (v. 6 above).

Have you thought of this? If your sins are many, if you persecute Christians like Saul, or start a world war like Hitler, what damage does that do to God? Does the flame of His fiery glory lose its spark? How could the depraved actions of corrupt creatures influence an incorruptible God? It's not possible to harm God. When God, in His mercy, extends grace for our salvation, who are we to argue that our sins are too great for His pardon?

"If you are righteous, what do you give to him?" (v. 7 above).

On the other hand, no man stands better or more righteous or more worthy than another before God. The breath in every life comes from the same source: God. When He looks upon us, it's because the love brimming from within turns His head toward His needy creation, not because we merit His attention or have so impressed Him that He looks upon us in praise.

> "Your wickedness only affects humans like yourself, and your righteousness only other people" (v. 8 above).

When you study the Bible, attend church, serve as a deacon, tend children in the nursery, and tithe faithfully, you benefit yourself and those in your sphere of influence. You don't contribute anything to God's grandeur. He is beyond being embellished by our works. When God makes demands of our character, it's for our own good, to conform us to the image of Christ, that we may one day share in His glory (Rom. 8:17). Christ's righteousness produced in us also blesses those we influence (Job 35:8). For this, we will be rewarded (1 Cor. 3:13–14). God makes demands to inspire us to act, not to compel us to comply.

Man's righteousness cannot bolster God's reputation. God's glory emanates from inside Himself, wholly self-sustained. No measure of sacrifice, service, or song can contribute one speck more to the glory of God. God is so great and so greatly to be praised that He *will be* praised for all eternity, by men (Rom. 14:11), angels (Rev. 5:11–12), animals (Rev. 5:13), mountains, and trees (Isa. 55:12). Entering His presence will be so overwhelming that His glory will elicit automatic praise from His creations.

The salvation of the world doesn't rest on the shoulders of Christians but on the shoulders of one man, Jesus, who is more than able to seek and save the lost. His power, purpose, and authority are at work and will not be hindered. Souls won are recorded to His tally sheet. It is our privilege to be swept up in His mission as joyful servants, oblivious to cares or counts.

Where Could This Lead?

I've never been a fan of the word "fate." It has always had a dirty, four-letter-word ring to it. During my early adulthood, reality seemed to strive so hard against me that it forced me to consider the possibility that God might be overriding some of the choices I made.

First, it must be said that God permits us to sin. The consequences of sin are written into the way the world operates. So that explains half of where our lives end up, but what about the healthy paths we pursue with vigor, which end up having shorter lives than a dud firecracker? What about the pursuits that die on the vine just because the path was not meant to be? Was fate at work?

In review of my life, it appears I spent my twenties wandering through a maze with high, rigid walls. I sprinted full steam ahead in one direction only to run straight into a dead end, turn, and start all over again aiming somewhere else. Sometimes, a path worked for a while and then ended, forcing me to turn right or left. Some paths diverged from others. My life seemed to be defined by one thing for a season, and then a year or two later, it was something completely different. In retrospect, I wonder why doors closed in some directions. Was a Master Controller at work?

As Christ-followers, we try to discern God's will as we make major life decisions. We apply scripture and welcome the advice of fellow believers. We pray and trust God's providence to keep us on the path He prefers. Later, we review the unfolding of events. Whether reality played out according to or contrary to our wishes at the time, it's usually apparent why things occurred as they did; God reveals His purpose and brought about the greatest good.

However, some events never make sense no matter how hard you try to analyze them. After many such dead ends, I couldn't avoid confronting the likelihood that God might be circumventing some of my decisions. I asked, "God, why did you deny me that good thing? You promise to work everything together for good, but I don't see it in this case." I reasoned that if He wasn't going to give me what I wanted, then the least He could do was tell me *why*. If I could require Him to tell me, and He answered, then He would prove to be within reach of my persuasion.

I repeated the accusation, camouflaged as a question, demanding to know what was going on, but God wouldn't repeat what His Word had already told me. Since God is good (Joel 2:13), and He works out all things together for my good (Rom. 8:28), then my irritation did not stem from God's lack of transparency but from my lack of submission. I knew that I was intensely frustrated, but I didn't perceive the subconscious tug-of-war taking place.

What's worse than a "no" answer to prayer?

Silence is worse.

What do you do if He's sought, yet silent?

What do you do if your prayer intensity is at an all-time high, and yet God remains distant?

Do you wait and try again later?

Do you rephrase the question?

I confess, my reaction was anger. Our relationship had been a steady diet of dialogue, and I wanted feedback. I got angry and stayed angry *for years*. I held out for God to answer me.

"Tell me why, God," I demanded. "Why didn't you nudge me this time? Why didn't you warn me? Why did you allow me to believe my request was in sync with your plan, only to allow reality to contradict it?" I rephrased the question a hundred different ways, but the dynamic was still the same. I refused to cooperate any further in our relationship until I got answers.

(nothing)

(nothing)

(nothing)

God can wait forever.

(nothing)

(nothing)

(nothing)

He can hold out longer than I can.

(nothing)

(nothing)

(nothing)

Eventually, my question changed.

"God, why won't you *answer* me!?"

When He spoke, He said,

"**Because I am God, and I don't owe you an answer**."

It was the conversation-ending, parental, "Because I said so" response. The discussion was over.

If we set up shop in the middle of our bitterness, God will allow it. He won't relieve a misery rooted in obstinacy. God can break down rigid attitudes, but there must be some thread of agreement between the two of you before He'll undertake the task. You must want to relinquish the thing that's destroying you before anything will change. Until you *want* God to change you, God *won't* change you.

Could I accept His final answer, or would this display of His authority put an end to my spiritual passion? Were my wants, needs, and demands the only substance behind my faith, or would my love for God stand even if He never blessed me with another thing, if He never answered another prayer, if I never felt His presence again?

Yes, it could. I would still choose to believe.

Until God confronted me with silence, I didn't know how much I loved Him. I didn't know the depth of my faith because the pursuit of blessing had always been between us. Now I believe because He is worthy of belief, not because He can bless me. The blessings He chooses for me may not suit my preferences. If I am a true disciple, then I will accept that portion and be just as passionate.

Even though Christians try their best to do everything right, the plain truth is:

A good thing that's not a God thing is a bad thing.

And we can't tell a good thing from a God thing. It's *always* possible that we're laboring toward a wrong result. There's no fault in this. When we do our best with the information we have, we can't be blamed for the outcome. And God isn't to blame for letting us learn the hard way. He aims to implant wisdom permanently in us, and experience is often the means He uses. Even our ignorance and our failures can honor Him if they result in a right relationship between the two of us. He doesn't have to explain Himself, and we don't need to understand, for God to be using every single scrap of our lives. Detours, which look like mistakes to us, can be intentional teaching moments along the path to His ultimate will.

God gives us evidence of this in the journey the Israelites took out of Egypt after four hundred years of captivity. "When Pharaoh let the people go, **God did not lead them** on the road through the Philistine country, **though that was shorter**. For God said, '**If they face war**, they might change their minds and **return to Egypt**.' So **God led the people around** by **the desert** road toward the Red Sea" (Exod. 13:17–18, NIV).

God led His chosen people the long way around the desert (the country of Jordan) instead of straight into Israel on the opposite side of the Red Sea. There were giants along the most direct route, and the threat of war could cause them to return to Egypt. God wanted them free from slavery, but freedom would cost them a longer period of hardship, because they didn't have the faith to stand up to giants. We too desire to reach a good destination, and God wants us to get there, but we may need to be protected from dangers we know nothing about.

It makes sense to flee obvious evils that draw us away from God, but it's hard to let go of things that appear to be good. What about the man who's willing to devote his life to foreign missions, but God doesn't provide a way? What about the woman who wants to have a child, but God closes her womb? Or the person willing to donate a kidney, but God declares, "*You are not your own, you were bought with a price. I have not given you permission to dismantle that which I created.*"

There are a lot of *good* things that God in His grand purposes denies, on occasion, not because they're sinful, but because they're out of sync with the unseen work He's orchestrating. He doesn't have to let us in on His plan. He has the right to guide our lives among good options just as much as He takes responsibility to steer us away from bad.

Take, for example, a jar of fresh peanut butter sitting on a shelf. In it lies the potential for sustenance and satisfaction. In its natural condition, it appears like a very good thing. Feed it to me, and I will enjoy it, but feed it to my brother, and it will send him into anaphylactic shock because of his life-threatening allergy to peanuts. That which appears perfectly good in the asking may be harmful in the receiving.

If we pursue something seemingly good because we can't see the bad in it, even after God has impressed on our conscience that we are to distance ourselves, then we're just as guilty of sin as if we had continued in a bad thing. If we ramp up our giving or our serving to make amends for obedience that we refuse in another area of our lives, then we insult God as much as if we had ignored Him entirely. Don't give God your left hand when He is asking for your right.

The closer we get to what we want, we find that the discipline we thought we could rely on can be threatened. Consider the temptations in a romantic relationship, for example. The excitement of pushing small boundaries makes you feel alive. Your self-image improves, and you like the new you, the desirable you, the "worthy" you. Attention and affection from another human being can be very good things, but the devil loves to corrupt a blessing. He suggests that it's enough to uphold the sexual boundaries we decide God *should* require rather than the standards He has actually set. We have no trouble justifying lenience because it feels good, but *feeling* good is not proof of *being* good. Good can be bad in disguise. I've heard that you can put a frog into a pot of water and slowly increase the temperature until the water is boiling, and the frog won't jump out. I think it's easy to behave like frogs when what we want is within our reach. We would be wise to ask for God's opinion on the things that matter to us, lest we be blind-sided.

Our desires are fertile ground for temptation, yet God promises us a plan of defense. People love to say, "God will not give you more than you can handle." This saying stems from 1 Corinthians 10:13; however, the verse doesn't declare a limit to suffering, but a limit to temptation. God does *not* promise maximum load limits on pain, grief, despair, or helplessness. Observe a mother receiving news that her child has died, a prisoner of war being tortured, or a drug addict undergoing detox, and you'll see someone enduring more than their human strength can bear. A circumstance that exceeds our ability to manage is the definition of a crisis. Our world is full of them. Crises are often used to draw out our dependency on God. However, God *does* promise that He will not allow more temptation than we can bear.

"No **temptation** has overtaken you **except such as is common** to man; but God is faithful, who **will not allow you to be tempted beyond what you are able,** but with the temptation **will also make the way of escape**, that you may be able to bear it" (1 Cor. 10:13, NKJV).

Notice the word used to weigh your present degree of temptation: it says you're not facing anything which is not "common." Your case is not special, extreme, or permissible. You don't get a free pass to sin just because temptation presses on you with a heavy hand. God's plan A is that you resist sin.

James 1:12 says, "**Blessed** is the man that **endures** temptation: for **when he is tried**, he shall receive the **crown of life**, which the Lord has promised **to them that love him**" (KJV).

God wills to reward those who resist temptation with a crown of life. When I read "crown," I think of royalty, and when I read "life," I think of eternity. To me, this sounds like royalty for eternity in exchange for successfully weathering run-of-the-mill, everyday temptations. God doesn't remove temptation entirely because it's part of His grand incentive package.

What about severe cases when our need outweighs our logic, and our willpower under performs? Sometimes, we are just too weak, and sin is just too accessible. The Creator is never at a loss for options. God's plan B is that you escape sin. "...But with the temptation **will also make the way of escape**, that you may be able to bear it" (v. 13 above).

In the sin arena, escaping is considered a success in God's eyes. Sometimes, it's the only lifeline we have left. Temptation is the ultimate "fight or flight" scenario: fight if you can resist it; flee if you cannot.

Dodging obvious sin is usually easier than resisting the urge to overindulge in a good thing. A love of sports, family, your job, physical fitness—anything can rival God's place as your ultimate love. None of these things are bad in themselves, but try to surrender one at God's request, and you'll discover what reigns as your highest priority. It's always an effort to keep what you love from becoming an idol. The line between a blessing and an idol is blurred. When we've crossed that line, or are about to cross that line, God puts His foot down, and His foot is heavy! If you've asked Jesus to be the Lord of your life, what might seem like fate treating you unfairly could be your loving heavenly Father establishing a barricade to protect you.

If you rush a baby to be born before it's fully mature because you love it so much that you just can't wait to meet it, then you risk permanently damaging God's fragile project. Likewise, an overeager farmer who reaps his fields prematurely will jeopardize the entire harvest. God knows when our flesh just can't handle the temptation. Under such circumstances, He may call time-out as a safeguard. For the Israelites, it looked like forty years of wandering in the desert. Those forty years saved future generations from slavery in Egypt. In your life, God's intervention may also feel like exile. Exile can be an instrument of mercy, one way God provides an escape from irresistible temptation.

How Deep Are You Today?

"How deep are you today?" is the question I use to gauge how I'm feeling day by day. I correlate the power of depression with the ocean, because depression is pressure, and most people can comprehend the pressure of the ocean. In the ocean, you experience a power stronger than yourself pressing you down, working against you. You are suspicious of it. It's unpredictable and may become unmanageable at any moment. Fear and vulnerability rise, the deeper you go. You can't stop pushing back or you'll be swept away by the current. You give all that you have in effort against it, until you have nothing left to give.

My usual responses are:

a) "Today, I'm barely treading water. Only my face is above the surface."

b) "Today, I'm waist deep. I'm going to have to give it all I've got."

c) "Today, the water is to my knees. I'm okay."

d) "Today is a good day. There's hardly any water at all."

Depression presses on your physical strength. Your stamina is shot. Your grip strength is nonexistent to the point that even your handwriting suffers. Your neck can't support the weight of your head, so you must prop it up most of the time. Breathing is hard work, like when wearing the lead apron at the dentist's office during x-rays. Sometimes, I hold my breath so

I don't have to breathe as often. My limbs always feel weighted down and difficult to lift, like they do after donating blood. These common physical feelings are why I'm tired all the time. I function on caffeine and prayer. I need a lot of sleep because my waking hours are steadily exhausting, no matter how much or how little effort I exert.

A depressed person's desire to function is choked by fatigue. You're defeated physically, emotionally, and mentally (and in that order, for me). At its worst, you can feel each heartbeat thump against your chest wall. These symptomatic sensations aren't imagined; they're as real as a headache or nausea. You can't see the sickness, but you can feel it. It waxes and wanes in intensity but never disappears.

Could I Be the Problem?

Human beings are really good at fixating on something specific and chasing it nonstop for years, blocking out discouraging feedback and refusing to face reality. I once read a quote on a decorative wall plaque in Las Vegas that described me perfectly. It said, "I Refuse to Let Reality Cloud My Fantasies." I thought it was so clever that I came home and painted this quote on a tile trivet.

We refuse to accept the signs pointing out our misdirection because we take exceptional care to select the perfect desire for our long-term fixation. And we pick something good—something really good—something obvious to the eyes of everyone that our lives would be marked as "blessed." Empowered by righteous ideals, we interpret scripture to our favor and dismiss the historical hardship that often accompanied the fulfillment of God's promises.

It's possible to establish your life in pursuit of something valuable only to find years down the road that you were misguided and misappropriated all your energies. I did this and suffered a good deal because of it. Had I been more receptive to an alternative other than my own will, I would have accepted the reality God dealt me sooner and learned a lot faster.

The following verses were the crux of my great misinterpretation.

Philippians 2:13 says, "For it is **God** who **works in you to will** and **to act** according to his good purpose" (NIV).

What a beautiful verse! God is the source who deliberately transforms our will and moves within us to carry out deeds according to His plans. How awesome is it to consider that God distributes yearning and not solely the fulfillment of that yearning?

When paired with Psalm 37:4, my interpretation grew even more slanted. It states, "**Delight** yourself also **in the Lord**, and **He shall give you** the **desires of your heart**" (NKJV).

To the best of my reasoning, I determined that if I looked into my heart to see what upright desires were there, then I could credit God for placing them there and count on His favor to bring them to pass. I executed this philosophy with uncompromising fervency. Aiming to cooperate with His Word and invest in the outcome of future events, I kept my fixations in check with two distinct tests.

Test number 1: Does my desire pass the Philippians 4:8 test? Is it true, honest, just, pure, lovely, of good report, virtuous, or praiseworthy (KJV)? If it passed this test, then I would move on to test number 2.

Test number 2: Does it violate any of God's written commands? I know God's Word, and I know what lifestyle choices are off limits to me. It isn't difficult to construct life pursuits within the confines of His precepts. I know better than to presume God will sanction any sin.

So, if my desire passed tests number 1 and number 2, then I would assign God the credit for planting the desire in my heart, label that insistence "faith," and pursue the stated goal with gusto. I thought this was the recipe I could use to guarantee that my wishes would be granted. Once I labeled my desire *faith*, I wouldn't compromise an ounce of my dream for fear of sabotaging it with doubt.

At every turn, reality disputed my philosophy, but I held firm. I reasoned to myself, "God *must* be instilling me with this desire in my heart. My motives are good, the quest is biblically appropriate, and I desire a God-glorifying result; therefore, I give credit to God for the origination of this dream. And since He placed it there, then He *must* see it through to completion. His power *must* bring it to pass."

Good intentions gave birth to an ugly sense of entitlement. I tested this hypothesis over and over and reaped little success in support of it. My selection of a college major passed tests number 1 and number 2, as did my first career in social work, subsequent jobs, and relationships I entertained. Most of my decisions passed the two tests of virtue, but the results of these attempts amounted to no more than failed pursuits and wasted effort.

If you can relate to my experience, then you know that it feels as if some definable "good thing" exists only for others but is off limits for you. The fantasy turns into a nightmare because the absence of something singularly dwelt upon becomes an empty, stinging hole.

What do you do?

Do you wake up every morning at the bottom of the pit to stare at the walls and complain that fate is keeping you down?

Do you try to move past it, only to find that the void has its own gravitational pull?

Do you broaden your mental timeline to expand the possibility of the dream coming true?

When one tactic doesn't solve the problem, another rises up and sustains you for a while. I sat in the bottom of that hole for years taking turns between these alternatives.

After twenty years of working to further God's kingdom and paying my dues in the ring of morality, I felt entitled to a return on my investment. I believed that God is the giver of all good things, just as scripture teaches us. I knew only God could grant my heart's desires; therefore, I agreed to play by His rules. Yes, I wanted to obey God because I loved Him and was indebted to the cost of the cross, but the flesh half of me wasn't serving or loving or sacrificing without anticipation of reward. By my definition, that meant simple pleasures, reasonable happiness, safety, security, provision, and good health. I was convinced that since He loved me enough to die for me, why wouldn't His perfect will for my life be comfortable and painless?

Until we are denied our desires, we don't know how entrenched we are in self-will. As reality played out, neither my dreams nor my backup plans transpired as I expected. A godly husband was not provided, so there were no children, either, and my only dog got cancer. A stable, stimulating job didn't come without trying and failing eight times, returning to college for a second go-round, and forfeiting years of leisure for hard work, followed by an abrupt season of unemployment. When my best friend was widowed at thirty-one years old and literally lost my figurative dream, I could no longer deny that what I had committed my whole adult life to acquire could be lost as soon as it was attained.

I had always believed marriage would be the turning point at which my life would start. But then, I saw clearly that there was no security in acquiring a husband. The heartbreak I felt having never experienced reciprocal love could be magnified having lost husband, father, home, and future. At least in my heartbreak, I had lost none of those things. Where was escape from the pain in any direction?

My coping skills failed as I reached the conclusion: What have I been doing all this for? Everything I'm living to attain is worthless. What do I have if I ever get the things I'm working and waiting for? And if I ever do get them, I can lose them in a second. Apparently, you have changed the rules on me, God. I don't want to play this game your way anymore.

I locked myself away in my own little hovel and surrendered to my despair. All the while, God remained ever patient, waiting on me to return to a place of desiring Him again. He never left me, although I did everything to shut Him out. He didn't return my treatment of Him with the banishment I deserved. In a gracious gesture of love, He extended a lifeline to me so that I could see the precarious state of my heart and come to understand the foolishness of my ways.

He ministered to my heart with this understanding: *I have not answered your prayers because you have asked for things I reserve only for heaven. You have anticipated a husband who can-*

not die, a dog that cannot get sick, and a job you cannot lose. I have made you no promises at all, because I refuse to make promises I don't intend to keep. Until you understand that earth possesses only temporary blessings, then you are always praying, believing, and living outside of my will, and I cannot meet your requests. I will not grant kingdom promises on earth. That is what heaven is for.

If God performed according to my expectations, then what difference would there be between heaven and earth? If my definition of security had always been broken and would always be broken, why keep clinging to it? Navigating the shards of my shattered dreams was no longer creating only surface scratches. The only way to stop the bleeding was to gather up the pieces and toss them out.

Jeremiah 2:13 portrays this experience through metaphor: "My people have committed **two sins**: **<u>They have forsaken me</u>**, the spring of living water, and have **<u>dug their own cisterns</u>**, broken cisterns that cannot hold water" (NIV).

Yes, I had dug my own cistern. I had drawn a map of an imaginary world and committed my life to the hunt for it. *How foolish!* The book of Jeremiah identifies the people who are susceptible to this foolishness; it calls them "my people," God's people. People just like me. He says I have committed two sins.

I had dug my own cistern. I formulated my own life plan. I projected the life I deemed ideal and invested all my energies in it. I did this for a long time, and it was sinful because I disdained all other options, including His design, the life that I presently know. All those failed attempts were intended to show me that my plan was of my own unskilled construction. It never held water. It couldn't; it was flawed. A broken cistern isn't worth living for.

I had forsaken the spring of living water. I vetoed that God had rights to my future. He is the spring of living water; therefore, His path is a life-yielding one. There's a lot of life out there to invest in that is beautiful, eternal, and significant. It might not be a child who looks like me. It might not be a husband's last name to take. But it sure is beautiful.

I had been living my life for a reality that didn't exist, while the reality that did exist was pretty darn good. It was as if God had carried me to the top of the Swiss Alps to show me the view, yet I refused to look up, insistent on staring at the weeds beneath my feet. Who can compare the view from a mountaintop to the view overlooking the ocean? Forgive me, Lord, for holding in contempt the view where you have placed me because it isn't the view I wanted to see.

There's one thing on earth I can celebrate today that I won't lose tomorrow: God is on His throne keeping all things aligned with His plan. Although there's a lot left unknown when fixating on the spring of living water, the change of vision comes with a promise, the promise of life (living water) and abundance (the spring). I'll take life and abundance in whatever package it comes over broken glass.

The time had come to follow through with relinquishing my dreams to God for good.

I was working my way through letting go of my fixations when I bought my first house in April 2010. My lovely one-story ranch came with some very unlovely eight-foot shrubs stretched along the fence-line. These things were massive, mature, healthy, and dark green with appendages pointing out in every direction. And there were twelve of them. They reminded me of the sea monsters from the 1970s Sid and Marty Krofft children's show, *Sigmund and the Sea Monsters*.

My neighbors said these beastlike shrubs hadn't been trimmed in fourteen years. I decided one day I had had enough of Sigmund and his friends, so I got out the ladder and the electric hedge trimmer and went to work. It felt good hacking away at Sigmund. Not only did Sigmund need a haircut, but he needed a diet, too. I took about two feet off the top and at least a foot off the front all the way down the perimeter of my backyard, using a handsaw when the branches were too thick for the clippers. When the work was done, I was pretty satisfied with myself. I had tackled a job only Edward Scissorhands could contend with and turned those sea monsters into well-behaved shrubs again.

I admired my work for several days and imagined how the undergrowth enjoyed the sun exposure after so many years. "Any day now, I'll start seeing new growth sprouting out in brilliant neon green," I thought. But that didn't happen. The previously dark green limbs grew brown and brittle. What? Dying? Why would it die just because I trimmed it back? I went outside to investigate.

Wouldn't you know, I hadn't done such good a job of shaking and raking out all of the clippings. Loose leaves and cut branches were still clinging to the live tree, giving the whole shrub the appearance that it was dying. It was hard work reaching in and pulling out all the dead branches. Then it became clear to me how I had been handling the task of relinquishing my heart's desire.

"Cut it off, Lord, but let me keep it."

I had always prayed, "Have thine own way, Lord," but still held a tight grip on my dreams. To drive home this understanding, my mind wandered to what relinquishment may look like for others who struggle with it:

"Absolve my debt, but I'll keep my spending habits."

"Clean up my criminal record, but
I'll keep my social contacts."

"Restore my marriage, but I'll keep my wandering eye."

"Put an end to our family feud, but don't touch my attitude."

"Give me forgiveness, but I'll keep the guilt."

Partially surrendering to God is like trimming back a shrub but leaving all the dead branches intact. You may have accepted Christ at some point. You may hold a ticket to eternal life and admittance to heaven, and your roots may be very much alive, but you look and feel as dead as those who have not, if you're still identifying yourself by the dead stuff. It wouldn't be smart of me to think my shrubs would look great if I leave the debris where it was cut off, so why do I apply that logic to my life? Why ask God for His best and then hold back from surrendering to Him?

If the examples listed above are some of the only remaining pleasures you have to keep on living, then I don't want to paint them as something you can choose to relinquish simply by seeing them with new clarity. If anything in your life is too vital for you to relinquish that you cannot do so without wanting to end your life, then please seek medical treatment so that doctors can help bring your brain chemistry into balance. Before adequate medication, there was an intuitive force field that I sensed between myself and the rest of the world, similar to looking through the fine metal mesh of a window screen. Something perceivable had cut me off. Everything I thought, every task I performed, and every conversation I had was conducted from behind this invisible partition. I couldn't have described it this way until medication removed it, and the change was startling. I think this perception is what leads depressives to believe that the world wouldn't miss us if we were no longer in it, because we have a keen sense that we're disconnected from the world. If you feel this way and talk of relinquishment feels threatening, please seek professional medical care. There *is* help. You can heal to the point that relinquishment of harmful strongholds becomes feasible.

Only in retrospect have I been able to perceive my flawed interpretation of the scriptures that were such stumbling blocks for me. In regard to Philippians 2:13, the scripture says that God works in us to will and to act in order to fulfill His good purpose. It says *His* good purpose, not mine. I am capable of constructing my own good initiatives independent of anything God has instilled in me. Just because I have a biblically appropriate desire doesn't mean God put it there. When God does plant a desire in me, it will be consistent with scripture, but the latter doesn't obligate the former. I had that backward.

The ability to interpret this verse accurately lies in discerning what *God's* good purposes for me are. What career, volunteer services, ministry efforts, mission trips, family, or lack of a family does He will for me? I don't have the answers for you or for myself. His ways are not my ways, nor are His thoughts my thoughts, so my logic can't calculate what He's up to. There is no formula. Not knowing compels me to have faith that He will provide *His* will for me, whatever that may be. I can only seek Him, listen, and follow as He reveals new things on a daily basis. Reality is a pretty good indicator of God's sovereign will. He doesn't thwart His children when they're attending to His agenda. In order to listen, I must remain quiet, yet responsive. In order to follow, my leader must be moving. I should not exert my own creative efforts when I get restless; I must wait on the Good Shepherd. I must be patient, and then I must be obedient, no more, nor less.

In regard to Psalm 37:4, the requirement of God instilling and fulfilling desires hinges on delighting in Him. Have I ever authentically delighted in Him alone, barring any ulterior motive? Is my concept of delighting in Him a mediocre, watered-down version that doesn't measure up to His purified concept of delight? I imagine that God has a refined measurement of delight, which I should not assume I have ever reached. I must strive to delight in Him to the best that I can understand it, and let Him alone judge when I meet that standard. To delight in Him, I must focus on who He is, what He has done, what He will do, and love Him with all of my heart.

What Does God Desire from His Creations?

I sit at home in my pajamas this evening, having skipped church today and not feeling the least bit guilty about it. I assess the stillness of this house, the quiet; there is nothing but the sound of the dryer running and the birds chirping outside after a long silence due to an afternoon rain. The late day sun is just breaking through the clouds for the first time, warming my cheek through the window. This is the beginning of adoration. Adoration begins where everything else ends. No agenda. No noise. No duty. No distraction. Just stillness. Alone with God.

For a while now, I've been restraining my Type A personality to sit and wait on God. I want to see what He will do if I let go of the reigns. My goal has been to force my Martha personality to sit still beside Mary for a while. What will God do when I stop busying and barking? What will He say when He has my full attention?

I'm still waiting on a great revelation, some booming call I've been too self-consumed to receive. Like the prayer of Jabez (1 Chron. 4:10), I'm waiting for God to expand my territory. So far, my territory is still small and unimpressive. When the temptation rises to forsake this waiting, I remind myself that it truly is God's job to make the most of me, my life, and the resources He has placed at my disposal. I'm good at making plans, but what would He prefer to do with all of this? At last, I've relegated myself to the watchtower and refuse to move without His permission.

Remembering the scene between Mary, Martha, and Jesus convicts me that I haven't yet evolved to interact with my Lord the way Mary did. As I sit at His feet, I'm reminded just how much it pleases Him to be adored.

Luke 10:38–42 says, "As Jesus and his disciples were on their way, he came to a village where a woman named Martha opened her home to him. She had a sister called Mary, **who sat at the Lord's feet listening to what he said**. But Martha was **distracted** by all the preparations that had to be made. She came to him and asked, 'Lord, don't you care that my sister has left me to do the work by myself? Tell her to help me!' 'Martha, Martha,' the Lord answered, 'you are **worried and upset about many things**, but only **one thing is needed**. Mary has chosen what is **better**, and it will not be taken away from her'" (NIV).

Have you prioritized action over adoration? I have.

Action comes naturally to me. I assumed adoration could be inferred from my actions. Yet Jesus says only one of the two is "needed." One of the two is "better." According to Bible, service is encouraged, advised, and appreciated, but it isn't imperative. Only adoration is imperative. Adoration isn't to be inferred through acts of service but prized above service, regardless of whether service ever catches up. Serving is leagues behind adoration in warming the heart of God. In my human zest for efficiency, how can I continue to dismiss adoration by devoting all of my energy and emotion to service? This has been my track record.

We serve God and man because Luke 10:27 says, "**Love the Lord** your God with **all your heart** and with all your **soul** and with all your **strength** and with all your **mind**"; and "**Love your neighbor as yourself**" (NIV).

Yes, this is exactly why we feel impassioned as well as obligated to take action. This is why I don't enjoy inactivity, sitting and waiting, even if what I'm waiting on is God's leading. I'm eager to act.

In the same chapter where Jesus lays out the two greatest commandments, loving God and loving man, He follows that instruction with the scene where He tells Martha that her service to Him is not "needed." Why is this? Could this be because her work lacked love? Jesus identified worry and stress as her motivations.

Maybe Jesus tells us work isn't needed to love God and love man because He sees our hearts and knows how infrequently our actions are motivated by love. Maybe the motive behind our service isn't love but a sense of accomplishment or a self-esteem boost. Maybe our motive is a flight from boredom or toward social affiliation. Maybe we fill our schedules so full of service that we squeeze all the adoration out of them.

Can you see yourself taking someone a home-cooked meal when they lose a loved one or have a baby, and then later you make an ugly comment about them? Can you see yourself giving someone's child a ride home from school, and yet you judge them for their lifestyle choices? Where is love in your act of service?

I am capable of generous actions that appear selfless but are motivated by my quest for self-worth. Jesus wants to convince me that my worth isn't measured by my actions. My value is measured by the price He paid for me. Do I believe Him? Will I stay seated at His feet long enough to discover my self-worth in His gaze? Can I crucify my gnawing urge to act long enough to encounter true adoration?

When I get restless in inactivity, I replace my negative thoughts with this one:

A day spent praising God is not a day wasted.

What does loving the Lord your God with all your heart look like? Must it look like a preacher behind a pulpit in a three-piece suit with shiny cuff links or a missionary dressed in the traditional clothing of the country where she serves? No. Sometimes, it looks like Mary, sitting at Jesus's feet soaking up every second of His presence, having no other priority, not saying a word, not asking questions or making petitions, just listening and adoring.

What does loving your neighbor as yourself look like? Must it look like the man outside mowing his neighbors' yard while they're on vacation or the woman shopping for school supplies to donate to the underprivileged? Sometimes, it looks like that. But it also looks like the elderly gentleman on his knees in private grief over his prayer list, loving uninterrupted.

Oh, how misled we are by what our eyes see. God sees the heart where love lives. To answer the question, "What does God desire from His creations?" we need look no further than creatures who abide in Him.

"I [Jesus] am the vine; you are the branches. **If a man remains in me** and I in him, he will bear much fruit; **apart from me you can do nothing**" (John 15:5, NIV).

It's a simple scenario, yet a complicated practice, to abide in the Lord. I don't know of any tomato plants that have gone rogue and yielded bananas; it's a ridiculous image. And yet we strain so hard to do just that: to depart from the vine, which produced us and possesses all the nutrients we need to prosper in the identity we were designed to fulfill. God's will for us is as stress-free as the requirement of abiding in Him, remaining actively passive, hungering for everything the vine wants to pump into us in an attitude of receptivity.

The following quotes pieced together from *The Practice of the Presence of God,* by Brother Lawrence, paint a picture of how action can crowd out adoration. I must strive to become a worshipper first above any call to action.

> "It is, however, necessary to put our whole trust in God, laying aside all other cares, and even some particular forms of devotion, though very good in themselves, yet such as one often engages in unreasonably, because these devotions are only means to attain to the end."

"I have looked on God as the Goal and End of all the thoughts and affections of the soul."

"That the end we ought to propose to ourselves is to become, in this life, the most perfect worshippers of God we can possibly be, as we hope to be through all eternity."

What Will I Gain?

I stepped up to the coffee shop counter and placed my standard order, a medium mocha made with nonfat milk and no whipped cream. After handing over my credit card, I noticed the barista's eyes shift away from mine high above my head to the customer behind me. I followed her eyes to see who had captured her attention. Immediately, I recognized the six-foot-five, perfectly built, dark-skinned man with a gleaming white smile. His clothing was understated: a plain black tank top, shiny black gym shorts, a baseball cap worn backwards, and flip-flops. I couldn't help disclosing that I recognized him.

"You are ______," I said aloud to him, momentarily star struck but maintaining my composure.

"Yes," he replied, broadening his super white smile just for me.

"It's nice to see you," I said, returning the smile.

"It's nice to see you, too," he followed politely.

I turned back toward the counter to retrieve my credit card and then slid down to the other end to wait for my coffee. After he placed his order, he propped himself on a barstool and directed his focus to the cell phone in his hands. I noticed two teenage girls at a nearby table eyeballing him, whispering, and jostling their phones. He had apparently attracted their attention, as well. His order was completed before mine. The girls motioned for him to come over to their table. He complied. They exchanged words. He flashed his pearly whites and nodded. The girls jumped from their chairs and enthusiastically followed him out the door. This struck me as unusual, so I asked a bystander who overheard their conversation what the girls had said.

"They asked if that was his decked-out BMW in the parking lot," the customer answered.

I shook my head. The girls following him outside made sense. With cellphones in hand and an exceptional interest in his car, I assumed they wanted close-up, possibly even interior, photos of the car to post to their social media newsfeeds. "How could their admiration be so misdirected?" I thought. "If they only knew who they were talking to, they would forget all about that car."

I grabbed my coffee and exited the coffee shop as the two giddy girls returned from the far corner of the lot, celebrating the photos they could now publicize.

"Don't you know who that was?" I asked them, eager to expose their oversight.

"No?" they questioned. Their faces went blank, and their eyes grew large.

"That was Cullen Jones, an Olympic gold-medal swimmer."

The girls let out a squeal and turned to each other with both hands on the sides of their faces and mouths open. They spun around abruptly to capture the significance of the moment, but the opportunity had passed. The striking black BMW edged its way out of the parking lot.

As I drove off, I replayed the sequence of events in my mind. How had the girls missed seeing what was so clear to me? How did Cullen feel knowing he had gone unrecognized while his car received the attention he deserved?

A sermon illustration presented itself. How often am I caught in a spiritual stalemate because some *thing* stands between me and God? When I pray, I rattle off a laundry list of requests, all the while disregarding the fact that I have God's undivided attention. I allow unresolved hurts and unanswered questions to weigh me down as God lingers nearby, desiring for me to fix my eyes on Him instead of on my problems. God convicted me that I treat Him just as the teens had treated Cullen.

He also consoled me that I am not the only person guilty of this. He reminded me of Jesus's encounter with the Samaritan woman at the well.

John 4:10 says, "Jesus answered her, '**If** you knew the **gift of God** and **who it is** that asks you for a drink, **you would have asked him** and he would have given you **living water**'" (NIV).

"If you knew." That is the biggest *if* I have ever heard.

Jesus knew of the woman's deep need for salvation. Her priorities were so singularly focused that she could only attend to water she could collect, drink, and enjoy. If she only knew she was talking to the Messiah, then she would have forgotten all about that water.

If she knew the gift of God, which is eternal life, then she would have forsaken the pattern of sin she had been perpetuating.

If those girls knew they were speaking to an Olympian, then they would have asked to be photographed with the man instead of with his car.

There's a reality occurring among us more real and more profound than our faculties comprehend. The Spirit of God is ever present. He is available. Are we seeing Him? Are we hearing Him? God wills to overhaul our natures, consume our thoughts, and empower our actions. Are we engaging Him? I don't want to keep going through the motions, ignoring the most important part of my day: my relationship with the V.I.P. In order for this to happen, I must harness my focus and grant the Lord my undivided attention.

The heart wants things it should want, things it shouldn't want, things it will attain, and things it will never gain, but it doesn't know the end result when it fixes itself on an object. The heart exposes itself to great risk in hope of great return. It's incredibly vulnerable.

God is generous to bless through visible, tangible gifts. Where I to list all the ways God has blessed me, my memory would fail me. I realize I can never account for all His goodness toward me, and yet in the quiet moments when the past seems distant, and the future is a fog, I'm held captive in the present where my fickle emotions reside.

"After these things the word of the Lord came unto Abram in a vision, saying, '**Fear not**, Abram: **I am** thy shield, and **thy exceeding great reward**'" (Gen. 15:1, KJV).

There's a fear embedded in every dreamer's private dreams. The Lord instructed Abram to "fear not" because he, too, experienced deep longing. We realize some things just won't materialize according to our design. In the midst of all the dreaming, the asking, the hoping, and anticipating, we yearn for security. God proclaims that He is our shield. He guarantees us a return on hope.

When needs go unmet, this may sound like a far-fetched grasp for relief, but if you'll consider the impact of such a reality, then you'll understand that a personal relationship with the living God can compensate for unfulfilled dreams and delayed answers to prayer.

God is our exceeding great reward.

To be *thy* exceeding great reward means that He is *mine* to claim. He has portioned Himself out just for me. He knows my name; He blots out my sins; He attends to my needs, and no one stands between us.

To be thy *exceeding* great reward means that however great a reward can be, He *exceeds* even that. He exceeds great!

To be thy exceeding *great* reward means that my portion of God's goodness is immense. Any comprehension of Him, as reserved for my benefit, is an underestimation.

To be thy exceeding great *reward* means that God is a valuable asset to me, greater than any prayer request, profit, or pleasure. He is the substance who brings depth to my life, bears my burdens, and brightens my path. He is a benefit in the here and now and in eternal life to come.

Psalm 34 testifies to the intimate relationship the Lord has with His children, an intimacy experienced through spiritual communion. The psalm praises God's listening ear, His watchful eye, His attentiveness to prayers, His closeness to the brokenhearted, and His promise of deliverance. It is one magnificent revelation after another about the God who responds personally to us.

Do you send out prayers like a boomerang motivated by a distinct, desired return? Are your prayers so focused on your wants and needs that you neglect the *who* you're praying to? When a desired return is the substance of prayer, then the prayer sender becomes the center.

What if we reverse this order? What if our primary intent becomes engaging God, the person on the other end of the line? We would discover that the relief we most need lies in experiencing His greatness, His holiness, His mercy, and His sovereignty. He is our exceeding great reward.

Roger Palms, author of *Enjoying the Closeness of God,* explains:

> God should be our focus, not the act of praying. Prayer doesn't have to "work." God answers prayers because he is God, not because we have to see answers... But we keep on going [to Him] in trust because he doesn't have to give us every answer. He is God; that is enough. He repeats in his Word that he is near. That's what we believe in—his promise, not our definition of results. When we are dealing with the omnipotent God, the word "result" is a puny word. God is much, much bigger than just what we want. God is big enough to want for us what he wants... When the focus is right, the reference is right, the obedience is right, and the relationship is right, we will no longer have to wonder, "Does prayer work?" or ask, "What if prayer doesn't

work?" For we will no longer be looking at prayer,
we will be looking at God.

When we determine that experiencing God is the greatest reward we can pursue, then all risk disintegrates. No matter how long or painful or desperate a prayer plea is, one constant among all outcomes is the cumulative revelation of God's character. Knowledge of the Holy is a progressive relationship. You never lose ground getting to know God. Understanding only grows.

Imagine God's message to you is this: *I heard your prayers. I received your wish list. Follow the star in the sky to Bethlehem. What you seek awaits you there.*

When you arrive at the stable, the baby Jesus is placed in your arms, and God's voice echoes,

"**I am your exceeding great reward**."

To My Eternal Valentine

Dear Valentine,

1. How could I ever overlook you? I am merely compacted dust disguised by a thin skin shell. I appear strong and capable, healthy and young, but it's an illusion. At the snap your fingers, I would disintegrate into a heap, and the wind would carry me away. As soon as this body floats into oblivion, my soul will return to the One who made me, and I will lay eyes on my place of origin at last, where my soul once was before I lost all recollection of that divine place and your divine face.

2. You ordained my existence for glory's sake. When my parents had no plan of me, you began your weaving. To their surprise, you ordained a life they had not considered. You wove and wove, designing my height, my voice, my eye color, and my body shape. You accented my face with dimples. You constructed these short fingers and deep ribs. Not a detail went unchosen. You are the artist and architect behind what the world now sees as me.

3. You have contrived a master plan and spread the script across my entire life—every hour building a day, every day prospering the plan, with monumental peaks approaching in the coming days and distant future. You capture my tears in a bottle. Nothing is wasted. Not a moment's rest, quiet, or heartache. Everything factors into your plan. Your perfect plan will not depart from me until you finish your work.

4. You are alive and well in my constant company. How can I neglect to acknowledge you every moment? How can I ponder thoughts of the future while you and the intricacies of your weaving in this very hour are more than I can comprehend with all my concentration?

5. You are not deaf. I have a direct line to your ear at the mere mention of your name. I will not fail to come to you in prayer, confident of the power emitted, striving to surrender to your sovereignty.

6. You make your commandments known. I will anticipate divine guidance and trust the simple instructions you deliver me. I will measure my days by how attentive I was to your leading.

7. You are not absent. Your presence commands my observation. Let me collapse here at your feet forever, for what strength does dust have to lift herself?

8. You never abandon me. I am never misunderstood. I am always someone's favorite. These truths grant me inexhaustible gratitude.

9. Everything I see with my eyes is in place at the command of your spoken word. It is only by your divine management that the hands of the clock click one more notch, that the sun's fuel has not yet exhausted, that gravity holds my feet to the surface of the earth so that I don't fly away.

10. I am aware that you have numbered my days. I'm appointed a day to die. This is no fearful thing. My last day will be as intentional as my first, and you did a fine

job that day without assistance. Your very breath causes my lungs to rise and fall.

11. How can created man not perceive how powerless he is? Man cannot even command his own heart to beat once more! *What helplessness!*

12. Oh, Lord, give me a constant awareness of your weaving. Allow me to perceive all encounters, every conversation, smile, and exchange, as an intentional fiber running precisely though your tapestry. I will take inventory of every moment. All things carry your signature. Nothing exists outside of you.

13. All that I have is yours. What have I to fear in this sea of unanswered prayers? Since the hour is yours, how can the burden of the hour not also be yours? My desires are yours; you accomplish exceedingly above all I can ask or think. My resources are yours; every good gift comes from you. Do with them what you will. Help me to release everything at the foot of the cross. You are a trustworthy steward of my worries. Nothing slips through your fingers. Keep my heart in this position, for I have wayward instincts.

14. You always care more, not less, than I do. You always have a greater agenda than mine, which is bringing glory to yourself, and you are far more creative with the details. Thank you for letting me hitch a ride, a speck of dust clinging to the hem of my Savior's garment.

15. In your magnificent handiwork, would you appoint a special place for me to shine? Would you anoint me with the spark of everlasting life so that I might always hint at heaven while I'm here? If it pleases you, make it so, Lord.

My Whole Heart Is Yours.

D. M. H.

Note: Numbered references at the end of the book indicate the scripture verses that inspired the reflections in each paragraph.

What Is God Up To?

If you can remember being a kid, you may recall having overused the retort, "But, Mom!" when you were asked to do your chores or your homework. Motivated by the same knee-jerk reactions, we give God a similar response. He could be telling you to serve on a committee at church, and you reply, "But, God! I work too hard all week as it is. I don't have time to volunteer." Or He might be asking you to commit to a consistent prayer time. "But, God! I'm just too tired." Or He may press upon you to increase your giving. "But, God! I don't have a dollar to spare," you say while sipping a $4.50 cappuccino. We need to be watchful for a "But, God!" attitude and curb it before it starts making decisions for us. A "But, God!" attitude is a cancer in the life of a Christian, but a "But God…" attitude is a lifesaver.

Hudson Taylor, a missionary God used to evangelize the country of China in the 1800s, lived a lot like the apostle Paul, forsaking everything in order to spread the gospel message. He lost his wife and three of his children to disease, his own health and safety were jeopardized, and riots and rebellion threatened his life, but nothing halted his calling. Taylor had a "But God…" perspective. His story is captured in the book, *Hudson Taylor's Spiritual Secret.*

After the death of his first child, an eight-year-old daughter, Taylor wrote, "Pray for us. At times, I seem almost overwhelmed, *but God* has said, 'I will never leave you or forsake you,' and 'My strength is made perfect in weakness.' So be it. I would not have her back again. She is far holier, far happier than she could have ever been here."

Regarding the most trying time of his life, Hudson said, "I strove for faith, but it would not come; I tried to exercise it, but in vain… Unbelief was I felt the damning sin of the world; yet I indulged in it… *but the Spirit of God* revealed to me the truth of our oneness with Jesus as I had never known before… It is a wonderful thing to be really one with a risen and exalted Savior, to be a member of Christ! Think what it involves. Can Christ be rich and I poor? Can your right hand be rich and your left hand poor? Or your head be well fed while your body starves?" Hudson's "But God…" perspective opened the door to his spiritual restoration, and his ministry flourished as a result.

When his wife and newborn baby died of cholera, Taylor wrote, "A few months ago my home was full, now silent and lonely… Is it real, and not a sorrowful dream, that those dearest to me lie beneath the cold sod? Ah, indeed it is true! *But* [God has promised] there is a homecoming awaiting me which no parting shall break into, no tears mar… Love gave the blow, which for a while makes the desert more dreary, but heaven more homelike. [Jesus said] 'I go to prepare a place for you'; and is not part of the preparation peopling it with those we love?" Hudson's "But God…" mindset kept his eyes focused on heaven.

Please notice that hardship does not fall more softly on the Christian than on the non-Christian, but God lifts the weight of our burdens if we allow Him, which makes the impossible task of continuing with life possible. Complete reliance on God enables Him to prove Himself as the Promise-Keeper, Comforter, and Master Sustainer. We won't experience that God inhabits these qualities unless we clear the stage for Him to display them.

In 1956, Jim Elliot, along with four other missionaries, was speared to death by a tribe of Ecuadorian natives they were attempting to befriend. Jim was survived by his wife, Elisabeth, and a ten-month-old daughter, who remained in Ecuador another two years and finally succeeded in ministering to Jim's killers. In *Secure in the Everlasting Arms*, Elisabeth wrote, "Jesus did not promise physical safety for His disciples. He did not expect it for Himself… Satan was given permission for a while. Satan is allowed to do appalling things today, too. For a while… But in the meantime, the world must be shown. There has to be living proof that some men and women today actually love God and will do exactly what He says."

God softly and tenderly wants us to open our hearts and minds to the "But God…" reality occurring in our midst. Life isn't only what we can see and feel. Anything He plants, He perfects, and the culmination of that perfection is resurrection.

"Jesus replied, 'The hour has come for the Son of Man to be glorified. I tell you the truth, **unless** a kernel of wheat **falls to the ground and dies**, it remains only a single seed. But **if it dies**, **it produces many seeds**" (John 12:23–24, NIV).

Death reeks of loss, pain, and sadness, but who among us grieves for the apple seed, which falls into the soil and dies? None of us do, because the result of that sacrifice produces measureless pleasures. The fruit is worth more than the seed. Can we not look at death and loss on this earth in a similar way?

What happens when the lumber industry clears a plot of land for the trees? Do the trees not replenish themselves? And what happens when a hard winter comes, stripping the earth to barrenness and dryness? Does spring not arrive like clockwork a few months later? What happens when you cut your hair or burn your skin? Does it not return to you after a period of slow or painful waiting? How can we human beings not recognize, through all the signs and wonders we see, some occurring even in our own bodies, that a huge part of God's personality is resurrection? How can we experience so much resurrection on a consistent basis and yet underestimate the most dramatic resurrection to come?

"And **he** [Jesus] is the head of the body, the church: who **is the beginning**, the **firstborn from the dead**; that in all things he might have the preeminence" (Col. 1:18, KJV).

Firstborn from the dead.

"Firstborn" indicates that more will follow. Jesus resurrected in the flesh from the grave after defeating death with the purpose of being the *first* of *many*.

Sin became real the day Adam defied God's warning not to eat from the tree of the knowledge of good and evil (Gen. 2:16–17). Upon Adam and Eve's decision to defy God, sin and its consequences flooded human nature, and Adam and Eve began to age, the process that leads to death. Romans 6:23 eloquently states, "For the **wages of sin is death**; but the **gift** of God is **eternal life through Jesus Christ our Lord**" (KJV).

If the wages of sin is death—if death only exists where sin exists—what should happen to a man who has never sinned when He is executed?

"But God raised him [Jesus] from the dead, freeing him from the agony of death, because **it was impossible for death to keep its hold on him**" (Acts 2:24, NIV).

Without sin, Jesus had no debt of His own to pay, no penalties accrued; therefore, death could not keep Him in the grave. The Lord exercised His mighty power, and Jesus's body rebounded. If anything testifies to the sinlessness of Christ, it is the fact that His physical body resurrected in addition to His Spirit. Death had no authority over Jesus's body.

First Corinthians 13:5 states that love keeps no record of wrongs. Because a list of our sins stood against us, proving that we deserved damnation, Love allowed Himself to be nailed to a cross. The blood Jesus shed was so deep red that it thoroughly painted over the record of our wrongs. Jesus's crucifixion erased the report.

"**Blotting out the handwriting** of **ordinances that was against us**, which was contrary to us, and **[Jesus] took it** out of the way, **nailing it to his cross**" (Col. 2:14, KJV).

Therefore, what can we expect to happen to *our* natural bodies if our sins are blotted out, taken out of the way, and nailed to the cross?

Jesus was the first among us to rise from the dead, and by the way He went, we, too, shall go. He died to bar our descent into hell and then resurrected to grant us access to heaven. It's the Holy Spirit, who resided in Jesus and is transferable to us, who will unite all those in God's family.

"But **if the Spirit** of him **that raised up Jesus** from the dead **dwell in you**, he that raised up Christ from the dead **shall also quicken your mortal bodies** by his Spirit that dwells in you" (Rom. 8:11, KJV).

How marvelous it is to envision the day of resurrection! I can't think of anything more uplifting. With so many difficult days to face, sometimes the promise of resurrection is the only thing that sustains. We need that precious assurance. Praise Jesus; He has secured it for us.

I taught Sunday school at our local jail for a couple of years. The prayer request of a student in my class one Sunday was, "Pray that God would select me, that I would be found among His selection."

Coming from a group of women who prayed unanimously for speedy court dates, a merciful judge, and mild sentences, one can understand why Jesus pardoning their sin wasn't easy to believe. Hearing this misconception about God's mercy triggered a detour of our lesson to the topic of acceptance.

As blessed as we were in the United States in 2012, every one of my eight students had a free copy of the Bible in her hands. It took my breath away to witness such unhindered favor, and yet, even with doors wide open to my visit and a free copy of God's Word in each lap, they still couldn't believe that God desired them.

We presume that something as valuable as salvation must be complicated, but the truth is, salvation boils down to two simple realities:

1. The *fact* that God's Word is true, which conveys the act of Jesus's sacrifice.

2. The *acceptance* of that fact, which is called "faith."

Doubting God's promise of a pardon from sin isn't exclusive to individuals with criminal records. The self's last-ditch effort to resist surrender is coddling the doubt that God's Word isn't one hundred percent true. When shame camouflages itself as humility, we own our shame instead of rejecting it. Indirectly, we deny the grace that Jesus died to grant. The requirement on our shoulders is to accept forgiveness with such trust that it decimates shame.

Do you realize that you call God a liar when you doubt His written Word? There are times when I have read the Psalms, and the devil has whispered to me, "Aren't those pretty words. Too bad they are only pretty words." Yes, I understand doubts. But I also see them for what they are: lies from the lips of the devil.

Hebrews 6:18 says, "**It is impossible for God to lie**" (NIV).

Do you accept that God cannot lie? Jesus is so faithful and true that these titles even replace His first name in Revelation 19:11, which reads, "I saw heaven standing open and there before me was a white horse, **whose rider is called Faithful and True**. With justice he judges and wages war" (NIV).

Every single letter of God's Holy Word is true. If He said He came to save sinners, then He came to save you (Luke 5:32). If He said He desires all to come to repentance, then He desires you (2 Pet. 3:9). God does not show favoritism (Acts 10:34), meaning, He doesn't discriminate. He knows that all have sinned (Rom. 3:23); therefore, He compensated for *all* sin, without exception. Allowing yourself to doubt God's Word is an offense to God's gift and a hindrance to salvation. Acceptance is key.

Ephesians 2:8 tells us, "For it is **by grace** you have been saved, **through faith**—and this not from yourselves, it is the **gift of God**" (NIV).

Grace is imperative for Jesus's payment to cover my debt. My acceptance of that gift completes the transfer of ownership. Faith is required for the gift to become more than a pretty present on a shelf, but a fully unwrapped gift transferred to me upon me claiming it.

Can you imagine your daughter refusing to open gifts at her birthday party because she insists they belong to the boys and girls who brought them? Yes, Jesus brought the gift to the party, but to give it away, not to keep it for Himself. Jesus doesn't need a pardon; we do. There's a vial of Jesus's blood portioned out with your name on it. Have you taken the gift in hand?

Herein lies the secret to God's selection, which my student prayed for:

God selects those who *accept* His gift of grace.

Where are you along the path to acceptance? One foot out the door and one foot in? Halfway around the block? Or have you crossed the finish line, completely and irrevocably convinced that God's Word is the unshakable bedrock of your life? Full acceptance completes the transfer of righteousness from Jesus to you. This is affirmed when the Holy Spirit takes up residence in your heart.

"**When Christ** who is our life **appears**, then **you also will appear** with Him in glory" (Col. 3:4, NKJV).

Resurrection can't be dissected from God's personality; it is His personality. He didn't create us to forfeit us, but to perfect us. His plan to resurrect His people and His creation from the jaws of death is imminent. The foundation has been laid. Death is only a temporary pit stop, a phantom victory for the enemy. So when we pray, "Our Father which art in heaven," remember that He reigns supreme over the earth but not on the earth. We are still on the earth; we are not yet in heaven, and the earth has its proper place contrary to heaven.

And when we pray, "For thine is the kingdom, and the power, and the glory for ever," know that His kingdom isn't this fading one. This earth and all of its pain will pass away, but His power and His glory can be praised even now! Let us praise what is worthy to be praised and not objects of illusion. Striving to capture and preserve this life is nonsense. It will be gone tomorrow, no matter what we do or how much we may wish otherwise. Cling to the reality that never fades: Christ crucified and the victory won! May this resurrection plan already in motion be a comfort to those presently enduring death's brief blow.

Here Comes the Rain Again

I think two tiny rainclouds have grown behind my eyes. They are always heavy and about to burst. Sometimes, I think the only way to control them is to fall asleep. It's them or me, so I close them to shut them off.

My lower eyelids quiver, forcing me to fight back tears. My mind may be completely clear, but the crying compulsion overwhelms me from out of nowhere. Crying signals to my mind that something must be wrong, and I must feel bad even if I haven't figured out why. Trying to convince yourself everything is okay while crying feels like a lie.

Even when the sun is shining warmly on my face, and I can attend to the simple pleasures of the day, it takes very little to summon the rain. Just give me a moment to think of my absolute aloneness. Just say the name of a lost love. Just leave me to disappear in a tender song or quiet fantasy, and tears will drip.

They drip when I'm driving in to work. They drip during the credits of a movie. They drip when the object of my affection closes the door behind him. They drip when I'm alone at work. They drip in the shower. They drip when I lie in bed. I spend all day, every day, restraining the natural outpouring of my soul.

Is that what they are? My tears feel like my soul pouring out of me. They feel like my heart in liquid form leaving my body. After all, to keep it inside will contaminate all of me with sadness and heaviness. If they come out, maybe things will lighten up. Maybe I'll be able to dwell on something else. Maybe.

How Can I Go On?

Lamentations, chapter 3 (NIV):

> "I have been deprived of peace; I have forgotten what prosperity is. So I say, 'My splendor is gone and all that I had hoped from the Lord'" (v. 17–18).

Sometimes, Death works extra hard to make its presence felt. Many precious people are left behind to rebuild their worlds in the absence of a loved one they never imagined having to exist without. I have been there, forced to redefine my universe after tragedy. Oh, the unstable footing, the confusion, the oppressive fog of despair! It's a most bitter sentence.

> "I remember my affliction and my wandering, the bitterness and the gall. I well remember them, and my soul is downcast within me" (v. 19–20).

Why do my days keep climbing when some are called home at six years old, some sixteen, some thirty? How long will my days keep counting, or the days of my parents, my siblings and friends, the support I cannot imagine living without? When will the roster cycle around again, and I return to bat, to swing blindly at redefining my universe after loss? How can I prepare? How can I reach out to steady the arm of my neighbor who is currently under fire of the merciless pitcher, Death?

> "Yet this I call to mind and therefore I have hope:
> Because of the Lord's great love we are not consumed,
> for his compassions never fail.

They are new every morning;
great is your faithfulness" (v. 21-23).

When you are deprived of peace (v. 17), when all remembrance of prosperity has fled (v. 17), when splendor has vanished (v. 18), and hope has shriveled and died (v. 18), this *one sliver of hope* can be called to mind (v.21):

**"Because of the Lord's great love
we are not consumed**" (v. 22).

You are not consumed! *You are not!* You may feel utterly crushed. It may look as if your life is in shambles. The voice in your head may tell you that all is lost. But you are not consumed. You are still breathing.

Maybe you aren't doing much more than breathing, and that's okay. You have permission to do nothing but breathe. Sleep. Wake. Continue breathing. Do it again tomorrow. When rational thought returns to you, take your first swing at living armed with this encouragement: "**His compassions <u>never fail</u>**. They are **<u>new</u> <u>every</u> morning**" (Lam. 3:22–23, NIV).

Motivated by compassion, God redefines your life daily as if He were starting creation from scratch just for you. God doesn't define life by what *is not*, but by what *is*. Luke 20:38 boldly claims, "He is **<u>not</u>** the **God of the dead**, but of the **living**, for to him **<u>all are</u> <u>alive</u>**" (NIV).

Those who no longer live among us on earth live alongside the Lord in heaven (or stand apart from Him in hell). Death has been overpowered by life. Our present benefit is only limited by the degree to which we believe in that triumph. God's compassion will swallow the stench of death, which hovers over the earth, if we allow it into our lives through faith.

Redefining a personal universe after loss is a shapeless pursuit because we can't create structure around an absence, no matter how hard we try. We want to preserve a hole in our new world shaped like the departed loved one, but God says, "*No. I am not the God of the dead. Your loved one lives; I have simply relocated him. My compassions do not accommodate death. Today's definition of life for you is new. Then when you lay your head down tonight, let that definition go. I will wake you to new compassions and introduce you to a different life tomorrow.*"

Death becomes a most formidable enemy when it claims someone in the prime of their life. The wound is immeasurable. Oh, how we want to grab Death by the neck and shake it, to throw every grenade, rock, dagger, fist, and bomb within reach at it! But we cannot. This is the point where Jesus appears as the only one within arm's reach of Death. When the passing of someone compels the living to confront their own mortality, Jesus is close at hand. He finally becomes a very near reality among all that is practical.

Heaven grows more desirable, and its welcome seems more personal, because our view of heaven changes into one that contains familiar faces. And yet, Jesus has always resided in heaven, we have always known Him to live there, and His love for us has always been secure. But has that mattered? Had our relationship with Him always been as relevant as it can be, then no new addition could ever increase heaven's loveliness.

In *God is the Gospel*, John Piper asks, "If you could have heaven, with no sickness, and with all the friends you ever had on earth, and all the food you ever liked, and all the leisure activities you ever enjoyed, and all the natural beauties you ever saw, all the physical pleasures you ever tasted, and no human conflict or any natural disasters, could you be satisfied with heaven, if Christ was not there?"

This is one of the most important questions we can ask ourselves. In this life, we will either grieve or be grieved, die or say goodbyes. Compounded grief is the by-product of a long life. This inevitability is all the more reason why Jesus *must* become our sole fixation. Our emotional stability depends on it.

James 4:14 says, "For **what is your life**? It is even **a vapor** that **appears** for a little time and **then vanishes** away" (NKJV).

Awareness of this truth is intended to strengthen and stabilize us. Unless we develop a sensible opinion concerning the temporary condition of our physical bodies and the mortality of those we love, grief will destroy all of the thriving in our surviving. We must cooperate with the Holy Spirit to impose mental and emotional boundaries around the allowances grief is permitted to have. God will accomplish this work in us, for us. We cannot do so on our own power. But He waits to do so until we hunger for an eternal perspective of death.

Although pain inches by slowly, after it passes, time seems to have been a blur. Your recovery from trauma may go on for days, weeks, possibly years, yet the hands of the clock will circle around the dial at the same rate whether you're in a season of mourning or blessing. Without notice, a new reality will replace the former one, and the season of mourning will pass (2 Cor. 4:17).

I'm not saying your joy will be restored to the degree it was before the traumatic experience. Nor am I saying that your naivety will return, and you'll see the world as you did before exposure to intense pain. With age comes wisdom, and with wisdom, there is increased sorrow (Eccles. 1:18), but the hours shall pass. There's some small comfort in this: the pain won't go on forever. Everyone you love and lose, if they're born again with Christ as their Lord, is just around the corner. Once you see them again, it will be as if you'd never been apart.

Heaven isn't just a place, but a destination, and it isn't those we've lost who are displaced, but it's actually we who remain who are displaced. Ecclesiastes 12:7 says, "**the dust returns to the ground** it came from and **the spirit returns to God** who gave it" (NIV). The spirit of a man could not "return" unless it departed from a source of origin before coming to earth. See how it is we who remain who are displaced? See how you're already on track to join those who have gone ahead?

Had there been a time-traveler present with Mary and Martha at the time of Lazarus's death during the three days before Jesus arrived to proclaim, "Save your grief! Lazarus's death is an illusion! He will rise!" could a prophet have prevented even an ounce of the family's pain? I doubt it, because they wouldn't have believed him. How could they believe while preparing the body, rolling back the stone, and placing Lazarus in the tomb? But it *was* true! And we are foretold the exact same thing, yet it does nothing to lessen our pain, either. Death is done for! Help us, Lord, to be more sure of you than we are of our feelings. Slay the emotional allegiance we forfeit to Death. Let your compassions show up in our ability to *believe you more*!

God defines life by the day. The changes are often subtle but not so subtle that we can't discover them. Desire to see. What is today's new compassion? How has God defined your life differently today than yesterday?

God doesn't distribute His compassions in universes for us to clutch but in days for us to spend. He doesn't allow us to construct our own universes, either; no wonder the effort is futile. Life isn't defined by what is not but by what is the substance of today's mercies. Tomorrow, with the sunrise, His compassions will be new, and therefore, the definition of your life will also be new. Dwell on your fresh dose of life as God has prescribed you for today. Then wake up to a new life tomorrow. It's a challenging mindset to embrace, but it's the secret to coping, surviving, and thriving as an eager recipient of God's compassion.

Why So Much Pain?

It has not escaped my attention that the Bible affirms mourning and grieving over joy and celebration. In the believer's punch list of recommended behaviors, James 4:9 includes, "Be afflicted, and **mourn**, and **weep**: **let** your **laughter be turned to mourning**, and your **joy to heaviness**" (KJV).

Ecclesiastes 7:1–3 espouses a similar sentiment: "A good name is better than precious ointment; and the day of death [is better] than the day of one's birth. **It is better** to go to the house of **mourning**, than to go to the house of feasting: **for that is the end of all men**; and the living will lay it to his heart. **Sorrow is better than laughter**: for **by** the **sadness** of the countenance **the heart is made better**" (KJV).

It requires a lot of ruminating to convert a natural heart into a hard heart. A hard, insensitive, griefless heart is impenetrable to the Holy Spirit, but a grieving heart is vulnerable and sensitive. When we're sensitive, then we're pliable. When the walls are down, we're more receptive to supernatural intervention. Those who harden their hearts run to evil and risk never returning to a proper relationship with God. Perhaps this is one reason why we're advised to "let" mourning come upon us. Do not reject or despise it; do not guard against it. The consequences of hardening your heart exceed the benefits of preventing pain.

Laughter is a momentary lift, a fleeting delight, but the intimacy experienced through communing with our Creator in times of sadness affects the heart for the better in the long run. Sadness leaves a permanent thumbprint behind, one of fellowship with Great Love.

In her book, *Not Good if Detached*, Corrie Ten Boom paraphrases, "Moody once said, 'In the valley of the shadow of death there must be light, otherwise there could not be shadow.' Jesus is our light."

In my experience, the times I have been most sensitive to God's nudge or whisper were times when I walked in the valley, lonely or afraid, looking for Him to keep me company. Distractions were few, because sadness was prominent. God's presence was easy to perceive.

Yet times when I distanced myself from Him and hardened my heart, I cared for nothing and shunned His approach. When the search for gratification was my driving ambition, God was an interference to my agenda. During those times, my emotional state wasn't overly sad or overly happy. I was callous and numb.

If mourning is "better" than not mourning, then why are there no tears in heaven (Rev. 21:4)? The heart while on earth is in an evolving state, constantly undergoing reconstruction, but the heart in heaven has fully evolved. No imperfections remain to be "bettered," and no objective remains for the mourning process; therefore, mourning will be discontinued. No tears, only full, perfect hearts shall be our inheritance.

Perceived pain forces a rigid mind open to the hope of something more. Yearning, seeking, then discovering God on an intimate level *is* that something more.

"Though he [God] brings grief, **he will show compassion**, so **great** is his **unfailing love**. For **he does not willingly bring affliction or grief** to anyone" (Lam. 3:32–33, NIV).

If God doesn't willingly bring affliction, but He sends it anyway, then only for the rich end product of that affliction does He do so. It isn't His will that we hurt, but it is His will that we benefit from hurting. There's a downpour of divine compassion distributed with every affliction. Pain, like a pulley, draws God nearer and nearer.

"The **Lord is close to the brokenhearted** and **saves** those who are **crushed in spirit**. A righteous man may have many troubles, but the Lord **delivers him from them all**" (Ps. 34:18–19, NIV).

I have a Lord, who in divine perfection, ordained my suffering and my restlessness in this life that I might aspire for more—more than this present reality, more than this temporal experience. His purposes are deliverance (Ps. 34:19), freedom (Rom. 8:21), and glory (Rom. 8:21). All of these point to His grandeur and mercy. A sad face transforms the heart of a person into one that's confident in the source of all glory.

Isaiah 48:10–11 says, "See, **I have refined you**, though not as silver; **I have tested you in the furnace of affliction**. For my own sake, **for my own sake, I do this**. How can I let myself be defamed? **I will not yield my glory** to another" (NIV).

How Can a Good God Allow Bad Things to Happen?

It's 1:00 a.m. I just woke up for the umpteenth time to pull furry little paws off my back so that I don't roll over and crush my dog in my sleep. My fourteen-pounder is oblivious to my size, my weight, my strength, and power to crush. She can't comprehend that I would ever hurt her, because she knows how much I love her, and she trusts me. She's right to trust me. I'm the one who sleeps gingerly, worrying about her well-being, while she sleeps undisturbed. When she wakes to discover the distance I have created between us, will she think I love her less when it's actually a sign that I love her more?

Our routine repositioning reminds me of when Moses asked to see the Lord's face. How close Moses wanted to be to God. He just wanted more of God. That must be a good thing, right? But God refused. Sin can't exist in the presence of holiness. Moses was still in human skin, woven throughout with sin. If the sin in him disintegrated, then he too would disintegrate. God was too good to allow Moses's premature death.

"And the Lord said to Moses, 'I will do the very thing you have asked, because **I am pleased with you and I know you by name**.' Then Moses said, 'Now show me your glory.' And the Lord said, 'I will cause all my goodness to pass in front of you, and I will proclaim my name, the Lord, in your presence. I will have mercy on whom I will have mercy, and I will have compassion on whom I will have compassion.' But, he said, '**you cannot see my face, for <u>no one may see me and live</u>**'" (Exod. 33:17–20, NIV).

Do you believe God wanted to grant Moses's request? He had announced,

"I am pleased with you."

"I know you by name."

Do you believe God was able to grant Moses' request? He offered alternatives,

"I will cause all my goodness to pass in front of you."

"I will proclaim my name in your presence."

"I will have mercy."

"I will have compassion."

"I **will not** give you what you ask."

"I will," "I will," "I will," "I **will not**."

How should Moses respond to this "no" answer? Kick and scream? Proclaim his entitlement? Recount the faithful labor he had done in God's service to merit his request? Delicately, or not-so-delicately, remind God that He is supposed to be good, implying that a good God would be more generous?

This is how I behave when God tells me "no." If He denies what I ask for, which I'm sure is absolutely, unquestionably good, then He must not be.

Yikes. When did the basis for good become my human logic? My motives? My "pure" heart? My thirty-something years of experience and insight?

Stop the presses! I need to reset my definition of good.

Moses's request is an important example of how a good God behaves and why. He always has a sensible reason for saying "no." In this situation, God revealed His reason. Evidenced by the extent God went to accommodate Moses, it appears that it was no more fun for God to say "no" than it was for Moses to hear it. God compensated with His goodness, His voice, His mercy, and His compassion. God continued to fulfill the desire of Moses's heart within the confines of Moses's best interest. Saying "no" actually meant more work for God. The verses that follow tell that God constructed a substitute for Moses. He hid Moses in the cleft of a rock, covered Moses's eyes with His hand, and then removed His hand so that Moses could view His back.

Let me pause to sync up my plight with Moses's. An all-knowing, all-powerful God is pleased with me, knows my name, tells me "no" only when protecting my interests, and then obliges Himself to compensate me for denying my request.

Heaven help me for ever daring to suggest that God might not be good.

I hear some of you saying, "But God hasn't compensated me. He took my husband's life, or my child's, or has shortened my own life with an incurable illness. God can't compensate me now; therefore, He can't be good. No compensation equals no good."

Then I must ask you, would a good God crucify His only Son? Can you see any good in that? If you can wrap your mind around the goodness that sent Jesus to the cross, then I beseech you to realize that the same brand of good is making decisions for you, too.

Also, I would dare to say that you have been compensated for your suffering. If you have accepted the blood of Jesus for your sins and asked Him to be the Lord of your life, then you won't spend eternity in hell. You have been more than compensated. I have been more than compensated. I must remember this.

Would a good God draw Satan's attention to a blameless man named Job and allow Satan to torment Job, only to reveal Himself and restore Job to affluence, making Job an inspiration for all mankind? Yes, a good God *would* display His preeminence that way, and a good God *would* compensate the sufferer that way. Job's story wasn't one flawed exception to God's reputation of good. It displayed exactly how a good God operates: He brings glory to Himself and draws the masses toward eternal life by way of that testimony. The terms He executes often don't make sense in the snapshot of one lifetime, but the result makes perfect sense over the course of all lifetimes.

Long ago, I embraced the definition of "truth" as the person of Jesus Christ because John 14:6 taught me, "Jesus answered, 'I am the **way** and the **truth** and the **life**. No one comes to the Father except through me'" (NIV).

And I embraced the definition of "sin" as what the Bible calls sin because Romans 7:7 taught me, "I **would not have known** what **sin** was **except through the law**. For I **would not have known** what coveting really was **if the law had not said**, 'Do not covet'" (NIV).

It's time for me to recruit "good" into the ranks of concepts measurable only by biblical definition.

Scripture says, "And we know that **in all things God works for the good** of those who **love him**, who have been called according to his purpose" (Rom. 8:28, NIV) and "Do not conform to the pattern of this world, but be transformed by the renewing of your mind. Then you will be able to test and approve what God's will is—**his good, pleasing and perfect will**" (Rom. 12:2, NIV).

My definition of "good" should no longer be subjective, quantified by my judgment, or gauged in degrees of painlessness. From now on:

Good is what God does.

What Does God Want from Me?

"So I say to you: **Ask** and it will be given to you; **seek** and you will find; **knock** and the door will be opened to you. For **everyone** who asks **receives**; he who seeks **finds**; and to him who knocks, **the door will be opened**" (Luke 11:9–10, NIV).

Many of us are familiar with these verses. It's the lure that whets our spiritual appetites. The Bible is a guaranteed source of food for the soul; however, with every appetite comes the capacity for both feast and famine.

This Luke passage is a promise we rightfully claim. After all, each of us fits into the "everyone" category. We all desire to walk away from God's table of blessing with something in hand. This promise is our golden ticket. It says, *"Welcome to the banquet. There's a place-setting with your name on it. Come and be filled."*

So you gleefully arrive at the banquet with your Luke 11 invitation in hand and pull your chair up to the table. You settle in, make yourself comfortable alongside your companions, and watch for the double kitchen doors to swing open any moment.

Would it surprise you if the one preparing the meal kept you waiting?

Until the wait becomes uncomfortable, you weren't aware that your appetite wasn't all you brought with you. You also brought expectations and selfishness, among other things. And so you sit, still seeking, still hungry, still clutching your invitation, and growing more uncomfortable with each passing minute.

The longer you wait, the hungrier you get. You wonder, "Did I come to the wrong house at the wrong time or on the wrong day? Has the patron run out of food?" As your stomach growls, you think, "My appetite has now evolved into a genuine physical need. I no longer sit here waiting to be indulged. I can be satisfied with the bare minimum. Just give me enough to silence my aching stomach. I must be fed. I may faint on the spot."

How do you react when waiting on God gets uncomfortable?

Do you entertain doubts about the legitimacy of the invitation and the reliability of the patron?

Do you justify your needs to the point that you consider other remedies?

Does the noise of other guests pulling away from the table sound appealing?

As the chairs empty, the loneliness makes the waiting worse. If the growling stomach hasn't gotten to you, will the loneliness provoke you to leave?

What a tenuous circumstance it is to find yourself besieged with need at a time when God appears distant. You grow painfully aware that you, too, have the freedom to jump ship.

The patron, God, will not let you starve to death, but He will permit your painful waiting. How much is He worth to you? How bad do you want what He has to offer? The wait will reveal it. The promise He made in Luke, chapter 11, will be granted to those remaining at the table when the appointed time comes.

God first pursued you. How else can you explain the invitation in your hand? He never withdraws His love but will, for a season, withdraw evidence of Himself to see how you respond.

Will it be, "**Out of sight, out of mind**,"

or "**Absence makes the heart grow fonder**"?

God led the Israelites out of slavery from Egypt with a pillar of a cloud by day and a pillar of fire by night (Exod. 13:21). When the intangible God removed His tangible signature, the people reacted in rebellion, refusing to uphold faith once God made Himself invisible. There would be no seeking after the One who had sought them, so they resorted to manufacturing idols that could be seen and held in hand. Do you likewise turn away from God to get your needs met in seasons of discomfort?

Jeremiah, chapter 2, reads, "This is what the Lord says: 'What fault did your fathers find in me, that they strayed so far from me? They followed worthless idols and became worthless themselves. **They did not ask, "Where is the Lord**, who brought us up out of Egypt?"' '**The priests did not ask, "Where is the Lord?**" Those who deal with the law did not know me; the leaders rebelled against me. The prophets prophesied by Baal, following worthless idols'" (v. 5–6, 8, NIV).

The Israelites had no need to ask, "Where is the Lord?" while He was still visible. Likewise, we have no need to seek Him while we're feasting. The purpose of famine, waiting, silence, and invisibility is that man should seek after God.

When God hides Himself, He listens for the faithful to cry,

"WHERE IS THE LORD?"

This cry doesn't displease God. It doesn't declare that we have no belief. On the contrary, it testifies that we indeed believe and have expectation in His existence, His goodness, His blessing, and His companionship. The question reveals that His absence is felt, and His presence is missed. The question doesn't state that He's nowhere to be found, but somewhere we want to be.

When we lose something valuable, we search for it, even to the point of asking for directions. "Where is the Lord?" is a plea for directions. In all regards, this lament honors God.

When in doubt, need, and discomfort, take to stalking God. This is what He desires.

So stay in your seat at the banquet table. Let your stomach growl. God permitted Job and his friends thirty-five chapters of the Bible to commiserate. Job didn't fail to cry, "Where is the Lord?" (Job 23:3), nor did he depart from God's table (Job 14:14). Thirty-five chapters later, deep into the misery of Job's suffering, God answered Job with grand authority, followed by grand reward. God's silence isn't golden; it is temporary.

What Is This Going to Cost Me?

"And he [Jesus] said to them all, 'If any man will come after me, let him **deny himself**, and **take up his cross daily**, and **follow me**. For whosoever will save his life shall lose it: but whosoever will **lose his life for my sake**, the same **shall save it**'" (Luke 9:23–24, KJV).

Take up your cross daily and follow me.

I suspect you're familiar with this essential instruction from Jesus. Yes, we know the words, but they're more than words. We can hear them, but hearing doesn't make them understandable. We can agree with them, because Jesus accomplished them before our eyes, but agreeing with them doesn't make them personal. We can study the passage, ponder it, and wish with all our human knowledge to embrace what is being asked of us, but without something tangible to forfeit, such as the pursuit of wealth or a preferred career path or a sinful lifestyle, we can't make heads or tails of what in the world we're personally being asked to deny.

Are we to abandon the blessings God generously gives us to live on pennies in poverty out of a raw exercise of selflessness? I don't think that's what denying yourself means, because it treats gifts from God as harmful and undervalues His generosity. Certainly, He calls some individuals to live this way, but not the majority. His Word says He grants *good* things to His children. God doesn't call good things bad just because they're earthly. So is it our sinful and self-centered instincts that we are to deny? Why, yes! *Absolutely!* We are to deny ourselves participation in sinful attitudes and actions even to the point of pain—agonizing pain, if it comes to that.

Hebrews 12:3–4 says, "For **consider him** [Jesus] that endured such contradiction of sinners against himself, **lest ye be wearied and faint** in your minds. **Ye have not yet resisted unto blood, striving against sin**" (KJV).

Consider Jesus, in all of His torment, sorrow, infinite suffering, separation from His heavenly Father, and life sentence on this filthy, fallen planet surrounded by heathens who did nothing but mock, beat, and crucify Him, to keep your position in perspective. Can you see Him in the garden of Gethsemane, prostrate on the ground, His friends asleep in the distance, His agony forcing the very blood from His veins through the pores of His skin? Only this vision will fortify your constitution regarding your own predicament. You haven't gone to such extreme lengths to resist sin. I haven't, either, but it isn't too much for God to require of us since He required it of Jesus. No matter how bad the imprisonment of body (perhaps for you) or mind/emotions (depression for me), we haven't suffered to that extent. The requirements on us are steep, but not nearly that steep.

When we focus on Jesus, His endurance impresses a determination upon us, like *The Little Engine That Could*, who chants, "I think I can. I think I can. I think I can," to herself as she chugs up a tall hill pulling another heavy train that has broken down. Our climb may be just as vertical and burden-laden as that, but it's doable when powered by divine strength.

In *The Paradoxes of Jesus*, Ralph Sockman wrote, "When he [Jesus] stood before Pilate at his trial, he seems restrained by an inner compulsion rather than by the power of the Roman law or the Jewish mob."

Jesus was often restrained by an inner compulsion. He did not "take up his cross" only on the day when the crossbeams were laid upon His shoulders to be carried beyond the city gates to Golgotha. As He spent forty days in the wilderness fasting, praying, and being tempted by the devil, He denied Himself. As He stopped and gave gentle attention to those who needed healing, He denied Himself. Even as He tenderly washed the feet of His disciples, He denied Himself. Since He expressed that we are to take up our cross *daily*, perhaps gestures of this sort are what He is asking of us.

The following restatement helps me to take up my cross when all I can see before me are ordinary opportunities:

Be restrained by an inner compulsion,
silence your human nature today,
so that God may have His way with you.

Taking up one's cross is hard to accomplish because it means costly personal sacrifice. This struggle is depicted in the encounter between Jesus and a rich, young man in Mark 10:21–22. When the young man asked Jesus what he must do to inherit eternal life, "Jesus looked at him and **loved him**. '**One thing you lack**,' he said. 'Go, **sell everything you have** and **give to the poor**, and you will have treasure in heaven. Then come, follow me.' At this the man's face fell. **He went away sad**, because he had great wealth" (NIV). The almighty dollar (ever wonder why it's called that?) was keeping the man from granting Jesus lordship over his life. Because he refused to depart from the idol of money, he walked away a sad slave to it.

When the Holy Spirit comes knocking, each soul innately comprehends the gravity of the commitment being asked of it. He looks inside us and points to where we challenge His authority. Deep down, each of us has a hint of a god complex. We want some part, or parts, of God's identity for ourselves. What lies at the root of your jealously—is it the urge to possess? Or what's behind your pride—could it be a hunger for power? Are you easily angered—do you carry out the role of judge and executioner in your mind? The Holy Spirit peers in and says,

"*That's it. That's your core sin—the throne from which you refuse to step down. I want that throne. When you are ready to give it up, I am ready to be your Lord.*" Receiving the Savior costs us our god complex, the most expensive part of our identity. We must relinquish the throne in order for Jesus to fill it.

C. S. Lewis describes this most important life decision in *Beyond Personality*. He says:

> I think that many of us, when Christ has enabled us to overcome one or two sins that were an obvious nuisance, we are inclined to feel that we are now good enough. He's done all we wanted Him to do, and we'd be obliged if He would now leave us alone... Of course, we never wanted and never asked, to be made into the sort of creatures He is going to make us into... That is why He warned people to "count the cost", before becoming Christians. "Make no mistake," He says, "If you let me, I will make you perfect. The moment you put yourself in My hands, that is what you are in for. Nothing less, or other, than that. You have free will, and if you choose, you can push Me away. But if you do not push Me away, understand that I am going to see this job through. Whatever suffering it may cost you in your earthly life, whatever inconceivable purification it may cost you after death, whatever it costs Me, I will never rest, nor let you rest, until you are literally perfect—until my Father can say without reservation that He is well pleased with you, as He said He was well pleased with me."

Is anything holding you back from welcoming Jesus into your heart? His holy presence needs a holy space. He will identify the thing, or things, which need to be removed to make

Him welcome there. To what or to whom are you most loyal? Your job? Your looks? Possessions? Alcohol? An affair? What constitutes the line drawn in the sand, which you would refuse to cross should Jesus ask you to do so? The answer to this question could be the key to your salvation.

The most costly thing the Lord required from me before He would enter my heart and secure my salvation was public identification as a Christian through water immersion in the Baptist church. Baptism is not mandatory for salvation, but it was for me, because God knew I would not go to that extent for Him. I wanted to be saved, and I wanted Him as my Lord, but not at that price. I deliberated with God over this requirement for five years before the Holy Spirit seared my conscience with Matthew 10:33, which reads, "But **whosoever shall deny me before men**, **him will I also deny** before my Father which is in heaven" (KJV).

The Holy Spirit required me to override my pattern of denying Jesus as Lord through this public demonstration of my faith. Confronting my fear of being exposed as a believer, walking the aisle of the church all alone, and putting my allegiance to Jesus on display for all the world to see secured my salvation because until that moment, my anonymity as a closeted Christian had been more important. When I exchanged self-preservation for a living Lord over my life, my independence died, and Jesus was elevated to His proper place. That initial death killed the identity I clung to while living independently from Him. I was born again: given a new identity and the power to live the lifestyle of surrender I had chosen for my future.

Are you also refusing God in some subtle way that only you and He know? Please consider this important question. There is a death to be accomplished, and without death, there is no resurrection to eternal life.

We must meet Jesus half way, or His sacrificial blood *cannot* cover us. For Jesus to die on the cross in our stead, He needed the help of another man to carry the cross to Golgotha. When Jesus was devoid of physical strength due to blood loss, Simon of Cyrene was forced by the Roman authorities to partner with Jesus in bearing the weight of the cross. Figuratively, we too must know what the weight of the cross feels like. Jesus will pay the penalty for our sins—He has already done so—but He did not make it to Golgotha alone. If Jesus's crucifixion had been intended for your salvation alone, but it required your help to share the load in getting Him there, would Jesus's blood have ever been shed? Have you met Him half way?

Here are some examples of how it occurred in the lives of certain disciples:

"Now as Jesus was walking by the Sea of Galilee, He saw two brothers, Simon who was called **Peter**, and **Andrew** his brother, casting a net into the sea; for they were fishermen. And He said to them, '**Follow Me**, and I will make you fishers of men.' Immediately they <u>**left their nets**</u> and followed Him" (Matt. 4:18–20, NASB).

When Simon and Andrew took up their cross, their livelihood died since they were fishermen and left their nets to follow Jesus.

"Going on from there, he saw two other brothers, **James** son of Zebedee and his brother **John**. They were in a boat with their father Zebedee, preparing their nets. **Jesus called them**, and immediately they <u>**left the boat**</u> and <u>**their father**</u> and followed him" (Matt. 4:21–22, NIV).

When James and John took up their cross, their attachment to possessions and family was demoted because they abandoned their boat and their father in order to follow Jesus.

Taking up your cross isn't always as dramatic as the initial hearing of the command suggests. It doesn't necessarily imply persecution, martyrdom, or secular ruin, but it will mean that in some way, you must choose His will at the expense of your own. Taking up your cross is an active, personal choice and requires concessions day by day. It's uncomfortable. It's deliberate. It's the act of a sincere servant and the example of Jesus.

As children, my brother learned he could manipulate our sister with the simple phrase, "If you loved me, you would." Most often, the statement followed some request to bring him something when he was already comfortably tucked into bed: one of his blankets, a glass of water, or the pinnacle of all brotherly requests, a "prepared" toothbrush. Yes, he managed to sweet talk our sister into bringing him a wet toothbrush precoated with toothpaste and a cup to spit into so he could brush his teeth in bed. It was downright comical how he could get our sister to serve him.

He had her wrapped around his finger in a way only a little brother could, and she delighted in spoiling him. She still loves to spoil him, and "If you loved me, you would," always does the trick. His plea works like a charm, because in essence, it's absolutely true. When someone loves you, it's reasonable to expect certain behaviors from them.

Words can be honest or dishonest, misinterpreted or misunderstood, but actions don't lie. They reveal motives and uncover priorities. It's dreadfully painful to face the truth of another person's feelings for you through what their actions proclaim. Talk all you want, apologize, beg, or flatter, but nothing spoken can carry the weight of a single act of betrayal. Actions preach.

Try to argue away conclusions like these:

"If you loved me, you would try harder
to provide for our family."

"If you loved me, you would reciprocate
my expressions of love for you."

"If you loved me, you would honor
our marriage commitment."

All true statements!

How can we help but entertain these haunting one-sided conversations in the sanctuary of our inner thoughts? The most damaging aspect is that these conclusions don't stop at defining the terms of the two-person relationship but penetrate deeper to define the self-worth of the wounded. Their inner voice whispers, "If he/she doesn't love me, then I must not be worth loving." And it's all downhill from there.

I say, "I love you," frequently because I realize I may not get another opportunity. I realize the significance of the moment may be lost if I don't ping the ear of my friend that he or she is a treasure to me. Because I say it often doesn't mean that I say it flippantly. It always means one consistent thing, which is:

"**I will sacrifice for you**."

How can love mean anything else? This is why the heart-wrenching realization of love denied pelts self-esteem like a hailstorm. There's suffocating pain in recognizing that someone you love refuses to sacrifice for you.

John 15:13 says, "Greater **love** has no one than this, than to **lay down one's life** for his friends" (NKJV).

Sacrificing your life for another person is the greatest display of love possible, as was demonstrated by Jesus our Lord. Genuine love is always recognizable by a twin degree of sacrifice.

Do you think you love and yet you withhold sacrifice, putting yourself above those you claim to love? Does someone tell you they love you but no evidence of sacrifice can be found? Where there's no love, there's no sacrifice, and where there's no sacrifice, there's no love. Love and sacrifice give rise to one another. I caution you not to misinterpret anything devoid of sacrifice as love. It is a lie.

Jesus said, "**If you love me**, **keep my commandments**" (John 14:15, NKJV). Keeping Jesus's commandments requires sacrifice. He measures our love by the payments we make.

"And to Simon Peter, He [Jesus] said to him the third time, 'Simon, son of Jonah, **do you love Me**?' Peter was grieved because He said to him the third time, '**Do you love Me?**' And he said to Him, 'Lord, **You know all things**; **You know that I love You**.' Jesus said to him, '**Feed My sheep**'" (John 21:17, NKJV). Knowing that Peter loved Jesus was not enough; He required sacrifice to confirm Peter's profession.

And to us, Jesus departed this world saying, "**A new commandment I give to you**, that you **love one another**; **as I have loved you**, that you also love one another. **By this all will know** that you are my disciples, **if you** have **love** for **one another**" (John 13:34–35, NKJV). Loving one another as Jesus loved is evident through sacrifice. The requirement to love sacrificially rests on our shoulders.

So what will salvation and the gift of an internal Helper cost you? The answer is active faithfulness, which emulates the Master once Jesus becomes your chosen Master. Faithfulness that never again says, "Why me?" but instead, "Why not me?" Faithfulness that says, "If God can use me to the fullest by placing any demand upon my life, then I consent." Is this a hard pill to swallow? Yes, it's the hardest pill! The Word calls it losing your life (Luke 9:24)!

Paul says, "It is no longer I who live, but **Christ lives in me**" (Gal. 2:20, NKJV). And this is how we get there: we make everything available for His purposes—the hour at hand and the next one and the next one until God removes His breath from our bodies. We no longer demand answers, we elect a "thy will be done" attitude. You must agree for your life to be reduced to this size.

Detaching your sense of self from the things of this world and seeking your identity wholly in Him is what is meant by your life must be "reduced." Seeking your identity in Him means that you allow Him to define who you are, who you will become, and how He will use you. When you are operating in His will, life revolves more around receiving than pursuing.

A life poised to receive is a life of freedom, surprises, and profound significance.

Can you hear His sweet voice? The soft, gentle request says simply,

“**If you loved me, you would**.”

What Should I Say?

What do you have to say for yourself? Open your mouth, and it will reveal your heart. The world is listening.

Matthew 12:34 says, "For **out of the abundance of the heart the mouth speaks**" (NKJV).

We can peek into a person's heart by listening with observant ears. Maybe this is why professing faith in Jesus Christ with your mouth is essential to salvation. If Jesus lives in your heart, then evidence of Him can't help but come out of your mouth. When spoken sincerely, confessing Jesus as Lord seals the deal.

Romans 10:9–10 reveals that our mouths play an active role in salvation. It says, "That **if** you **confess with your mouth** the Lord Jesus and **believe in your heart** that God has raised Him from the dead, **you will be saved**. For with the **heart** one **believes unto righteousness**, and with the **mouth confession** is made **unto salvation**" (NKJV). There's a direct link between what resides in the heart and what is spoken from the mouth.

I always thought that the purpose of confession was repentance, but this text indicates that salvation is also established by these means. Where there's an active Lord over a life, then there are verbal expressions of praise, thanksgiving, declaration, and testimony. The public will hear whom our voices profess as Lord.

If Jesus is your Lord, then you have a testimony.

Giving your testimony aloud can be an intimidating prospect, but it need not be a lengthy, articulate, or entertaining speech. We assume that our whole life story must be told before an audience can grasp how one infidel becomes a Christian, but an effective testimony is much simpler than that. The plotline is always the same: a sinner in need of a Savior by the name of

Jesus. Proclaiming Jesus as Lord is the *only* thing needed for a testimony to register in the ears of a listener.

Revelation 19:10 says, "And I [John] fell at his [the angel's] feet to worship him. But he said to me, 'See that you do not do that! **I am your fellow servant**, and of your brethren **who have the testimony of Jesus**'" (NKJV).

Who knew that angels have testimonies? I suppose this makes sense, seeing that 1 Corinthians 6:2–3 tells us that angels will be judged alongside the world; they, too, must give an account to God. The angel speaking to John reinforced that he had the same testimony that John and the other disciples shared, which is, "*Jesus is Lord!*" Only the profession of Jesus as Lord qualifies as a testimony.

When considering creative angles for evangelism, ministries often overshoot the runway. The gospel doesn't require graphics, loud music, or laser lighting to touch hearts. Seekers simply need Jesus, au naturel.

"So then **faith comes by hearing**, and hearing by **the word of God**" (Rom. 10:17, NKJV).

There's no sure-fire method of expanding your faith outside of *hearing* God's Word. I am an avid reader and enjoy writing down my thoughts (as I'm doing now), but I'm keenly aware of the insufficiency of human communication. I can share personal stories, divulge my weaknesses, and empathize with your hurts, and perhaps these exchanges will create camaraderie between us, but shy of quoting God's truth over a situation, talk lacks power. Let me not waste too much time; let me proclaim the Word of God!

"For **the word of God is living and powerful**, and **sharper** than any **two-edged sword**, piercing even to the division of soul and spirit, and of joints and marrow, and is **a discerner of the thoughts** and **intents of the heart**" (Heb. 4:12, NKJV).

Are there things in your life that need a little reshaping, like a potter taking a scalpel to a mound of clay? The Word of God divides like a sword.

Some Christians seek an alternative to the Bible to share the message of salvation if their listener disputes the divinity of scripture. Good luck finding another resource that's living and powerful and sharper than any two-edged sword. When you bypass God's Word in evangelical conversations, you do no more than entertain one another with debate. You have removed all power to persuade. Can human insight discern another's thoughts? Can human words interpret another's heart? Nothing I say is infused with life and power except for scripture, which thankfully, He has equipped me to recall.

The Bible has an agenda. You'll find its instruction serves to help you isolate thoughts and motives that are harmful to you. Which ones should stay, and which ones should go? Could a new concept you've never considered be the breath of fresh air you've been missing? How else will you discover where opportunity for personal progress lies unless wisdom shines its spotlight into you?

"Is not **my word** **<u>like a fire</u>**?" says the Lord, "And **<u>like a hammer</u>** that **breaks the rock** in pieces?" (Jer. 23:29, NKJV).

Are there harmful things in your life that you need to break free from? The Word of God breaks like a hammer.

As you practice what the Bible teaches, it will help you break free of strongholds that have taken hold of you. You may have never recognized these strongholds, but the Word of God will reveal them. If sorting through thoughts and emotions doesn't meet your need, God's Word is equipped to perform a clean break. Breaking can be painful, but it's only a transitional phase. Freedom like you have never experienced is just beyond the breaking. God must free you from the old self and the old life. Like Eustace, in chapter 8, your new skin will feel sensitive at first, but it will grow strong.

And if you find yourself in a corner, where the breaking phase has not accomplished a full revolutionary work in you, then strengthen your commitment. Hold tighter to the Word of God. Honor it with all of your determination, and God's holiness will burn away any unrighteousness remaining in you. The Refiner's fire is set on purification. The Word of God burns like a fire.

God's Word was not given to humanity to point out aspirations that can't be achieved. God made His Word able to wage *and win* wars within you. Let the Word do its job of dividing, breaking, and burning. Just take in as much of the Bible as you can.

Our conversion from sinners into saints is a process that requires different tactics, sometimes dividing, sometimes breaking, and sometimes burning. Those are three serious jobs, and when you need any one of them done, having the proper tool for the job is a must. Some things are soft and can be separated with a knife, like cutting fat away from a steak. Some things are harder and need to be broken off, like a dentist chips tartar from teeth. And some things, well, there's just no good left in some things, and a fire is necessary to burn the past away completely, like clearing land of a dilapidated house so that a new one can be built on fresh soil.

When studying or quoting scripture, we have assurance of its advancement. God's Word is *always* a rod of influence. Isaiah 55:11 says, "So shall **My word** be that goes forth from My mouth; **It shall not return to Me void**, But **it shall accomplish** what I please, and **it shall prosper** in the thing for which I sent it" (NKJV).

Let us recount His Word all day long. Let us meditate on it day and night. Let us hide it in our hearts so that we will not sin. And let us echo His Word aloud for all to hear, so others may witness our testimonies and increase their faith, too.

God's Word never comes back void. It is the magnetism that created the world (Gen. 1); therefore, speak it, preach it, teach it, and live it out! Only *it* is alive. Only *it* pierces hearts. Only it convicts while simultaneously pardoning. Only it convinces that grace is personal, pervasive, and powerful over sin.

No other approach can touch a soul with laser-point accuracy. Only our Creator speaks the universal language of His creation across all cultures and generations. Only God can press revelation into minds and hearts. No matter how hard we try, humans can never enter territory where only the Holy Spirit can go. We are simply messengers called to bring the gospel directly to the doors of hearts. May we courier His Word faithfully and cheerfully. All other deliberations are merely sidebars from the fact that sin has separated man from God, and God has provided the remedy in Jesus.

What If You Never Heard the Name of Jesus?

"**<u>Everyone</u>** who **<u>calls on the name of the Lord</u> <u>will be saved</u>**. **How**, then, **can they call** on the one they have not believed in? And **how can they believe** in the one of whom they have not heard? And **how can they hear** without someone preaching to them? And **how can anyone preach unless they are sent**? As it is written: 'How beautiful are the feet of those who bring good news!'" (Rom. 10:13–15, NIV).

This passage is a step-by-step portrayal of how the Great Commission is accomplished. The stages are like squares of a quilt, individually inadequate but collectively complete. When read in reverse order, the foremost action is that God (1) sends. Once the messenger receives the call to go, he (2) preaches. As the messenger preaches, the ears of listeners are primed to (3) hear. Active hearing triggers hearts to (4) believe. Believing hearts prompt mouths to (5) call upon the name of Jesus. Once Jesus is invited to enter a heart, then salvation is secured.

Salvation begins with God calling a speaker to relay His message and ends in a believer professing the name of the Lord. See how salvation begins and ends in God? The Great Commission is a marvelous sequence of inspired parts. The gospel messenger bears a gift so good that carrying it makes even his feet beautiful!

It's a legitimate concern to wonder how people receive salvation who have never heard the name of Jesus. How do those who died before Jesus was born get to heaven? How do individuals with mental handicaps get saved if they can't understand the consequences of sin and their need for a Savior? God hasn't neglected to address these situations.

The Bible conveys that salvation depends on hearing the message sent by God. After God sends a preacher and the message is delivered, responsibility to accept the message then rests on the listener. God doesn't take responsibility for the hearer's response. Everyone who hears the gospel is obligated to receive Jesus as Lord in order to be saved. John 14:6 states, "Jesus said to him, 'I am the **way**, the **truth**, and the **life**. **<u>No one</u> comes to the Father <u>except through Me</u>**'" (NKJV).

It's only by the righteous sacrifice of Jesus, God's only Son, that the power of sin was defeated and the penalty of death was paid, once for all. Because all humans have sinned, we all need the victory over sin that Jesus's blood accomplished. Embedded between the end caps of human history, the timing of that once-in-history act doesn't threaten the full victory it accomplished. The final judgment has not yet occurred when the payment for sin will come due for all people. The victory won by Jesus is sufficient to cover all those who stand before God to be judged when that day arrives.

"Therefore as by the offense of one [Adam] **judgment came upon <u>all men</u>** to condemnation; even so by the righteousness of one [Jesus] the **free gift came upon <u>all men</u>** unto justification of life" (Rom. 5:18, KJV).

The free gift of grace was made available to *all* men, not only those who have lived in the A.D. years. Jesus says to have seen Him is to have seen God the Father (John 14:9). The two aren't separate but the same; therefore, to know, honor, obey, and serve God the Father is to know, honor, obey, and serve the Savior Jesus. All those pardoned at the judgment will be marked by the saving blood of Jesus, because His righteous blood is the only sacrifice sufficient to cover sin. Those who lived during Old Testament times may claim the blood of Jesus if they based their faith on the promise of a coming Messiah. The fact that they didn't know His name or the date of His arrival doesn't negate that they lived by faith. Conversely, we who live following New Testament times believe that Jesus was that promised

Messiah. Our faith is founded on His promise to resurrect us to eternal life. We both center our lives on God's Word concerning a future event. It is the same faith requirement and the same obedience requirement, we just see different angles of the same God. They saw the sun rise. We see the sun set.

Since God takes responsibility to send out preachers, He also takes responsibility to reach those whom no preacher reaches. God instills all people with at least three gifts that promote an awareness of His existence, so that all people for all time have the opportunity to accept Him as Lord.

1. *A conscience* – the perpetual voice inside man that differentiates right from wrong.

"For not the hearers of the law are just in the sight of God, but the doers of the law will be justified; for when **Gentiles, who <u>do not have the law</u>, by nature <u>do the things</u> in the law**, these, although not having the law, are a law to themselves, who **show** the work of **the law <u>written in their hearts</u>, their <u>conscience</u>** also bearing witness, and between themselves **their thoughts <u>accusing</u> or else <u>excusing</u> them** in the day **when God will judge** the **secrets** of men by Jesus Christ, according to my gospel" (Rom. 2:13–16, NKJV). The conscience serves as God's speaker where no formal preaching, teaching, or written text is available. He makes eternal truths plain to the minds of men.

2. *A measure of faith* – the necessary basis for spiritual comprehension.

Hebrews 11:6 says that without faith, it's impossible to please God. Ephesians 2:8 says that it's by grace we are saved through faith. Because faith is essential for salvation, God equips every person with the only faculty we need to accept His grace.

"For I say, through the grace given unto me, to every man that is among you, not to think of himself more highly than he ought to think; but to think soberly, according as **God hath dealt to every man the measure of faith**" (Rom. 12:3, NKJV).

In *Knowing God*, J.I. Packer further explains, "For our faith, which from the human point of view is the means to salvation, is from God's point of view part of salvation and is as directly and completely God's gift to us as is the pardon and peace of which faith lays hold."

"But **the natural man does not receive the things of the Spirit of God**, for they are foolishness to him; **nor can he know them**, because **they are spiritually discerned**" (1 Cor. 2:14, NKJV).

A leaning toward spirituality is initiated by the Holy Spirit. A person who's only interested in living an atheistic life won't entertain spiritual philosophies at all. If you look to your inner life and find an interest in knowing God there, then God has opened the floodgates of your understanding. Any fragment of Christian belief is evidence of the Holy Spirit's work upon your comprehension.

3. *An awareness of creation* – God's visible masterpiece is used to reveal the Creator.

"For the wrath of God is revealed from heaven against all ungodliness and unrighteousness of men, who suppress the truth in unrighteousness, because what may be known of God is manifest in them, for **God has shown it to them**. For since the creation of the world **His invisible attributes are clearly seen**, being understood **by the things that are made**, even **His eternal power and Godhead**, so that **they** [people] **are without excuse**" (Rom. 1:18–20).

Helen Keller, both blind and deaf by two years of age, testified that she had an awareness of God before ever being taught about the Bible. Multiple online sources summarize her confession as follows:

> In one of her letters, Helen told Bishop Brooks that she had always known about God, even before she had any words. Even before she could call God anything, she knew God was there. She didn't know what it was. God had no name for her–nothing had a name for her. She had no concept of a name. But in her darkness and isolation, she knew she was not alone. Someone was with her. She felt God's love. And when she received the gift of language and heard about God, she said she already knew.

The gifts of a conscience, a measure of faith, and an awareness of God through creation are inalienable birthrights of all people, given to draw even those who never hear the name of Jesus into an intimate relationship with their Creator. Birthrights are granted without merit but may be forsaken at will. A man may deny, defy, or reject his birthrights, but only by deliberate effort will he succeed in purging these resources from his life. No birthright will ever restrain a man to remain faithfully in his father's house, as was conveyed through the parable of the prodigal son (Luke 15:11–32).

Because these birthrights are inherent, we should always assume that these seeds remain alive and active in a person, working to woo that soul to Christ. The hearer may argue that none of these elements remain in their possession, and this may be true at the point in time of the conversation, but the seed of all three once did. A person may go so far as to rebuke these birthrights. In such cases, God may relinquish that person to the hardening of their heart (Josh. 11:20; John 12:40). But believers can never know, nor should we dare speculate, when God has discontinued His pursuit of a soul (Rom. 1:24, 26, 28). That is not a liability we want on our accounts.

What Rules Must I Live By?

I cannot reconcile the propensity for confrontation that ensnares some Christians with the peaceable spirit that Jesus demonstrated. Nonbelievers are treated as threats rather than children created in the image of God. Shouts of, "Forsake your sin or go to hell!" are met with, "Who are *you* to tell me what I should do with my life choices?" The activist wins no one, and the nonbeliever runs away faster. It's a sad scenario.

God is our Creator. He can and should require us to behave in ways that please Him. Because He is holy, His standards are going to feel unnatural to us, but that doesn't mean they're intended to be punishment. They're intended to enable intimacy between sinful men and a holy God. Jesus came that we might have life and have it more abundantly than we could manage on our own (John 10:10). Mostly out of love for us, God provides the guidance we interpret as "rules." They aren't meant to hamper us but to enable us.

Sin is defined as that which is offensive to God's holiness or superiority. Sins that are offensive to God's holiness are the same for everyone, but transgressions that are offensive to His preeminence vary between persons, cultures, and generations. Our God is a God of three persons in one. As with any three persons, there are distinct differences. Herein lies the custom design capability of the Christian faith. It opens the door to variations in what God permits among people. If Christians understood this better, it would make us more humble, approachable, and gracious.

First, there is God the Father who defines when sins *are* the same for everyone. God the Father penned the Ten Commandments. He is the voice that resonates, "Thou shalt not steal, murder, commit adultery," et cetera. God the Father is the Creator who designed the laws of gravity, time, and aging, and bound every living thing to them. You may just as well defy His authority as you may defy needing to breathe in order to live. He is the author of order, of causes and their effects. He is uncompromising and unchanging. But neither the Christian faith, nor God Himself, begins and ends in God the Father alone without Jesus, the Son, and the Holy Spirit.

The second person of God is Jesus, who is completely human yet completely divine. To illustrate the role that Jesus arrived on earth to perform, I invite you to visualize three people in a row holding hands: God the Father on the left, Jesus in the center, and you on the right. Jesus is the mediator between a Holy God and sinful man. Without Him in the middle, there would be nothing but distance between God the Father, who is holy, and man, who is unholy. Jesus permits there to be unity. Jesus translates God the Father's black and white laws into a functional message, which man can carry out. Jesus's fresh interpretation of God's laws states, "'**Love the Lord** your God with **all your heart** and with **all your soul** and with **all your mind**.' This is the **first** and **greatest** commandment. And the **second** is like it: '**Love your neighbor as yourself.**' **All the Law** and the Prophets **hang on these two commandments**" (Matt. 22:37–40, NIV).

In Jesus's synopsis, where is the central focus on sin which resounds from God the Father's proclamations? The focus on sin is gone. It has been nailed to a cross and buried in a tomb. We no longer have a sin enemy to wage war against. We have the Lover of Souls to introduce to people! It's as if Jesus has loaded down our pockets with Valentine's Day cards and has told us to give one to every child in the classroom. Everyone gets a valentine! *Everyone!* The commands of "thou shalt" and "thou shalt not" are no longer as important as the *reasons* behind them. If you're stealing, murdering, and committing adultery, then you aren't loving God ultimately and people secondarily. The thou-shalt-nots are merely the how-to guide.

Loving God first and others second is a lot harder than it sounds because that puts us in third place. It's not always apparent how to rise above our instinctive selfishness. Jesus personified, *"I know it's hard to live life in a godly manner, as if you weren't human. Let me show you. Watch and listen."*

In the New Testament, He teaches us how to be Good Samaritans, to forgive seventy times seven, and to be about our Father's business at all times. He redefines the church to be the congregation of believers, urges us to seek out the needy, and shows us the refuge we have in our heavenly Father when this world is too much for us.

Jesus didn't spend the majority of His time on earth warning people about the consequences of sin. He came to help as many as possible *escape* their sin debt. Bearing the good news of salvation through faith was His central message. Why do Christians spend so much energy splitting hairs about what is judged a sin rather than celebrating the victory over sin that Jesus accomplished?

Would you mind returning to the visual of God holding hands with Jesus who then holds hands with you? If God were to transfuse His blood wrist to wrist with Jesus, and then Jesus were to transfuse His blood wrist to wrist with you, you would then share enough of the Father's likeness that you two could join hands and the circle could be completed. The Holy Spirit is that unifying life force within, the adapter who binds you to God's goodness and purpose for this world. He transforms you from within, making it possible to bond intimately with a holy God. He enables your mind to comprehend wisdom and your body to prevail over a sin nature, which would otherwise be impure. He transforms your emotions and will, motivating you to replicate the actions of Jesus. Because of Christ's victory on the cross, the rejuvenation is perpetual. God the Father never runs out of power, Jesus never runs out of grace, and the Holy Spirit never runs out of instruction. They live and operate in unison to accomplish God's will in you.

God personalizes His works, including His commands to us. There has only been one Jonah, one Billy Graham, and one Corrie Ten Boom. God told Jonah to go to Nineveh, but Jonah headed to Tarshish instead, and it was a sin because he disobeyed God. But God hasn't instructed me to go to Nineveh, so I haven't sinned by not going there.

Romans, chapter 14, explains God's stance on questionable topics—is this a sin or is it not a sin? The answers are "yes," and "yes," depending on how the Holy Spirit directs you to best love God first, people second, and yourself third in every situation.

"**Accept** the one whose faith is weak, **without quarreling over disputable matters**. One person's faith allows them to eat anything, but another, whose faith is weak, eats only vegetables. The one who eats everything **must not treat with contempt** the one who does not, and the one who does not eat everything **must not judge** the one who does, for **God has accepted them**" (v. 1–3, NIV).

Accept others. You'll have different opinions about what behaviors are permissible. The Holy Spirit convicts people differently for a reason, or for a season, in order to reach all people.

"Therefore let us stop passing judgment on one another. Instead, make up your mind **not to put any stumbling block** or obstacle **in the way** of a brother or sister. I am convinced, being fully persuaded in the Lord Jesus, that ***nothing* is unclean in itself**. But if anyone regards something as unclean, then **for *that* person it *is* unclean**. If your brother or sister is distressed because of what you eat, **you are no longer acting in love. Do not** by your eating **destroy someone for whom Christ died**" (v. 13–15, NIV).

Sin has been defeated. Therefore, "nothing" possesses the same condemnation that it did before Christ was crucified. We have a new priority, a higher law—love. Anything is sinful which brings hurt, harm, or offense to another person. Love is gentle. Love is kind. Therefore, always make your decisions in the best interest of the weakest person among you. You wouldn't watch a horror movie in front of a four-year-old, but you would invite him to spend time with you even if the activities needed to be different from what you would do when a child wasn't present.

Conviction is key. The Holy Spirit is deliberate with the intuition He places in your heart. Listen to Him. Honor Him. If peace (the Holy Spirit's favorable impression upon you) permits you to participate, then you're free to follow through. But if conviction (the Holy Spirit's reprimand) forbids you, then it would be a sin for you to disobey.

"Let us therefore **make every effort** to do what **leads to peace** and to **mutual edification. Do not destroy the work of God** for the sake of food. All food is clean, **but it is wrong** for a person to eat anything that **causes someone else to stumble**. **It is better not** to eat meat or drink wine or **to do anything** else **that will cause your brother or sister to fall**. So whatever you believe about these things keep between yourself and God. Blessed is the one who does not condemn himself by what he approves. **But whoever has doubts is condemned if they eat**, because their eating is not from faith; and **everything that does not come from faith is sin**" (v. 19–23, NIV).

Everything not done in full confidence that your conscience will allow it is a sin.

The Holy Spirit calls out different requirements, depending on who in the group is vulnerable. Sometimes, the most vulnerable person is you; therefore, your convictions may be the most rigid. There could be a future pitfall that God is protecting you from by developing a conviction in you now. It doesn't mean your conviction is the only right one, and all other derivations are wrong.

Don't belabor whether or not you have God's permission to do something. If there is doubt, then you don't. Accept the doubt as a "no."

Most of all, never prompt another person to sin.

With maturity and wisdom, your convictions may change over time. God knows when it's safe for you to experience more freedom. Walking on coals would destroy the feet of a child, but an adult with toughened skin could tolerate it.

"Anyone, then, who **knows the good** he **ought** to do and **doesn't do it**, **sins**" (James 4:17, NIV).

Each of us has different impressions as to the good we should perform. See how individualized the definition of sin can be? When you know to do good, it is the Holy Spirit who has made that obligation apparent to you. Because the leading of the Holy Spirit is a personal exchange, the sin committed when disobeying Him is a personal violation, as well. It isn't necessarily universal. The same obligations don't always apply to everyone.

If God's rules for me were written in a valentine, a love letter to me alone, I would see God the Father's message in **boldface type**, unmistakable to the eye. I would have no doubt interpreting exactly what He requires of me, and there would be a tone of warning to it. I would sense the implied punishment, or at minimum the implied consequences, were I to detour from it. If I compared my valentine to anyone else's, they would read exactly the same when coming from God the Father.

A valentine from Jesus would be in standard font, just as you're reading this, clear and logical. It would be wise and unlike the mindset I would have without His insight. The tone would be inspiring and encouraging. It would motivate without threats or promises. It would simply be full of wonderful ideas, which sound pleasant to implement. Comparing this letter to anyone else's would also read exactly the same, but we wouldn't all have the same emotional response. Some of us would respond with eagerness. Others would be unmoved. Each recipient's general personality, mind, and heart would determine how much they would desire to abide by its message.

A valentine from the Holy Spirit would be in fine print. I would have to look intently and hold the letter close to my eyes in order to make it out. Although there would be no obligation to keep it private, it would be intended solely for me. My letter would not read like anyone else's. It would be as distinct as my fingerprints. Its tone would be the voice of my conscience, which tells me the things I should or shouldn't do.

There's a vast difference between what I *could* do and what I *should* do. The voice in my head, which speaks of the things I *could* do, is the voice of my own ideas. But the voice that speaks of what I *should* do is the voice of the Holy Spirit.

"Anyone, then, who **knows the good** he **ought** to do and **doesn't do it, sins**." The keyword here is "ought." The difference between the voice of the Holy Spirit and myself is the difference between a suggestion (received from an outside source) and an idea (generated from within).

For example, I notice a coworker's cake carrier sitting on the kitchen counter, empty of the delicious cake that I enjoyed yesterday. Only crumbs and traces of icing remain.

I have the idea, "I could deliver the cake carrier to my coworker's office."

The Holy Spirit suggests, "You should wash it first."

I think, "Well, if it must be washed, then someone else can do it," and I walk away.

The Holy Spirit insists, "Anyone who knows the good he ought to do and doesn't do it, sins. Wash the container."

I relent.

I don't march through life automatically doing the things that I should. I need to be snapped into reality by the conviction of the Holy Spirit, warning me of the wrong I'm about to commit. It disappoints me how often the Holy Spirit must remind me to represent Christ well. I fear what my life would look like if He stops showing up. But His job is to show up, and I can rely on Him to do so. There's a custom set of instructions the Lord intends for me. I must pay close attention in order to hear them. He whispers to me through the fine print of my conscience.

Likewise, both your calling and the definition of sin for you are contingent on the fine print of your conscience. The Holy Spirit will remind you of all truth (John 16:13), including God the Father's **boldface type** statements and Jesus' standard font messages. God is three persons in one, not just God the Father who informs us what bad is, or only Jesus who shows us what good is, but also the Holy Spirit who reveals when good is bad in disguise and therefore a sin for some but not for all. Sin isn't the same definition for everyone. God leads us individually in order to use each of His servants to the full.

What Should I Do Differently?

Riding into work one morning, I saw a handful of energetic eight-year-olds on the train, eyes shining, smiles beaming, and voices several volumes too loud, as if each one had just downed a breakfast of gummy bears and Red Bull. I marveled at the freshness of their faces and their carefree natures. I asked myself how I would feel if one of them were mine. How would I arm them for the future? What have I learned on my journey that might help them?

My answer went like this:

Early in life, we conjure a life mission worthy of our self-investment, and we chase it day after day, year after year. Along the journey, we experience hurdles that are numerous and unforeseeable. A life mission is far more difficult than anyone ever imagines in his youth. A prolonged illness, an unexpected death, and unemployment are only a few of the challenges that can halt one's life goal. At the point when one's life mission seems impossible, depression, cynicism, or destructive decision-making can set in. After all, when what you're living for and working toward becomes unattainable, the sense of loss is riveting. It's common to strike out in anger when you're taunted by the thought that you have nothing left to lose.

Those who choose a more constructive reaction to hardship press forward. Life continues, and just when they can almost taste success, another brake-squealing difficulty stops them in their tracks, causing them to pause and reevaluate in order to gather the motivation to strive once more. If you're living, then you're striving, and if you're striving, then you're climbing, and if you're climbing, then you're fighting to keep from losing ground. The hurdles never cease.

Countless people come to the end of their lives unsatisfied, not knowing if they achieved their desired mission or quite confident they haven't even come close. Most of life is spent battling the hurdles, not living the dream that was chased all along. Should we determine the value of our lives by such ambiguous and uncontrollable terms? Could we go about it all differently?

Under the weight of reality, I grasped at wisdom. I concluded that I'd like to train eight-year-olds to think smaller, to lean more toward day missions than life missions so they could experience a sense of success more often.

I would ask them repeatedly:

Have you blessed someone today?

Have you been blessed today?

When we meet at the judgment seat of Christ, our thoughts and actions will be examined incrementally, not broadly. We would be better off to adopt that mindset now, if possible.

"Then the King will say to those on his right, 'Come, you who are blessed by my Father; take your inheritance, **the kingdom prepared for you since the creation of the world**. For I was hungry and **you gave me something to eat**, I was thirsty and **you gave me something to drink**, I was a stranger and **you invited me in**, I needed clothes and **you clothed me**, I was sick and **you looked after me**, I was in prison and **you came to visit me**'" (Matt. 25:34–36, NIV).

"The King will reply, 'I tell you the truth, **whatever you did for one of the least of these** brothers and sisters of mine, **you did for me**'" (Matt. 25:40, NIV).

"He will reply, 'I tell you the truth, **whatever you did not do** for one of the least of these, **you did not do for me**.' Then they will go away to eternal punishment, but the righteous to eternal life" (Matt. 25:45–46, NIV).

This conversation is one of the most convicting passages in the Bible. It runs contrary to logic that we are responsible to act even when we feel no personal connection to a need. It commands our attention and requires that we answer the question, "By neglecting the needs of your fellow man, have you failed to minister to Jesus?"

I once believed that secular service lacked eternal significance. I assumed that all the jewels in my heavenly crown would be made up exclusively of times when I overtly served in the name of Jesus. Through Matthew, chapter 25, we peer through a spyglass into eternity to see that the services mentioned are, in fact, secular: a need for food, drink, hospitality, clothing, care-giving, and visitation. For those who meet these needs, a kingdom is being prepared.

This teaching opened my eyes. I see the granularity of daily encounters and recognize how God blends His identity into every human life. Why shouldn't He? His very breath within keeps each person alive. It has become my daily initiative to discover where opportunities to bless others lie. Taking inventory at the end of a day and realizing how it measured is quite humbling. God makes His will evident through ordinary encounters.

There's something liberating about the three simple words, "God is love" (1 John 4:16), and that is:

Whatever you do in love glorifies God.

Take advantage of every opportunity to display love, for you never know which deed will earn you a platform in the life of an unbeliever. "**Let your light shine before men**, that **they may see your good deeds** and **praise your Father** in heaven"

(Matt. 5:16, NIV). This verse doesn't say that they may see your evangelical deeds or hear your evangelistic words; it says that they may see your *good* deeds. Good deeds glorify the Father without even a mention of His name. Isn't that motivating?

Growing up in the church, I cannot count the number of times I was on the receiving end of the inspirational speech, "Who are your role models?" The goal was to get us kids to slow down long enough to recognize who we were following and why.

There were a couple of older girls beyond my league of social affiliation whom I recognized as role models. There was one at school and one at church who made a profound impression on me. These two girls were beautiful, confident, well-dressed, and popular. They were prominent fixtures on the map of planet "Under-18," the well-defined, narrow world in which I lived. Within those borders, I was an underdeveloped, insecure, shy speck of a girl. I was dubbed "Dinky Donut" in the first grade, "Small Fry" in the sixth grade, carried around piggy-back by the boys in my class, and affectionately asked, "How is it down there in the land of the little people?" At the close of the seventh grade, the school weighed and measured us before summer started. I measured four feet eight inches tall and weighed seventy-five pounds. The pet names were warranted.

I got saved the summer after the eighth grade and was born again into a new identity in Christ. Immediately upon getting saved, the Holy Spirit initiated a demolition and reconstruction process. Being only thirteen years old, I didn't have a deep bed of sins for Him to dismantle. Instead, His first order of business was to change my personality. Believing in the Lord Jesus meant accepting who He said I was, which required disputing my prior self-assessment of insignificance. In junior high, I had been invisible among the normal-sized students, but not in God's eyes, nor in the eyes of those two older girls.

I studied the examples of my role models. The distinct difference about those girls was that they acknowledged me, not for being cute or abnormally tiny or someone's little sister, but as a person worthy of individual recognition and encouragement despite my miniature stature and lack of social status. They invested in my sense of self and were consistently kind. Their attention, as brief as it was, was sincere. I soaked it up and internalized what it was about them that I admired so much.

With my newfound confidence based on my relationship with Christ came aspirations of the person I could become, a vessel fit for His purposes. I entered high school, a wimpy, shrimpy freshman with a mission to mimic the two girls I looked up to. I remember coaching myself to approach and greet shy students. I remember telling myself to hold doors for people. I remember seeking out something in common with each person I met. At first, these efforts were forced, but it didn't take long for them to become second nature. It surprised me how easy it was to transform into a new personality, into a new person. As I practiced obedience in the small things, I evolved under the power of the Holy Spirit.

Many years have passed since the summer of 1989. I'm grateful I learned how to change from who I was into a new creature early in life. As I matured, God demolished and reconstructed other areas of my life: my priorities, time management, strongholds, sins, and desires. He's always working on something. Today, I find that once again the order of business is a change of my personality. It's been decades since we tackled this subject. I have different motivations to subdue this time, like ambition, selfishness, and the guarding of my established position on planet "Over-30." This time, I must dethrone myself in order to select new role models. I want role models who turn the other cheek, are quick to listen, slow to speak, and stand firm in faithfulness even in the face of death.

Worry, fear, and anxiety churn within us like alter egos competing for face time. These are the sorts of things that prevent us from experiencing rich lives. The things we truly want—to have value, to mean something to someone, to have a reason to live—are readily attainable. Your significance lies in the next conversation you have with the next person you meet and then in each encounter after that.

The July twenty-eighth devotion from Oswald Chambers's book *My Utmost for His Highest,* captures the change of perspective that finally brought me closer to peace:

After Obedience, What?

> We are apt to imagine that if Jesus Christ constrains us, and we obey Him, He will lead us to great success. We must never put our dreams of success as God's purpose for us; His purpose may be exactly the opposite. We have an idea that God is leading us to a particular end, a desired goal; He is not. The question of getting to a particular end is a mere incident. What we call the process, God calls the end.
>
> What is my dream of God's purpose? His purpose is that I depend on Him and on His power—now. If I can stay in the middle of the turmoil calm and unperplexed, that is the end of the purpose of God.
>
> God is not working towards a particular finish; His end is the process—that I see Him walking on the waves, no shore in sight, no success, no goal, just the absolute certainty that it is all right because I see Him walking on the sea. It is the process, not the end, which is glorifying to God.
>
> His purpose is for this minute, not for something in the future. We have nothing to do with the afterwards of obedience; we get it wrong when we think of the afterwards. What men call training and preparation, God calls the end.
>
> God's end is to enable me to see that He can walk on the chaos of my life just now. If we have a

> further end in view, we do not pay sufficient attention to the immediate present: if we realize that obedience is the end, then each moment as it comes is precious.

Measuring our moments could be the key to combating the defeatist mentality. Thinking smaller calls that big, scary monster that has blocked our path out from the shadows and shines a light on it to reveal that it doesn't have claws or teeth. It's big, it's bulky, it's a barrier, but it doesn't have to disable us permanently. It may block our path in one direction, but it can't block us in every direction. There's more around the corner, and maybe, like the game of Candyland, the good parts are woven in along the winding path.

I need to return to being eight years old and seeing the world the way I wish I could enable those children to see it: valuable in small deposits. Even dimes make up millions.

Catch Me, I'm Falling

I feel like I am standing on a tightrope, balancing thirty feet above the ground, teetering on the centers of my feet. My stomach is in my throat. I frantically clutch the wire with my toes and feverishly fight the bar, which is too heavy for my two hands. I think I have been living atop a high-wire most of my life. Everything is a delicate balance, juggling all I can carry in two hands, striving for the absolute maximum I can attain at any given moment.

There's a safety net far below me, but there may as well not be, because I don't trust the net to catch me should I fall. I am terrified. TERRIFIED. What if the weight of my body, combined with the momentum of the fall, plunges me straight through to the cement floor? I am convinced of this inevitable end. However, the net has caught many people before me. It's plenty big enough and designed exactly for that purpose, and yet, I operate as if there's no net at all. Just imagine the chronic state of anxiety of living atop a tightrope with no confidence in the net. Welcome to my world.

I only just realized why anxiety is the prevailing state of mind in which I live. I am constantly thinking, "What if I can't do it all? What if I miss a step? The altitude has gotten so high that it's hard to breathe up here. I am totally alone and solely responsible for myself. What if I fall? What if? What if!"

I finally came to understand that I unconsciously feed this frantic feeling by failing to trust the safety net, which is God's sovereign control over my life.

God says to me, "*My child, why do you insist on the terror of falling and losing everything, your future, your hopes, your dreams, your very life? Look below. I AM YOUR SAFETY NET. You don't have to fall in order to come rest in my arms. Cast aside that heavy load; crawl down the ladder and into the net. Lie down and rest completely. Let me hold you up. Wouldn't you rather climb down and rest instead of falling from unknown heights? Come down and rest.*"

The only way to experience functional trust is to actually release all control and test out the net.

I can. I will! Then I must wake up tomorrow and do it again. The net *is* safe. The net *is* comfortable. And I don't have to fall to find that kind of security. Yes, I will come down.

How Should I Handle Difficult People?

If I have come to terms with anything about myself, it's that I can be my own worst enemy. Stability isn't achieved so much by controlling what happens to me as what occurs within me. If I can fix my eyes on Jesus, then He will enable me to walk with Him on top of the chaos of life continually. I want that: to be free from being knocked around by every slight breeze.

It's pretty unsavory how needy I can be, and when it manifests, it looks a lot like irritability. As a psychology-communications double major in college, I took several family and interpersonal communications classes. A statement by one of my professors, Dr. Lawrence Rosenfeld, struck me as profound. He said, "The reason your family is so good at pushing your buttons is because they are the ones who put them there." It's in the early communal environment of the home and the initial intimate relationships with family that our triggers develop. This makes perfect sense, but learning this in the 1990s did not cure my short-fused tendencies.

I was in my thirties before I owned how selfish it was to explode and ruin family gatherings for everyone. After one too many early exits in tears, I decided my zero-to-ten outbursts weren't fun for me, either. I had become the person to blame if conflict broke out because I was predictably the first person to discard civility. So I decided it was better to adopt the bottle method. When I felt offenses mounting, I bottled them up, choosing to endure instead of react. If I wasn't at the center of the next conflict, then others could discover their own share of responsibility.

This strategy worked for a few years. I stopped being the instigator. My family enjoyed time together more. Unfortunately, the bottle method had side effects. I would return home to nurse my wounds and replay the offenses in my mind. Eventually, they would lose their sting, and I would let them go. Once, when my mental replay of hurt wouldn't wane, I placed a phone call to my parents and asked them both to stay on the line. I went through the list of infractions from our last visit. They listened calmly, empathetically, and apologetically, but before the call came to an end, they shared lists of their own where they had exercised grace toward me and harbored no hurt. Because I had blocked giving them grace, I had no perception of receiving their grace, which I highly desired.

There is such a thing as grace repellent. Like a deadly fume, it silently poisons relationships. When you refuse to give grace, you won't be able to perceive the receipt of any, but as soon as you choose to grant grace, you awaken to grace raining down on you, as well. And you know what else happens? You learn how to give grace to yourself.

I have tried on therapists like people try on shoes. I am so full of self-analysis that it bothers me to pay someone who has no more to tell me about myself than I already know. I never felt that I got my money's worth, until I met a therapist who simply gave me grace. I would leave her office without insight into the pathway out of my struggles but armed with a slow-growing willingness to accept myself in spite of it all. I didn't get what I came for, but I left with what I needed. This grace giver convinced me that I deserved leniency, foremost from myself. This was the beginning of my ascent out of the pit.

Grace is an extremely powerful tool in the life of a depressive. It's probably the one thing we need most from the people in our lives. It penetrates the darkness and truly convinces us that we have a friend in our corner. Active and evident grace spurs deep healing and teaches a depressed person how to become his own best friend. Practicing giving grace to others is a natural first step to developing a gracious attitude toward yourself.

There is also such a thing as love repellent. If you barricade your heart to protect yourself from pain, out of retaliation, or any other justification, you cannot perceive where love is already flowing into your life. But by choosing to *give* love, the lid must come off. When the lid is off, you're open to receive, and your tank fills.

We all have an emotional reservoir that needs filling, whether or not we're willing to admit it. We have needs, and those needs are valid, but most of the ways we go about getting our needs met are not. We run to the emotional storehouses of others and make demands or take what we want, which doesn't satisfy, because coerced validation is meaningless.

It's crucial to understand why certain emotional needs chronically ache. In order to do so, you must identify two parts of every need: the *what* and the *who*. First, *what* would you change about the closest relationship in your life if you could? The answer to this question could help identify your deepest unmet need. Common emotional needs include: affirmation of your sexual desirability, confirmation that you're a priority to your significant other, and assurance that your family values your membership. Second, *who* have you chosen as the ideal person to meet this need?

I needed assurance that I was worthy of love regardless of my marital status, fluctuating weight, unstylish clothes, bad habits, and dirty house. I needed to know that I was acceptable regardless of appearances because stress had driven me to the brink of collapse, and I indirectly sought permission from an authority figure I respected to discontinue the things that weren't making life easier. I debated with my chosen source of affirmation that I should reduce the demands I place on myself when my emotional stability is in jeopardy, but my source insisted that compromising my best was too risky. At the apex of these debates, in the spur of a moment, she ordered me to refrain from helping a blind man across a congested street in the capital city of a foreign country. Instinctively, I rebelled. I realized that her actions were dictated by fear. In that life-altering moment, I decided to reject her as my chosen source of emotional fulfillment, not because I loved her less, but because I didn't want to adopt her fear. I told myself, "She can't be my source for affirmation anymore, because she won't lead me properly. Jesus must be my source." Friends later prodded me, "You want her to accept you just as you are and communicate her unconditional love clearly, but what if she can't? What if she doesn't have that skillset? Can you give her the very thing you're asking for? Can you love her just as she is, even if *she* cannot change?"

After you've done all that you can to facilitate change in a relationship, there comes a point when your emotional well-being becomes solely your responsibility. No one is going to manage you for you. This was the point where only I could improve my emotional health. It required changing my perception of her from being the *source* of my emotional fulfillment to the *recipient* of my emotional regard. By His example, Jesus showed us how to love to our fullest capabilities while releasing the expectations that perpetuate unrest. This doesn't mean that the underlying needs go away, but it frees us to seek new, healthy outlets for getting our needs met.

To some degree, I think we all end up empty in relationships that should be sustaining because we're supposed to reach the conclusion that people can't meet all our needs. Like missing puzzle pieces, God designed us to find certain remedies only in Him. When we inspect our human sources of emotional support, we discover that they aren't Jesus, they're going to love us imperfectly, and the reason it hurts is because we keep going to dry wells for water. Becoming better caretakers of our emotional health begins by shifting our source for approval to Jesus alone.

Taking what another person needs, like disrupting a cooperative workday or always having to win an argument, isn't going to bring us closer to emotional rest. However, when we pursue filling someone else's tank, we begin refueling our own and encouraging reciprocation. In summary, we inspire the free gift we need most. God's Word gives us pointers on how to go about this.

"Let **nothing** be done through **strife** or **vainglory**; but **in lowliness of mind** let each **esteem other** **better than themselves**" (Phil. 2:3, KJV).

First, it declares, let *nothing* be done through strife. You can put a period on that and make it a complete sentence. When you're angry or resentful, hit the brakes on your actions. You don't have permission to act on it. "So how am I supposed to respond?" you wonder. Well, you don't respond. You sit on it. You sleep on it. You vent to God about your hurt. You cry out for help. You envision Jesus's tolerance and reaction to strife. It puts your offense into perspective. Ask God to work on your heart. Let Him show you how to turn your anger into sacrifice.

Once, while playing the mediator in an argument among Christians, the words burst out of my mouth, "Humble people don't get offended! YOU are the problem!" and I repeated, "You are the problem," as many times as it took to point directly at each person involved. The message rang true and brought the argument to an end.

When we truly embody a humble spirit, offenses cease to be offenses but instead become opportunities to treat others as better than ourselves. If you find yourself frequently offended, ask yourself why this keeps happening. Do you consider meekness a positive trait? Are you willing to agree with Jesus that it is? Perhaps these occurrences are being placed in your path as opportunities to practice humility that doesn't come naturally to you.

Second, let *nothing* be done through vainglory. Well, there goes the selfie culture. What good has vanity ever accomplished? It's an embarrassment to the vain and distasteful to witnesses. If God forbids actions motivated by attention-seeking, then we must check ourselves.

Philippians 2:3 gives us "don't do," "don't do," and "do" directives. Sometimes, the "do" step—esteeming others as better than ourselves—is so challenging that we must first figure out why others seem to be at the center of all our difficulties.

In *The Sense of the Presence of God,* John Baillie writes:

> I may do my best to ignore the claim my neighbor makes on me, as I fear I often do. I may act toward him as if he were merely a part of the world in which I dispose and not another disposer of it; merely within the circle of my own dominion and not another centre of it. I may treat him not as a person but as a thing… not an end in himself but as a means to my own ends.

This quote caught my attention from both the perspective of the speaker and the perspective of the neighbor. From the perspective of the speaker, when am I treating others as the means to my own ends? Since my neighbor and I are equally bought with the blood of Jesus, is my neighbor of equal worth as myself in my own eyes? If they aren't, then I must confess this sin and rethink my perspective. I must ask God to help me see them differently. I am to welcome opportunities to exercise actions contrary to my previous errant behavior.

From the perspective of the neighbor, is my coworker or classmate or customer treating me as the means to their own ends? Do they trample me as if I am disposable in their universe? If they aren't a believer in Christ, then they don't have the Holy Spirit working in them to show them any other way. They are merely responding to their own defensive instincts, the way

I used to do before I knew Christ. At least I understand why strife keeps flaring between us. Still, I acknowledge my obligation to treat them as better than myself.

One day, we will stand before God to be judged by the same terms we administer judgment to others. The Lord's Prayer clearly states, "Forgive us our debts, as we forgive our debtors" (Matt. 6:12, KJV). One way to protect our future forgiveness is to grow in graciousness toward others now. I feel that it's easier to be gracious than it is to forgive. If I set my threshold for being offended very high, then the less I'm offended, and the less there is to forgive. Half of the battle of being quick to forgive debtors is being slow to label others as debtors. The exercise of seeing others as better than ourselves aids that goal.

The verse that follows Philippians 2:3 proceeds toward an even greater responsibility: that of advocacy. It reads, "Look **not** every man **on his own things**, **but** every man **also** **on the things of others**" (Phil. 2:4, KJV). I'm not only obliged to be a good steward of the resources God has entrusted to me, but I'm also obliged to be invested in my neighbor's best interests, as well, regardless of their treatment of me.

Baillie's insight converts this duty into something a little more palatable. He says:

> My concern must not be merely for his [my neighbor's] desires, but for what is right in his desires; not merely for his desires but for his good; not merely for what is desired by him but for what, because it is good in itself, is good for him... they [others] embody for me, in my encounter with them, something greater than themselves, an intrinsic right and a universal good.

Baillie looks broadly at treating others better than ourselves in aim to define the "how" regardless of the "who." We should feel empowered to celebrate anyone's happiness, achievements, prosperity, stability, merits, strengths, and talents because all these things are good and right in themselves. I don't have to be a person's biggest fan to affirm the things they're doing right in their life. My neighbor has an intrinsic right to be here. God has a purpose for his life and desires an ultimate good for him; therefore, so should I. Because God loves and values him, I have the opportunity to manifest God's love and convey that value.

Recently, I pulled up to a stoplight and saw a woman in workout clothes and her daughter, perhaps seven years old, exercising along with her. The mom wore a loose-fitting, gray tank top and a baseball cap. The daughter's tank top was bright pink and her plentiful curls bounced high with each animated step. The little girl was obviously having a lot more fun than mom. Her joy warmed my heart. I'm sure I smiled behind the steering wheel. I smile now just remembering her.

"Isn't she precious," I thought.

"*That is how I see all of you*," the Lord whispered.

I used the rest of my drive to practice seeing people the way the Lord sees them. The next man was riding a professional lawnmower. I used my imagination to replace him with a nine-year-old behind the controls whose hands could barely reach. The next person was a man walking on the sidewalk, pulling his bicycle along. In my mind, he became a six-year-old boy, and the biked dwarfed him. The frail, hunched-over, elderly woman in a wheelchair at the bus stop with a dazed expression became a fresh-faced eight-year-old who looked as if she was sitting in a giant's chair. If we were to wear the eyes of God every day and see the precious soul in every life, then it would be easy to treat the people we meet with kindness, even those who need a little extra grace. All we need to do is ask God to alter our perception and soften our hearts.

There is no threat in investing in another person's best. No one has to fall in order for me to rise. If my day is spent prospering the interests of others while performing all my actions for the glory of God, then I'm already rising, and the waves beneath my feet are drifting further and further away.

Is God Done Working on Me Yet?

It's a typical Tuesday afternoon. You approach your locker/cubicle/vehicle at the end of the day, and find an envelope with your name on the outside and the most frightful letter inside. An anonymous note is written in heavy black ink and all capital letters. You don't recognize the handwriting, nor do you recognize the message of hate seeping out from between the alpha characters. A faceless voice inside your head screams at you as you read, "YOU ARE A WASTE OF SPACE. I HATE YOU AND EVERYTHING ABOUT YOU. I HATE EVERYONE YOU CARE ABOUT. I WILL GET YOU. THAT'S A PROMISE. BE AFRAID. BE VERY AFRAID."

Every day for the next week, a new note follows, each in the same handwriting, all with the same sentiment, and each subsequent threat is more specific in description of physical harm. You do as the notes suggest: you grow very scared, even to the point of nausea, and go home midday on several occasions because fear overwhelms you. Even after the notes cease, your fear doesn't. It cripples you and ruins your day every day for the rest of the year.

Nothing more ever occurs as a result of the threatening notes. You never put a face to the evil. Would you say that the person on the other end of the letters has sinned against you, even if they never touched you or anyone you care about? Which is worse: the act of leaving nasty letters for someone, which are nothing more than ink on paper, or the anonymous heart that contained those feelings? Where is the sin: in the act or in the motive behind the act? The heart of the perpetrator is diseased; his acts are merely symptoms.

I present this scenario to you because this is what Christians do. We conjure vile imaginations of revenge, humiliation, or sexual exploit, and then we exercise the social dignity to control our behavior. We indulge in these thoughts privately and presume that we're innocent before God because we never perform the acts, but an outward sin never exists without first an inward, incubating one. What does the action matter, when the sin within is evil enough? God examines the content of the heart.

“He [Jesus] replied, ‘Isaiah was right when he prophesied about you hypocrites; as it is written: “These people **honor me with their lips**, but **their hearts are far from me**”... ‘Don't you see that nothing that enters a man **from the outside** can make him “unclean”? For **it doesn't go into his heart** but into his stomach, and then out of his body’... ‘For **from within**, **out of men's hearts**, come evil thoughts, sexual immorality, theft, murder, adultery, greed, malice, deceit, lewdness, envy, slander, arrogance and folly. **All these evils** **come from inside** and make a man “**unclean**”’” (Mark 7:6, 18–19, 21–23, NIV).

It doesn't matter if you claim to be a Christian by your words or your deeds if your heart contradicts it. Cleanliness on the inside will lead to cleanliness on the outside, but to be filthy on the inside is to be filthy through and through. Since this is true, what of the opposite? What if a person acts righteously without spiritual training? Does he still please God? The Bible says, yes, his goodness counts toward his merit. Again, the heart is measured.

“(Indeed, when Gentiles, who do not have the law, **do by nature things required by the law**, they are a law for themselves, even though **they do not have the law**, since **they show that the requirements of the law are written on their hearts**, **their consciences also bearing witness**, and their thoughts now accusing, now even defending them.) This will take place on the day when **God will judge men's secrets** through Jesus Christ, as my gospel declares” (Rom. 2:14–16, NIV).

God prizes the content of man's heart just as He places supreme value in the heart of the earth. All precious stones and priceless metals lie buried beneath a rugged exterior camouflaged by age, dust, dirt, and weather, but their value is not diminished by the depth of their residence. Consider a small, insignificant oyster lying in isolation on the ocean floor. It's covered with barnacles and sea slime. It's ugly to the eye and nasty to the touch, but inside it holds a bright, flawless pearl of great worth. Is it any surprise that God deems the heart of man to be the substance of his value?

Work commitments, social activities, physical maintenance, and financial obligations demand our conscious energy during daylight hours. These responsibilities shout at us while the heart lies patiently waiting for attention. Let's examine our hearts and be mindful of what's brewing or dying inside, for what's inside is certainly on its way up and out.

God already knows your heart, but do you? Do not be deceived; your heart is calling the plays in deciding your destiny. The heart always follows its allegiance; therefore, be sure you are the master of your heart, always managing its contents to keep from being enslaved by any well-disguised sin.

I want to take an opportunity here to address what we Christians would consider a "lesser" sin, that of gossiping. We think of it as lesser because it typically doesn't run high with consequences, but there are no degrees of sin to God. "Everybody does it," we tell ourselves in defense. Surely, nearly everyone does, but that doesn't grant me a free pass. Personally, I want to go on record that I know better. I need to be held accountable.

First Peter 4:8 says, "Above all, love each other deeply, because **love covers over a multitude of sins**" (NIV).

The Holy Spirit uses this verse to convict me of gossiping. We've discussed treating others as better than ourselves whether or not they deserve it. The way we treat others is visible on the outside, whereas loving doesn't necessarily require action. Love can be just as real and powerful without display. Love begins internally.

Christ-like love desires to cover sin. Christ-like covering of sin is the refraining kind, the forgiving kind, the "go and sin no more" kind. It doesn't advocate collusion, which means to hide someone's sin by cleaning up their mess or lying in attempt to shield it. To do either would be a sin in itself.

Numbers 32:23 reveals, "You have sinned against the Lord; and **be sure <u>your sin will find you out</u>**" (NKJV).

When people sin, they have the consequences coming to them. God doesn't need any help correcting His kids. Do we care so little about our brothers and sisters that we want to spread their stink? What kind of coworker or friend or family member would that be? Let's be clear about this: gossiping doesn't heap additional penalties on the person being talked about; it's a sin of its own, perpetrated by the one gossiping. Your sin will find you out.

Since I have grown increasingly introverted, I tend to avoid unnecessary conversation. I internalize what I hear, and I talk to God about it. Have you any guess what He said to me on this subject? Our conversation went like this:

Me: God, just listen to them gossiping. Do they have any idea how unattractive that sounds? They are just doubling their frustration by commiserating.

God: And what are you doing right now, with me?

Ah-ha!

That's exactly what I was doing: gossiping to God about someone else gossiping. This chapter is about heart matters, so I must disclose that I still gossip in my heart and occasionally out of my mouth. Until I fix it in my heart, I'm still guilty. Unless the Holy Spirit called me out on this, I would continue to inflate my irritations this way. God desires to spare us from avoidable discomfort. He wants us to talk to Him about everything, but it would benefit us more if we would just let some things go. Gossiping is one of those things we need to let go.

What Should I Ask For?

"The **fear of the Lord** is the **beginning of wisdom**: and the **knowledge of the holy is understanding**" (Prov. 9:10, KJV).

One day, God offered to grant the wish of a young man. As you would imagine a genie-in-a-bottle's offer might come across, God asked, "What can I grant you?"

Solomon responded, "God, I want an understanding heart."

God replied, "What is that you say, Solomon? You desire *knowledge of the holy*? Consider it done."

I took some liberties with this retelling of their discussion as written in 1 Kings, chapter 3, by translating what Solomon said into what God likely heard, based on the definition of "understanding" in Proverbs 9:10.

Solomon asked for an understanding heart. Isn't that interesting? Most of us would assume that understanding is rooted in the mind, but Solomon didn't see it that way. Leading a great people like the nation of Israel was going to take more than information he could learn from a book. Head knowledge wasn't going to cut it; he needed heart knowledge. He needed supernatural depth of discernment to perceive the unseen and interpret the unspoken. He may not have referred to it as "knowledge of the holy," but that's how God defines understanding.

God was so pleased with Solomon's choice that He replied, "**Since you have asked for this and not for long life** or **wealth** for yourself, nor have asked for the **death of your enemies** but for discernment in administering justice, **I will do what you have asked**. I will give you a **wise** and **discerning heart**, so that there will never have been anyone like you, nor will there ever be. Moreover, **I will give you what you have not asked for**—both **riches** and **honor**—so that in your lifetime you will have no equal among kings" (1 Kings 3:11–13, NIV).

Through His relationship with Solomon, God revealed that a heart that pursues knowledge of the holy is a heart primed to receive abundant blessings.

Solomon received the following:

Wisdom and an understanding heart, riches, honor, kingdoms, authority, power, gifts, servants, livestock, food, dominion, a peaceful reign, fame, an audience, plus many other blessings (1 Kings 3:12, 4:21–34, 10:23–24). Solomon's story is an Old Testament example of the New Testament promise: "But **seek first his** [**God's**] **kingdom** and his **righteousness**, and **all these things** will be **given to you** as well" (Matt. 6:33, NIV).

The key word here is *first.* Solomon's foremost desire among the treasure chest of options was an understanding heart. Because he requested knowledge of holiness, it pleased God to grant his request and bless him with more. If Solomon's response had been anything else, do you think God would have extended the offer at all? If his response had been something self-seeking like wealth or the death of his enemies, do you think God would have fulfilled it? God replied, "*Since* you have asked for this *and not for*… I will do what you have asked." God's generosity was not a pre-scripted "yes" but "yes" in response to the depth of character displayed through Solomon's choice.

Solomon made his request for wisdom without God suggesting it, but the New Testament advises us to make the same request. James 1:5 says, "If any of you **lacks wisdom**, **he should ask God**, **who gives generously to all** without finding fault, and **it will be given to him**" (James 1:5, NIV).

That, my friends, is a promise. Ask for wisdom, and it will be given to you.

We are instructed to ask God for the very thing He is pleased to give, so our hearts may be transformed into hearts suitable for additional blessing. And God doesn't dole out small portions of wisdom, either. He gives generously and never reprimands a hunger for more.

After God granted Solomon's request for an understanding heart, God then delivered Solomon his first dose of wisdom in the form of a test. He announced, "And **if** you **walk in my ways** and **obey my** statues and **commands** as David your father did, **I will give you a long life**" (1 Kings 3:14, NIV).

Unlike the other gifts, the gift of a long life came with conditions. God said (I paraphrase), "*My decrees and commands are holy. Keeping them is wise. There is an expiration date on the extravagant life I have given you. Without obedience to my commands, I do not promise that these gifts, or your life, will last until tomorrow.*"

It's God's prerogative to set the conditions He deems appropriate on the length of our lives and the longevity of our blessings. It's wise to heed these conditions so that you may experience a full life, if He chooses that for you. Yet by choosing the hotbed of disobedience instead, you will likely find that the best stuff on earth has a shorter shelf life than a cup of coffee.

Promises uttered from the mouth of the Most High are an adequate incentive for me to keep walking a life of obedience. His words are more secure than a steering wheel gripped firmly in both hands, more personal than my given name, more apparent than the English language that I speak. Biblical promises are so concrete that they construct my reality.

So what if I can't perceive the time and location where my senses will catch up with His promises? Just because I've only viewed the moon for forty years doesn't mean that it didn't cast its glow on those who came before me. Just because I can't weigh the ocean doesn't mean it isn't heavy. Divine immensity by definition *should* exceed my minuscule comprehension. My sensory limitations actually support the legitimacy of His promises.

In his parting message to his people, Joshua reminded the Israelites of God's faithfulness. He said, "Behold, this day I am going the way of all the earth. And you know in all your hearts and in all your souls that **not one thing has failed of all the good things** which the Lord your God spoke concerning you. **All have come to pass for you**; **not one word** of them **has failed**" (Josh. 23:14, NKJV).

God has spoken His commitments in the Bible. He has programmed our three-pound brains with the ability to receive them. Although I love to simmer over His blessed promises, there's a grave oversight when reveling only in the pleasant ones. God keeps all of His promises, even the ones we don't want Him to keep.

Are we, His people, equally diligent to observe the warnings laid forth in His Word? Since He is a God who cannot lie, His warnings are just as enforceable as His promises. God keeps *all* His promises, both the lavish ones and the wrathful ones.

Joshua continued his advice to the Israelites with a twist, "Therefore it shall come to pass, that **as all the good things** have come upon you **which the Lord your God promised you**, so **the Lord will bring upon you all harmful things**, until He has **destroyed you** from this good land which the Lord your God has given you. **When you have transgressed the covenant** of the Lord your God, which He commanded you, and have gone and **served other gods**, and **bowed down to them**, then the anger of the Lord will burn against you, and **you shall perish quickly** from the good land which He has given you" (Josh. 23:15–16, NKJV).

Transgressing the covenant of the Lord is articulated as three sins in Joshua, chapter 23: (1) fleeing from God's presence, (2) worshipping a replacement rather than worshipping God, and (3) surrendering to another authority. These transgressions provoke God to anger. God will not relent until the transgressor of these acts is destroyed. I would prefer that God not keep this promise, because I don't underestimate the sins I'm capable of committing, but that's not my decision.

We must acknowledge that God makes negative promises (warnings) in addition to positive ones (blessings). However, none of His promises are without benefit to an attentive listener. He outlines boundaries for our benefit.

"Is it not **from the mouth of the Most High** that **both calamities and good things come**? Why should any living man complain when punished for his sins? Let us **examine our ways** and test them, and **let us return to the Lord**" (Lam. 3:38–40, NIV).

God's promises run in both directions. He keeps His sweet vows of undeserved favor, as well as His hard, uncompromising threats of justice for those who violate the treaty He established between God and man through the gift of Jesus as Savior.

The Joshua passage specifically states that God promises to destroy those who "transgress the covenant of the Lord." In the days of Joshua, the covenant of the Lord was the verbal law of God given to Moses, which included the Ten Commandments and required the blood of animal sacrifices to pay for human sin. The original covenant has since been replaced by a new covenant, salvation through the blood of Jesus.

"In the same way, after the supper he [Jesus] took the cup, saying, 'This cup is the **new covenant in my blood**, which is **poured out for you**'" (Luke 22:20, NIV).

"The **Lord is not slow in keeping his promise**, as some understand slowness. He is **patient** with you, **not wanting anyone to perish**, but **everyone** to come to **repentance**" (2 Pet. 3:9, NIV).

Thank you, Lord, for your negative promises, in addition to your positive ones, as all are intended for our edification. Thank you for staying your wrath, which is long overdue. As the deadline for repentance approaches, remind us of the destruction you promise should we continue to reject Jesus's sacrifice. Thank you for extending the window of opportunity for salvation. May we all be wise enough to take advantage of it through genuine repentance.

What Is the Point of All This, Anyway?

Can you imagine being granted god-like powers?

If everything was under your control to order according to your own design, what would you do? Would you trust yourself with those powers? Or would you be concerned that you might accidentally misuse them? How much do you trust yourself with god-likeness?

In light of the risks, if one option was deferring those powers to a greater, more trustworthy deity—one proven to embody all perfection, goodness, holiness, and justice—would you choose that option?

In reality, this scenario is the master plan God has laid before us.

This test has existed since the creation of the world. It's the very proposition that Satan failed. He was permitted the power to experience god-likeness to the degree that he indulged in self-love, pride, and greed. God granted Satan free reign for his desires to run amok. With power, beauty, and liberty, he was tested and failed. He challenged God's authority and rebuked subservience. The battle between him and God was, and continues to be, epic. God cast him to the earth until the day when eternal hellfire will become his permanent domain, and deservingly so (Ezek. 28:12–17; Rev. 2:13, 12:9, 20:10).

You and I have been offered the same proposition. Will we show ourselves to be little satans?

We are permitted so much freedom. I can take no credit for my own existence, nor can I control the moment of my last breath, and yet I am at liberty to do what I want, when I want, where I want, how I want. All of these freedoms are tests! I have the power to choose hate or love, selfishness or sacrifice, control or surrender. I have the option to be the center of my own world, my very own mini-god, or I can defer those decisions to another god, or God, of my choosing. Should I worship romance or perhaps a political platform? How about science? Should I join a cult or chase luxury? There's always something on the throne of our hearts. Who or what should I choose to worship? After all, the power to choose is all mine.

"From everyone who has **been given much**, **much will be demanded**; and from the one who has been **entrusted with much**, **much more will be asked**" (Luke 12:48, NIV).

I read these words and understand I have been given power and freedom in this brief life to prove myself. God grants me abundant opportunities to show what I will surrender back to Him. How I relate to His preeminence will be evident in my use of the powers I'm entrusted with right here, right now.

I am not a god. I'm a created being and a sinner. And sinners can't be trusted with power. But God has given me a lot of it. If I'm honest about the wretchedness of my nature, then I will opt for my good Creator to reclaim the power that He has entrusted to me. Freedom and power are always catalysts for testing. I'm not ignorant of this. If I select Jesus as Lord and put everything within my control at His feet, then I will prove that I can be trusted with eternal powers.

Yes, you heard me correctly. I believe God intends to elevate us to god-likeness in many ways. He's seeking those who, opposite of Satan, can be trusted with powers resembling His own. Before you suspect this is a one-way ticket to heresy, please hold on as I recount prophecies pulled straight from God's written Word. He wouldn't have divulged these promises to us without a commitment to fulfill them.

"Beloved, now we are children of God; and it has not yet been revealed what we shall be, but we know that when He is revealed, **we shall be like Him**, for **we shall see Him as He is**" (1 John 3:2, NKJV).

God's radiance and holiness are an all-consuming fire (Deut. 4:24, Heb. 12:29). First Corinthians 3:11–15 tells us we will enter the presence of God and "the fire" will try every man's work. When I see God as He is and approach His fiery glory in physical form, I will bring with me the manifestations of all my sinfulness, as well as the manifestations of Christ's righteousness produced in me. The fire of His very presence will disintegrate my corrupted parts, leaving only the righteous elements remaining. I will be reduced to only HOLINESS, LIKE HIM. All of the dross will be burned away.

"For now we see in a mirror, dimly, but then face to face. Now I know in part, but **then I shall know just as I also am known**" (1 Cor. 13:12, NKJV).

Upon meeting God face to face, His all-knowing mind will sear my flimsy faculties and convert my limited understanding into an OMNISCIENT MIND, LIKE HIS. I shall acquire a mind like God's, for I will immediately know as I am known.

"And just as we have borne the image of the earthly man, so shall **we bear the image of the heavenly man**" (1 Cor. 15:49, NIV).

Visibly, I will bear the image of God; I will take on His appearance. I will LOOK LIKE HIM.

"In a moment, in the twinkling of an eye, at the last trumpet. For the trumpet will sound, and **the dead will be raised** incorruptible, and we shall be changed. For this corruptible must **put on incorruption**, and this mortal must **put on immortality**. So when this corruptible has put on incorruption, and this mortal has put on immortality, then shall be brought to pass the saying that is written: '**Death is swallowed up in victory**'" (1 Cor. 15:52–54, NKJV).

My physical composition will change from corruptible (capable of decay) to INCORRUPTIBLE, LIKE HIM, and from mortal (capable of death) to IMMORTAL, LIKE HIM.

"Do you not know that the saints [the Lord's people] **will judge the world**? And if you are to judge the world, are you not competent to judge trivial cases? Do you not know that **we will judge angels**? How much more the things of this life!" (1 Cor. 6:2–3, NIV).

There are job openings in heaven to be filled: judges of the world and judges of angels. Who among us feels qualified to do either? It doesn't matter how inadequate we are now; when God purges our flaws and weakness, and casts our sins far from us, then He will deem us qualified for AUTHORITY, LIKE HIS, lofty enough to even judge angels, of which Satan once was.

"And [Jesus] **hast made us** unto our God **kings and priests**: and **we shall reign** on the earth" (Rev. 5:10, KJV).

Did you know you're destined for such an extravagant transformation? The height, depth, length, and breadth of God's good intent toward us cannot be fathomed.

God is on a mission to identify and prepare judge-worthy, king-worthy, and priest-worthy people to populate the new earth and reign over it. His idea of worthy is an abandoned heart that His Holy Spirit can fill. First, the blood of Jesus must blot out sins to sanctify a soul. Then the Holy Spirit's preparatory refining process begins. It's a process that's painful and lifelong but intentional and eternity-focused.

Who can God elevate? Who can be entrusted with holiness like His, omniscience like His, an image like His, incorruption like His, immortality like His, authority like His, and dominion like His? Not an abuser of power like Satan but one who surrenders all power at hand to its rightful owner, which is God. Remember, in chapter 30, I pointed out that the Holy Spirit requires us to relinquish our god complex to Him? Well, there is a reason He requires that we voluntarily give it up: to see if we can be trusted with similar powers permanently.

Only the one who surrenders completely can be trusted to reign righteously.

Who does that sound like to you?

In every case, Jesus modeled what God the Father requires of us, so the pathway is plainly laid for us to follow.

As I search the Bible for the different titles Jesus earned while on earth, my train of thought leads me down an interesting path. During His earthly life, Jesus was first a babe and heir of God, then a rabbi/prophet/teacher/healer, and finally, a Savior as of the day of His death. But when did He earn the title of Lord? Upon His resurrection, when He defeated the power of death forever, Jesus earned the title of Lord.

So when did Jesus earn the title of King? I believe we still wait for that day. Although Jesus is heir to the throne, He is presently at the right hand of the Father who remains on the throne. God the Father will reign until the time spoken of in Revelation, when Jesus will be named "King of kings" and "Lord of lords" (1 Tim. 6:14–15).

Who might those lesser kings and lords be? Could they be you and me?

Everything Satan coveted will be generously bestowed on us if we sacrificially refuse to covet any earthly thing. If we lay down our lives voluntarily, God will raise us back up. Resurrection is His motto. Jesus is proof!

How Do I Pray?

Oh, the irony of reading books about prayer!

Having read at least five myself, I realize five books later that each one left me beyond unsatisfied. What am I searching for when I read books about prayer that prayer itself doesn't generously grant? What can an author say to surpass the sanctity of solemn communion between just God and me alone?

If a position became available as a humble servant in the Lord's heavenly throne room, a behind-the-scenes job, would you want it? "Of course!" you say, "What a privilege and an honor!" The truth is, there's an opening, and there's no competition for the position.

"Let us therefore **come boldly unto the throne of grace** that we may **obtain mercy**, and **find grace** to help in time of need" (Heb. 4:16, KJV).

I confess, when I pray, I visualize God's throne room. I see a grand, open door that beckons me forward. I humble myself, block out the temporal world, and allow my faith to transport me into a throne room of brilliance. Once the open door is behind me, I stand in a room filled with warmth and light. I see the glassy floor, but the radiance in the room is reflecting off it so I can't see the color or the design on it. There are walls and high ceilings, but both are far beyond my peripheral vision, and I'm so enthralled by the glow emitting from the opposite end of the room that I don't steer my gaze away even for a moment to see how high or how wide the room is. I'm confident that within the exuberant light at the far end of the room the Lord sits on the throne with Jesus to His right, yet they can't be seen. His glory is so magnificent that I can only step a few feet into the room before I'm completely engulfed by it.

And then the magic sets in. I step into His glory, and He steps into me. I need not move one inch closer because the Holy Spirit within me rises up in union with the Lord on His throne. I find that the God in my view is actually closer than my own skin—His voice is in my head, His heart beats in my chest, His tears flow from my eyes. My body can't contain the intimacy of such holiness; I tremble and cry beyond control. As I speak my requests, I likewise experience His hearing of those requests, for my ears hear as He is hearing. It's as if we're fused together; I purge and receive simultaneously. If my burden is great, I see both my arms extended forward, palms open and outstretched, desperate to entrust the burden in hand to my helpful Lord, just as a frantic mother would charge forward with a gravely injured child in her arms as she enters a hospital emergency room. My heartfelt plea steals the Lord's undivided attention, and I am promised all will be well regardless of the outcome for my cry has not been neglected. And so, I am comforted. I cannot describe entering the throne room any other way.

"Do you not know that **<u>you are the temple of God</u>** and that **the Spirit of God <u>dwells in you</u>**?" (1 Cor. 3:16, NKJV).

I have no secret code, ticket, or key to grant you passage into such an encounter. I have only found myself in this place by God's generosity, which allows me to see through eyes of faith. But I can say that the invitation to "come boldly unto the throne of grace" is given to all of us. Without reading the Bible literally and developing an uncompromising faith in God's written Word, such encounters are impossible. Faith is the portal. I encourage you to prove to the Lord that He has no competition for your attention. Present yourself in private without reserve before His throne through prayer. No sin can be hovering over your head. No to-do list can be in the back of your mind. No time constraint can be tapping its foot at the door. Enter with trepidation, in an attitude of confession and in proper reverence. Hold nothing back.

"You will seek me and **find me** when you **seek me with all your heart**" (Jer. 29:13, NIV).

"In my distress **I called** upon the Lord, **and cried** unto my God: **he heard my voice** out of **his temple**, and **my cry came before him**, even **into his ears**" (Ps. 18:6, KJV).

"And I heard a great voice out of Heaven saying, 'Behold, **the tabernacle of God is with men**, and **he will dwell with them**, and they shall be his people, and **God himself shall be with them**, and be their God'" (Rev. 21:3, KJV).

Why Should I Pray?

In His management of the universe, God is discerning and deliberate. He is preeminent and purposeful. Despite the majesty of His work, He requests, even requires, that we participate through prayer. What a marvel this is to contemplate! Yet prayer doesn't always return a perceivable profit; therefore, it's easy for us to lose interest.

Many Christians find prayer unappealing and defend their decision not to pray with the following arguments: (1) God always wills to bring glory to Himself; therefore, why pray when God is guaranteed to execute His optimal will at all times regardless of what is voiced in prayer? (2) God knows what you're going to say before you say it, so why pray if you aren't bringing anything to the table that God doesn't already know? (3) God's will is impossible to discern; therefore, fifty percent of the time you get what you pray for and fifty percent of the time you don't. Fifty percent odds of being disappointed with the results are not motivating odds. Dealing with the circumstances God chooses to deliver is enough of an emotional rollercoaster without being doubly invested by praying ahead of time.

From man's perspective, these are sound objections, but logic alone doesn't make abandoning prayer the right thing to do. God gives us ample reasons to pray:

- Pray because God commands you to pray.
- Pray because it fosters an intimate relationship with God.
- Pray because God is listening.
- Pray because the Holy Spirit has a job to do.
- Pray because God desires for you to participate in your own destiny, for your own reward.

- Pray because man's input affects God's decisions.
- Pray because God has something to tell you.

Let's examine these reasons one at a time.

Pray because God commands you to pray.

"**Pray without ceasing**... Quench not the Spirit" (1 Thess. 5:17, 19, KJV).

I am convinced God commands us to pray and expects us to honor that command. My pleasing Him or not pleasing Him revolves around my compliance with this command, whether or not I understand anything further about the usefulness of the act. If we stopped our conversation right here, we know that the honorable action to take is to pray regardless of our emotions or the outcome.

Pray because it fosters an intimate relationship with God.

"But when you pray, go into your room, close the door and pray to **your Father**, who is unseen. Then **your Father**, **who sees what is done in secret**, will reward you. And when you pray, do not keep on babbling like pagans, for they think they will be heard because of their many words. Do not be like them, for **your Father** **knows what you need before you ask him**" (Matt. 6:6–8, NIV).

God knows our thoughts before we ask Him, so prayer doesn't educate God on what you need or what's going on in your life. But God is identified as "your Father" three times in this passage. By that title, we recognize an intimate relationship. Pouring out your heart to someone you trust, even if that person knows you so well that they can predict what you will say, fosters the bond between the two of you. God wants to be the ultimate love relationship in our lives; therefore, He commands us to pray to keep our relationship flourishing. This passage also emphasizes privacy and simplicity when praying, which are also benchmarks of intimacy. It doesn't condemn public prayer; it merely encourages private prayer. It says "when" you pray, not "if" you pray. From this, I conclude that God, who is my Father, has expectations about my behavior, just as my earthly father does. The more we talk and the more time we spend together, the more we mutually enjoy one another.

Pray because God is listening.

"**The righteous cry** out, and **the Lord hears** them; he delivers them from all their troubles" (Ps. 34:17, NIV).

"For the **eyes of the Lord are over the righteous**, and **his ears are open unto their prayers**: but the face of the Lord is against them that do evil" (1 Pet. 3:12, KJV).

His eyes and His ears are upon us! We have the Almighty's undivided attention, and yet we ignore Him as He watches and listens. We covet His attention in desperate times. Shouldn't we acknowledge His ear at all times, seeing as He is certainly giving it?

Pray because the Holy Spirit has a job to do.

Isaiah 55:8 tells us that our thoughts are not God's thoughts nor are our ways His ways. So, between the two of us, God has me completely figured out, and I don't remotely have Him figured out. I have sincere prayer needs that are short-sighted and emotional. I am compelled to pray, both out of my own desperate need for God's help, as well as in obedience to His direct command, but my pleas aren't spoken in God's language. They can't reach His holy hearing directly. Yet the whole point of prayer is to give and receive communication with God. An exchange must be achieved somehow. This is where the Holy Spirit gets involved.

Romans 8 says, "Likewise the Spirit also helps in our weaknesses. For **we do not know what we should pray for** as we ought, but **the Spirit Himself makes intercession for us** with groanings which cannot be uttered. Now He who searches the hearts knows what the mind of the Spirit is, because **He makes intercession** for the saints **according to the will of God**" (Rom. 8:26–27, NKJV).

God provides a translator, the Holy Spirit, to convert our flawed prayers into acceptable appeals. Our prayers are filtered through the Holy Spirit who converts them into a language acceptable to the ears of God. Can you see now how failing to pray quenches the Holy Spirit? He is striving to do His job. He relies on our commitment to pray no matter how infirmed those prayers may be. Neglecting to pray sabotages the Holy Spirit's work. Sins of omission are as dangerous as sins of commission. None of us wants to be found guilty of quenching the Holy Spirit by failing to pray.

Pray because God desires for you to participate in your own destiny, for your own reward.

Let's assume you have never seen the color purple and do not know its existence is possible. But God has a vision of purple and desires to bless you with it. So God commands you to surrender your blue paint by way of coming to Him in prayer. Without understanding why God has commanded you to surrender your blue paint, you obey anyway. The Holy Spirit contributes His red paint to the union, and God produces a perfect purple, which He returns back to you as a blessing. Of course, God could have created purple paint and given it to you directly, but there's more value for you in participating with

God's creative work. Our involvement in God's perfect plan contributes to our pleasure and our reward. He commands you to pray so that you are active in the destiny that He's weaving. He produces perfection through your obedience, no matter how insufficient your human contribution is.

In our example, you couldn't provide the needed red paint because you didn't possess any, but God compensated for your deficiencies through the Holy Spirit's input. When added to your prayer sacrifice, the Holy Spirit provides the missing pieces to produce a completed work of God's design.

I have often wondered why God instructs us to pray for laborers to harvest souls for salvation. God needs the help of no man to harvest a soul. No one loves a sinner more than Jesus who died for him. God reaches sinners through dreams, visions, angels, voices coming from burning bushes, and even talking donkeys (Num. 22:28). No human being assisted God in converting the chief of sinners, the apostle Paul. I could disappear right now and the number of souls granted entrance into heaven would still be the same; nonetheless, Jesus said, "The harvest truly is plentiful, but the laborers are few. Therefore [you] **pray** [to] **the Lord** of the harvest **to send out laborers into <u>His</u> harvest**" (Matt. 9:37–38, NKJV).

I think God commands us to pray for laborers so that our hearts will be moved to become one of those laborers. When I pray, I agree that the mission is an important one, and I develop a sensitivity to be called to it. By joining the mission, I reap the spoils of the harvest. If I don't labor for souls because I fail to pray as instructed, then I will have fewer rewards in heaven. Is my labor essential for people to obtain salvation? No, it isn't. God's plan cannot be thwarted, but my rewards would decrease.

Pray because man's input affects God's decisions.

"**Confess** your trespasses to one another, and **pray** for one another, that you may be healed. The effective, **fervent prayer of a righteous man avails much**" (James 5:16, NKJV).

God is listening to our prayers. He highly regards the Holy Spirit's support of those petitions; He cannot help but respond to His own Spirit, who actively intercedes as we pray. Righteous prayers avail much. Reading through the Old Testament, we learn that God rewrites the strategy of His plans in response to His beloved petitioners. Take, for example, a scene from the life of Moses: "And **when the people complained**, **it displeased the Lord**: and **the Lord heard it**; and **his anger was kindled**; and **the fire of the Lord burnt** among them, and **consumed them** that were in the uttermost parts of the camp. And the people cried unto Moses; and **when Moses prayed** unto the Lord, **the fire was quenched**" (Num. 11:1–2, KJV).

When God's anger was provoked, the prayers of his servant, Moses, spurred God to restrain His wrath. God also responded to the prayers of Abraham (Gen. 18), Jacob (Gen. 32), Phinehas (Num. 25), and Gideon (Judg. 6). The Bible is full of these accounts. Just because God has a fixed, ultimate will doesn't mean the range of scenarios He can use to achieve that will is limited. He is The Creator, after all!

Suppose He wills to bestow a gift of money on someone in need. He could inspire a praying donor to deliver the gift out of her abundance, for which the donor will be rewarded in heaven, or He could send the money via a tax refund where no donor is involved. Missions can be accomplished through multiple means. Prayer alters those means. Just because God is omniscient and knows when He will alter His strategy midstream, it doesn't mean that everything transpires just as it would have had no one prayed. Omniscience doesn't imply that God *controls* human actions; it means that He *foresees* human actions. He knows whose prayers will prompt Him to shift circumstances. He also knows how He would have carried out His will without those prayers.

Pray because God has something to tell you.

Jesus said, "**I still have many things to say** to you, but **you cannot bear them** now. However, when He, the Spirit of truth, has come, **He will guide you into all truth**; for He will not speak on His own authority, but whatever He hears He will speak; and **He will tell you things to come**. He will glorify Me, for He will take of what is Mine and **declare it to you**" (John 16:12–14, NKJV).

The same Holy Spirit who translates our prayers to the ears of God also translates God's words to our ears. There are powerful things to hear and see, which only the Holy Spirit can reveal. Without retreating to pray, we'll miss all of these fine revelations.

Personally, I think the perks of praying far exceed the emotional risk of investing in the unknown. The more you pray, the more you learn to trust the God you engage, and the less your vulnerability matters. We are privileged that these incentives are laid out so clearly. Any one of them can singlehandedly conquer the human tendency of neglecting to pray.

How Can I Recognize God's Voice?

I haven't always been good at hearing God's voice. Before I knew Him well, all I knew was His written Word. I mistook my knowledge *about* God for insight *from* God. I was so intentional about making biblical instruction my worldview that I failed to see that the eyes I was peering through were human and subject to human misinterpretation. As I pursued what I thought was God's will for my life, I found out the hard way that I was simply exercising my own will within the confines of biblical boundaries.

We are all amalgams—blends of the Creator's zest for life, man's proclivity to fail, the Spirit's pursuit of perfection, and base natural instincts. With so many conflicting currents within us, we can never bank solely on human rationale. The closest we come to arriving is embracing the fact that we will never arrive this side of heaven. Only God knows best.

Beyond the assumption that knowing scripture meant knowing God, another factor that hindered me from hearing His voice was my steady stream of outgoing prayers. I didn't mind hogging the microphone. God is a gentleman and exceedingly patient. He rarely interrupts.

As far as I could tell, I was following the proper plumbline in life. I expected God to do all the work of making Himself known to the degree that He wanted to be known. But He actually desires more. God spoke to Elijah in a "still, small voice" (1 Kings 19:12–13). Are you familiar with that voice? If not, have you considered why you've never grown acquainted with it? I didn't covet encounters with His still, small voice until I started having them. Hearing stirred a hunger for more.

God speaks to me in the free-thinking space of my mind, but I must make room up there and focus on Him in order to hear Him. I pray for God to break through my disjointed thoughts and speak to me. As often as I tell Him, I also remind myself that I'm giving Him my full attention. I ask Him to interrupt the noise of the day to fellowship with me.

It's in the free-thinking space of your mind where you'll hear Him. It requires liberating your mind to free associate while praying. Just imagine your mind is as expansive as a view of the Grand Canyon. Everything, in comparison to this view, is much too small to capture your attention. Push your focus off the edge and into the unknown. Your thoughts may drift from one unrelated subject to another. Basic, insignificant thoughts may initially occur to you. Just pass over them as you would if you didn't recognize any of the faces in a lineup. Move your focus along until a profound thought or phrase jumps out to you as valuable. Then concentrate on that thought.

You also need benchmarks to measure what you think you're receiving to confirm if it is, in fact, the Holy Spirit speaking and not your own ideas, or worse, the devil's suggestion. For a tactical manual on being led by the Holy Spirit, I recommend Henry Blackaby's book, *Experiencing God.*

Here's an example from my own experience. One night, I prayed, "Lord, please help me develop the skill of hearing you, recognizing your voice, and knowing it's you. Then grant me the conviction to carry out your will as passionately as I would have had you written it out for me." I prayed earnestly and continued to repeat this sentiment as long as my yearning remained. I opened my mind to free associate. Soon, a message arrived:

Quit acting without asking.

Why do I think this was from God?

First, because I directed my prayer to the God of the Bible as I am instructed to do. Second, because I am confident that hearing from Him is possible; I have faith that He inclines His ear to me. Third, because the statement I received was incongruous with my train of thought. It was something I couldn't have created because my mind wasn't there. Fourth, because the message came with understanding; as soon as I heard the words, in my thoughts, I knew exactly what they meant. The message was consistent with a specific passage from the book of Joshua I had read a couple of weeks prior.

The passage read, "Then the men of Israel took some of their [the Gibeonites] provisions; but **they did not ask counsel of the Lord**. So Joshua made peace with them, and **made a covenant with them to let them live**; and the rulers of the congregation swore to them" (Josh. 9:14–15, NKJV).

But God had a different plan for the Gibeonites. Had Joshua paused to ask before acting, God would *not* have allowed a treaty to be put in place between the Israelites and the Gibeonites.

"So they [the Gibeonites] answered Joshua and said, 'Because **your servants were clearly told that the Lord your God commanded** His servant Moses to give you all the land, and **to destroy all the inhabitants of the land** from before you; therefore we were very much **afraid for our lives** because of you, and **have done this thing** [instigated the treaty]'" (Josh. 9:24, NKJV).

Joshua used good human judgment to preserve peace and save lives, but he exercised poor spiritual judgment by failing to consult God. It was God's will to rid the earth of the Gibeonites, to give more land, plunder, and power to the Israelites. How could Joshua have known this unless He first consulted God?

When I read this, I noticed Joshua's negligence, but I didn't apply the lesson to myself. By instructing me to "Quit acting without asking," the Lord revealed that there was a personal message for me in the text. How many times have I stepped outside of God's will by relying on good human judgment without consulting Him? His announcement came with the understanding that I will hear Him more regularly if I pause to inquire of Him before I act.

Fifth, I believe the message was from God because the words were edifying. They were constructive words of correction to my character. If I obey, it will make me a better servant of Christ. Sixth, the statement was in the second person, like someone was speaking to me, not me conjuring thoughts in the first person to myself. And finally, the message was succinct. God gets His point across with brevity because His words are laden with power.

This is just one example of the many messages I feel I have received from God. I may not successfully maintain control over my free-thinking space well enough to block out all distractions and hear Him predictably, but I can strive to improve my concentration. Sometimes, when it's especially difficult to clear my mind, I imagine the inside of my head as an attic, dusty and cluttered. I ask God to sweep it out. I use my imagination to drag a broom across the floorboards from the top to the bottom in a zigzag pattern, pushing bulky trunks and cardboard boxes right through an opening in the floor. Then a squeegee follows, making additional zigzag laps, reaching into the crevasses, snagging all the scraps and particles that the broom left behind. I slowly replay these images until my mind is emptied so that I may hear Him speak.

There are times when I don't receive anything at all. It's His prerogative to speak or to remain silent. If my ears are open and attentive, there's no use fretting when a message isn't received. I don't pray twenty-four hours a day, nor does He speak twenty-four hours a day. But the practice of stretching toward Him is edifying in itself, regardless of an explicit instruction to take away from the meeting. Inclining to hear Him displays that I'm aware that He inclines to hear me. I reciprocate the gesture out of love and obedience.

It's always good to initiate conversation with the Lord no matter what subject is on your mind. You may not have a pressing question that needs an answer but rather a topic you want to share with your friend. When circumstances don't require a verbal response from God, a message may not arrive in words but in clarity. Clarity descends like a balloon gradually descends from the sky. When this occurs, there's a smooth transition between expressing your outgoing thoughts to receiving clarity from God on the subject. Pay attention to how the emotional atmosphere shifts as you go from taking facts to Him to feeling confident about your next step. You'll leave the prayer encounter with an assurance you didn't have before approaching the Lord in prayer.

As far as not acting without asking goes, I'm not suggesting that sinning is as narrow as failing to consult God before choosing things like Coke over Pepsi. But I think He enjoys helping me discern my best self, which may not be apparent to me otherwise. It's a lot easier to be your best self when God is telling you exactly what would please Him in the moment.

Does God Care about My Pain?

January 15, 1996, was an ordinary Monday night in Chapel Hill, North Carolina, where a large group of college students gathered for their weekly Fellowship of Christian Athletes (FCA) meeting in the Carmichael dorm. I was especially chipper that evening, seeing as it was my first FCA meeting since Christmas vacation. The reunion with my friends had me on an emotional high. I was smiling from ear to ear, bouncing around between friends, giving hugs, and catching up. Joy was in the air. The atmosphere was a welcome reprieve from the burden that wreaked havoc on my heart.

In standard fashion, we had a speaker that evening. Don Hartig was at least eighty years old. A white-haired man of small stature, he spoke with a feeble voice and walked with a limp. For about forty minutes, this gentleman captured our attention as he told stories of healing. He shared how he would come in contact with someone and would hurt in his body exactly where the person was afflicted. Through this sign, he would know what ailed the person and what the Lord desired to deliver them from. Story after story, we marveled at the way God supernaturally used this man to perform miracles. As you might imagine, a group of us congregated around Mr. Hartig after his formal presentation to interrogate him with our curious, collegiate questions.

I stood captivated, quiet, and smiling among a small group of eight or so students when Mr. Hartig shifted his gaze to me and changed the subject. He asked me, "Would you like to be baptized in the Holy Spirit?" A little stunned and yet eager, I replied, "I think I have been, but if I haven't, then yes."

He asked me to step forward and he placed one hand on each side of my face and leaned over my right shoulder to pray into my ear. Then he stopped. He pulled back, withdrew his hands, looked into my eyes, and said, "You have a broken heart. We have to pray for that first." Like a switch had been flipped, a tear streamed down each of my cheeks. My effervescent mask disappeared, and I wore my inside truth on the outside. I was visibly shaken. He prayed for my broken heart then followed by asking the Lord for the word of knowledge and discerning of spirits on my behalf.

Something profound happened that night, much of which I don't understand. My broken heart didn't go away, but it was bypassed so that I could be changed through his intercession. After the prayer, I developed firsthand experience with scripture. Don't you find it easier to recall the details of stories that happened to you rather than stories someone else has told you? Well, it's as if the Bible verses I read occurred in my presence. I experience them when I read them, and I retain them permanently. I presume this is how the "word of knowledge" manifests in my life.

As I have mentioned, I infer the emotions I expect others are having. Through instinct, I understand how to comfort or address them. I know what scriptures or testimony a person needs to hear just by listening intently to them in a frame of mind that's receptive to the Holy Spirit. This is why it's easy for me to minister in prisons, despite the fact that I don't share life experiences with my students. I yearn for my heart to connect with their hearts, and immediately a passage comes to mind that touches them or addresses a deeper issue, similar to what Mr. Hartig did for me. I think this is how the "discerning of spirits" manifests in me. These are the two ways that my Christian life changed after Mr. Hartig's prayer.

Mr. Hartig's insight into my broken heart parallels the story of the woman who was healed from a free-bleeding, blood disorder that plagued her for twelve years, told in

Matthew 9:20–22: "And, behold, a woman, which was diseased with an issue of blood twelve years, came behind him [Jesus], and **touched the hem** of his garment: For **she said within herself**, 'If I may but touch his garment, I shall be whole.' **Jesus turned about**, and **when He saw her**, He said, 'Daughter, **be of good comfort**; thy **faith has made thee whole**. And the woman was made whole from that hour'" (KJV).

This woman was afflicted by natural causes, and yet she was still in desperate need. None of us are exempt from needing some degree of healing. We don't ask for it because we think prayers for healing should be reserved for those in hospitals or therapy. You may need healing without a clear understanding as to why or what caused your pain. But God sees your need and can touch your hurt.

This woman had been openly and uncontrollably bleeding for twelve years. The Bible tells us, "The **life of the flesh is in the blood**" (Lev. 17:11, KJV). This woman's life was draining out of her body. She was dying slowly. I can relate to her sense of dying. Sometimes, the thorn in our flesh is so sharp and constant that we experience a foretaste of dying even as we live.

Notice how this woman approached Jesus: from behind. She knew her need. She recognized her source of help. She sought Him out.

Notice where she touched Him: on the hem, the bottom seam of His clothing. She was broken, weak, and lying on the ground within reach of His hem.

"For she said *within herself*, 'If I may but touch his garment, I shall be whole.'"

The woman began an internal conversation with herself, which Jesus responded to aloud, saying, "Daughter, be of good comfort; thy faith has made thee whole."

If someone touched the hem of your clothing without touching you, would you feel it? I doubt Jesus felt it because He had his back to her. It says that He turned to see her. I believe Jesus turned because he heard the woman speak within herself:

He discerned her spirit. We know this because He commented on her faith, faith that was only disclosed privately as she spoke within herself. Oh, how I long to know that every word spoken within myself is loud and clear in the ears of Jesus. This scene tells me that it is so.

What was the first thing Jesus did for the woman? He comforted her. "Daughter, be of good comfort," He said. When we are in pain, we underestimate how important it is to God that we be comforted.

Depression says to me, "You only feel like this because you don't trust God enough. You deserve to feel this way because you don't guard your heart enough." I blame myself for being emotionally weak. Instead, I should be embracing how deeply God loves me and how intimately He is acquainted with how I feel.

Jesus took responsibility for the woman's sense of peace. He comforted her *before* He helped her, just as He did for me through Mr. Hartig's prayer. Before I could be ministered to that night, first my pain needed acknowledgement. God penetrates the emotional undertow we're in before He meets our tangible need. Comfort is as much a miracle of God as deliverance is.

Finally, Jesus granted the woman's request for healing and she was made whole—no longer dying, restored to life.

It will be the same for us; God *will* bring wholeness. It may arrive in any number of packages, but it will be sufficient. It might not look like what we expect, but wholeness is en route. It will be deeply comforting. Although you may be enduring year one, two, seven, or twelve of your predicament, the faith in your possession is your compass to healing. Let faith arise in you. Relinquish your worry over needs you can't meet on your own.

When we doubt that God hears us or will help us, we think that our doubt is isolated to only a couple of situations, and if we could fix those situations, then doubt would disappear. This assumption is inaccurate. Doubt isn't incidental; it's an attitude. It's either permitted to enter your view of God, or it isn't.

Suppose you're driving along at moderate speed down The Path of God's Will Road when Doubt sideswipes you, turning you catty-cornered in the street and bending your axle. If you try to continue down The Path of God's Will Road with your wheels out of alignment, you won't be able to do it. You'll travel only a couple of car lengths before you're off the road completely. Doubt doesn't pelt you like a snowball that you can continue driving straight through if you just concentrate hard enough. It tilts you off your axis, distorting your vision of the whole scene. Doubt isn't randomly scattered along The Path of God's Will Road. If you encounter it, then you're on a completely different road. You must right the wheels and deal with doubt before you can reach your destination.

In *The Christian's Secret to a Happy Life*, Smith writes:

> Doubting is, I am convinced, to many people a real luxury, and to deny themselves this luxury would be the hardest piece of self-denial they have ever known. It is a luxury which, like the indulgence in some other luxuries, brings very sorrowful results; and perhaps looking at the sadness and misery it has brought into your own Christian experience, you may be inclined to say, "Alas! It is no luxury to me, but only a fearful trial." But pause for a moment. Try giving it up, and you will soon find out whether it is a luxury or not. Do not your doubts come trooping to your door like a company of sympathizing friends, who appreciate your hard case and have come to condole with you? And is it no luxury to sit down with them and entertain them, and listen to their arguments, and join in with their condolences? Would it be no self-denial to turn resolutely from

them, and refuse to hear a word they have to say? If you do not know, try it and see.

Punting My Emotions

A vibrant spiritual life depends on walking intimately with God. We each need divine insight into what about our personal life or inner self is displeasing to God and, therefore, harmful to us. Besides guidance toward holiness that everyone needs, those who struggle with depression possess additional complexities that clamor for divine aid.

A person who grows sad seeing others sad will stay sad forever if she allows herself to attend to the sadness in the world. The same can be said for a fearful person or an anxious person. Significant ground can be gained by a depressive who develops the ability to see which stimuli need to be banned from her environment and learns how to shield herself.

Part of Karmen's story (the dog I housed temporarily) that I haven't shared yet is how the flow of negative thoughts was eventually stilled. I spent more than a week addressing each moving part, but I couldn't balance all the emotions at once. There were too many considerations. As a last resort, I approached the Lord and said bluntly, "I can't do this. I can't be emotional about this anymore. You are going to have to be emotional about this for me." I gave Him my emotions and turned my mind off like you would turn off a television. I simply refused to give my thoughts over to the situation any longer.

Forgiveness for sin through the blood of Jesus introduces a powerful dynamic between God and man; intangibles are freely exchanged within that relationship. If Jesus can bestow His righteousness on me, then I can bestow my nervous dread on Him, and He will handle it for me. What's overwhelming to me is no match for Him. He sees the future from the present and has every resource at His disposal to navigate it. He can be trusted to care as much, or more, than I do about any challenge I am up against.

Trusting the exchange of intangibles that Jesus made possible is, indeed, a helpful tool when put into practice. If we learn the art of punting our emotions to Him, just as we would permanently cement a brick into place when building a house, then we'll discover all that's left to be dealt with are practical responsibilities.

Yes, I could drive Karmen to the veterinary clinic for surgery. Yes, I could pray for her. Yes, I could pay the bill. None of those tasks were too difficult for me, and that was all the Lord intended me to handle, anyway. He created Karmen, He loved her, and He knew what outcome He would provide for her. I could trust Him to execute His will over His dog. In Karmen's case, His will ended up being a benign mammary tumor, which was removed without complications, and a urinary tract infection, which was cured after a couple of weeks on antibiotics.

I have only been able to successfully follow through with constructive choices like punting my emotional distress to God after I became medicated. Long before I could implement any constructive strategy, my logic had no trouble agreeing with good advice. If you find yourself knowing how to help yourself but being unable to execute it, then please obtain the medication that you need. And if the medicine you have tried hasn't been helpful, please keep seeking the drug or combination of drugs that will help. Medicine is a gift from God. Pray for God to help you find the right match. He wants to help you grow strong enough to live out your faith.

What Is God's Will for My Life?

If God granted believers permission to ask Him one question, many would ask, "What is your will for my life?"

How can so many people desire an answer to the same question from a loving God and feel clueless as to His reply? God desires that His will be accomplished more than we're capable of desiring it, so why would He withhold that information? The truth is, God has already answered the question. He has written:

Love the Lord your God with all your heart, and with all your soul, and with all your mind (Matt. 22:37).
Have no other gods before me (Exod. 20:3).
Love your neighbor as yourself (Matt. 22:39).
Feed my sheep (John 21:17).
Deny yourself (Mark 8:34).
Take up your cross (Mark 8:34).
Follow me (Mark 8:34).
Love me (John 14:15).
Keep my commandments (John 14:15).
Submit yourself unto God (James 4:7).
Resist the devil (James 4:7).
Come near to God (James 4:8).
Cleanse your hands (James 4:8).
Purify your hearts (James 4:8).
Humble yourselves in the sight of God (James 4:10).
Speak no evil of one another (James 4:11).

God's will hasn't been kept secret from us. We have His ordinances in writing and Jesus as our example. We aren't ignorant. If we sincerely sought His will, then the entirety of the Bible would appease our curiosity and keep us busy working on character development for the whole of a lifetime. God knows that what we truly seek is for Him to reveal what the future holds for our personal lives. Yet fortune foretold is the opposite of faith. Since God desires great faith from us, we err when we yearn for revelation beyond what God sees fit to disclose.

James 4:3 says, "When you ask, **you do not receive**, **because you ask with wrong motives**, that you may **spend** what you get **on your pleasures**" (NIV).

Yes, we ask amiss. We want to meddle in our destiny or at minimum discover the path to prosperity with least resistance. It's likely that you'll never get an answer to the question "What is God's will for my life?" beyond the ample instruction already provided in the Bible. His will at any given time, under every circumstance, is that He be *ultimately glorified*. He won't shortcut the requirement to walk by faith.

Placing primary importance on our feelings is to dive headfirst into life's potholes. Feelings are so much a part of each experience that we're bound to lose hope if we give our feelings too much leverage. If we're brutally honest, many of our prayers are selfish, shortsighted petitions, which actually ask God to sabotage the future to relieve the present. The greatest disservice He could do us would be to give in to some of our demands. He did so with the Israelites to an unfortunate end.

"They [the Israelites] soon forgat his works; they waited not for his counsel: But **lusted** exceedingly in the wilderness, and **tempted God** in the desert. And **he gave them their request**; **but** **sent leanness into their soul**" (Ps. 106:13–15, KJV).

Tread carefully lest God grant your demands to your ruin. Let the realization of this possibility stabilize you when your prayers go postponed or denied. There's always room for gratitude. No circumstantial relief is worth leanness of soul.

There's an innate anticipation that motivates us to keep living. What is this elusive thing my soul recognizes? This appetite untainted by fear or impurity that only responds to the drumbeat of inspiration and pursuit? Living is a persistent wait for something unforeseen.

Because depression colors my view of everything, there are certain biblical concepts I struggle to personalize. Hope is one of these. My hopes have failed to materialize time and time again, so I do not trust them, yet hope makes a repeat appearance in the stories of those who achieved spiritual victory. They had very difficult journeys, as I do, yet they prevailed. If hope kept their faith secure, then I must press deeper to learn the difference between the way they hoped and the way I hope.

We stamp the term "hope" on our greatest needs: "I hope the cancer doesn't come back." Yet we toss "hope" around casually, too: "I hope it doesn't rain." And we use "hope" to express even minor preferences, which have no real bearing on our lives at all: "I hope the Panthers win." But throughout scripture, hope possesses a mysterious power, which doesn't sync up with our modern use of the word. What does God intend when He speaks of hope?

I have come to think of hope as a continuum. On one end, hope is intense. On the other, it's diluted. As our hopes vary in degrees of personal importance, they fall in different spots along the hope spectrum. The power found in biblical hope culminates in the "hope of salvation," which is hope in its most powerful form. Hope and salvation are wed together in scripture, and there's nothing more ultimately personal than salvation. First Thessalonians 5:8 describes the helmet we are to wear to protect our minds as "**the hope of salvation**."

I believe the "hope of salvation" means hope in *the realization of* salvation: a steady looking toward the day of receiving everything that a decision to accept Jesus as Lord secures.

Surrendering your life to Christ can be compared to purchasing a savings bond. You give the banker cash in return for a paper certificate, which represents the bond investment you made. You walk away from the bank with a paper receipt in hand, securing you a return on your investment at an appointed time. Collecting the return is a sure thing; you have assurance—paper assurance. When the note comes due, you return to the bank to exchange the certificate for your initial money plus the interest it has earned. In like manner, when you ask Jesus into your heart, you take your surrender, devotion, and obedience to Him. He grants you assurance of salvation right there in that moment. The Holy Spirit is the receipt you take with you, but your return on the exchange must wait to be realized. It has a future due date. So the hope of salvation is as secure as the gift of salvation itself: it's a done deal the moment that Jesus comes into your heart; it just awaits a future date to be cashed in.

Lamentations 3:25–26 says, "**The Lord is good** unto **them that wait for him**, to the soul that seeketh him. **It is good** that a man should **both hope** and quietly **wait** for the **salvation** of the Lord" (KJV).

Hope of salvation is the internal engine that gets us out of bed in the morning. It's our "Why?". As we live, work, and play, we sense a simultaneous waiting taking place. Would you like to hear a description of exactly what it is you're waiting for?

Isaiah, chapter 25, describes it to us: "The Lord of hosts will prepare a **lavish banquet** for all peoples on this mountain; a banquet of aged wine, choice pieces with marrow, and refined, aged wine. And on this mountain He will **swallow up the covering** [the shroud] which is over all peoples, even the veil which is stretched over all nations. He will **swallow up death** for all time. And the Lord God **will wipe tears away from all faces**, and He will **remove the reproach of His people** from all the earth; For the Lord has spoken. And it will be said in that day, 'Behold, **this is our God** for whom **we have waited** that He might **save us**. **This is the Lord** for whom **we have waited**; Let us rejoice and be glad in His **salvation**'" (v. 6–9, NASB).

The only thing we can hope for today, with absolute assurance, is salvation. As we place hope in other things, we gravitate away from concentrated hope toward things that are increasingly insecure. I need a working hope to keep me going each day, not an unstable hope at risk of failing me. Hope outside the context of salvation is shaky. As I desire lesser things, I must be mindful of where they fall along the hope spectrum to keep my mind straight regarding their fragility. Perspective is key to handling joy and disappointment. God is at the concentrated end of hope, safeguarding my salvation.

What Is It I Really Want?

"What is it you *really* want?" a stranger on an airplane asked me on August 17, 2007.

It was the day my best friend's husband was found deceased in a military helicopter lying on its side beneath a rocky precipice in California. I received a phone call around 1:00 a.m. east coast time that his helicopter was missing. Around 11:00 a.m., another call confirmed that the chopper had been found, and four of the five on board had perished. Seven hours later, I was on a plane to Arizona, where they were stationed.

As if this life-altering tragedy weren't enough, about ten hours before this news, I discovered that the marine pilot I loved was engaged. Two marine pilots lost on the same day: my friend's husband of seven years and the father of her six-month-old daughter, and my two-year dream, which never amounted to anything more than a hope unrealized. The depressed mind can't distinguish the pain of one loss from another. The distresses combined.

Separating the grief of the two losses was impossible for me. For seven years, I had lived vicariously through my best friend's happy marriage. I enjoyed the thrill of seeing her cross milestones I had only dreamed of crossing: getting married, moving away, buying a home, having a child. We both lost everything when Brad died; what she lost in reality, I lost in joy. The blow was compounded by the fact that just three years prior, we had buried her brother following a self-inflicted gunshot wound while Brad was deployed. We had already cycled through questions about God's sovereignty and worked through her radical change in family dynamics. It was too soon to lose someone so young and vital again.

My father drove me to the airport. I couldn't carry a conversation through tears and broken sentences. I knew too well the loneliness and quiet of Christian singleness that laid ahead for her. How could I console her? What could be said to alleviate the devastation of her daughter never knowing her father? How could I peel out of my own personal heartbreak to give her anything emotionally substantial? I was at the end of myself, and I had about five hours to pull it together.

The stranger next to me on the plane was more than gracious to hear my story. I gave him an earful, dissecting the drama of my personal love lost at warp speed, trying to discard my personal mini-loss during one plane flight's duration that I might make myself useful for my friend's cause upon landing. After hearing every excruciating detail of my heartache, he asked, "What is it you *really* want?"

I wondered how that question was going to make anything better, so I asked why that mattered.

"What is it you really want?" he asked again.

I collected my thoughts and said, "A godly husband, healthy children, and a happy sex life."

He replied, "You want a *pure* thing. He is not *your* pure thing."

Clarity bolted through me. I had fixated so intently on the provision of one person that I couldn't see how what I was asking for wouldn't lead to what my soul wanted most. I had prepared myself to receive a "redeemed and restored" thing, but God declared that the cry of my heart was for a "pure" thing. In my cyclone of prayers, I had attempted to blend oil with water, which only resulted in emotional chaos. It was time to let the truth settle and skim off the difference between what I thought I wanted from what I really wanted.

On the other side of desperate need, God is pursuing what we *really* want, even if it means denying the specific petition we beg for, even if it means we must walk through tragedy.

While Brad's helicopter was missing, I prayed hard for Brad to be found alive, but God dug into why I wanted Brad alive and answered that desire instead. I wanted Brad alive so that Julie would have her provision, her companion, her rock. I also wanted Brad alive so Catherine would have a godly father figure to guide her into the woman she should become, a daddy to tuck her in bed at night and hold her close. In four short years, God sent a man named Elliot into Julie's and Catherine's life. A man whose faith is deep and true, a faith that kept him a bachelor into his thirties, a faith that I have watched grow his whole life and have confidence in. Julie and Elliot are married and have a son, Ethan, who wouldn't be in this world without our extreme loss of Brad. God gave me what I *really* wanted in providing for Julie and Catherine, even though He took Brad up to heaven. And if the loss of Brad was instrumental to lead others to faith in Jesus, then we have another reason to be grateful.

I could tell you about other ways God has provided what's at the root of my needs rather than the solutions I specifically requested. There's an invisible list of earthly pleasures I'd love the Lord to grant me, but I choose not to ask for them. I talk to Him constantly and walk through each day with His companionship. When I pause to assess, I see how focusing on God instead of on my circumstances yields side effects of earthly blessing that I never felt worthy to ask for.

What motivates your prayer requests? Don't stop at face value. Ask yourself, "*Why* do I want this particular request granted? What is it I *really* want?" And when you come up with an answer, dig deeper by asking again, "And *why* do I want that?" Keep digging until the base need of your request becomes known. You'll see that what you *really* want is much broader than you thought, and the ways for God to meet those needs are limitless.

Make your base needs your new prayers and stop trying to coerce specific solutions from God. Give Him thanks that He can provide what you *really* want in any way and in any time frame He sees fit. God knows what motivates the deep cries of your heart even if you haven't figured it out yet. God knows how to identify what we really want better than we do. Believe in His good intent toward you.

It's important that we build confidence in God being a rewarder instead of on the rewards themselves because there's no timetable on which God must come through for us. We learn this through the tales of those who went before us.

Hebrews 11:38–40 reveals, "(Of whom [Isaac, Jacob, Joseph, Moses, Rahab, Gideon, Barak, Samson, Jephthae, David, Samuel, and the prophets] the world was not worthy:) they wandered in deserts, and in mountains, and in dens and caves of the earth. And these all, having obtained **a good report through faith, received not the promise: God having provided some better thing for us**, that **they without us should not be made perfect**" (KJV).

The Bible says that these honorable individuals died *without* receiving promises fulfilled this side of heaven. The rewards for their faithfulness are still accruing because people are still being blessed by them. Until everyone who will be blessed by their testimonies has been blessed, any redemption of their reward would be incomplete. The delay in rewarding them is making their full reward possible. If delayed gratification perfected the saints, then how can I prefer for God to apply a different approach toward blessing me?

The fact that God delays *some* promises by no means requires that *all* promises must wait for heaven. Nothing in scripture indicates such. Abraham and Sarah enjoyed the birth of a promised son Isaac. The Israelites occupied the promised land of Israel. Hannah received a son, Samuel. Elisabeth gave birth to John the Baptist at an advanced age. The Messiah was born of a virgin in the town of Bethlehem. Nonetheless, some promises must wait.

"These [Abel, Enoch, Noah, Abraham, Sara] **all died in faith, not having received the promises**, but **having seen**

them afar off, and **were persuaded of them**, and **embraced them**, and **confessed that they were strangers** and pilgrims **on the earth**. For they that say such things declare plainly that **they seek a country**. And truly, if they had been mindful of that country from whence they came out, they might have had opportunity to have returned. But now <u>**they desire a better country**</u>, that is, <u>**a heavenly**</u>: wherefore God is not ashamed to be called their God: for <u>**He hath prepared for them a city**</u>" (Heb. 11:13–16, KJV).

If we aspire to persevere as these did, it would be helpful to adopt similar survival strategies.

1. *Perceive the delay* of your rewards as permissible; they saw their promises "afar off."

2. *Meditate on the assurance of rewards* until you're fully convinced of their future reality; they "were persuaded of them."

3. *Experience pleasure in the present over future blessings*; they "embraced them."

4. *Confess your allegiance to heaven's ranks*; they "confessed they were strangers and pilgrims on the earth."

5. *Eject from your mind an attachment to the temporal*; "if they had been mindful from whence they came, they might have returned."

6. *Foster a passion for the eternal*; "they desire a better country, that is, a heavenly" one.

I can't grow in perseverance without examining these champions and their long-suffering. The extremes these leaders endured in order to convert their belief into sustainable faith enables me to comprehend what God could have in store for me. The goal is to make it through this life never letting go of faith and never returning to old ways without Him, no matter how long the tunnel extends.

We should advance through life anticipating earthly rewards but accept an indefinite delay, should God see fit. Delayed rewards possess a greater advantage, for they culminate in perfection. Without the wait, rewards are incomplete. God is good, and His promises will come to pass, but the fulfillment of His promises is not confined to the earthly time frame at hand. A delay doesn't diminish an absolute; it merely shifts the absolute beyond the parameters of our expectations.

You aren't at risk of missing God's will for your life if you're walking in obedience. His initiative to bring glory to Himself far outweighs your longing to be useful. The most radical thing you can do to fulfill your optimal role in His will is to pray for the sensitivity to perceive what He's already doing in you and around you. Eternal union with Him is His desire for you. God wants you close to Him forever. As soon as you learn to want that more than anything else, you won't have to wait until heaven for it. You can start enjoying it now.

Is It Better to Be Healed or to Be Well?

It has been said that every human heart has a "God-shaped" void, which can only be filled by the presence of the Holy Spirit. To a much smaller degree, I also feel that each person has a "dog-shaped" void. Who doesn't need a faithful friend, a warm touch, and an eager greeting on a consistent basis from someone who doesn't care how bad your hair looks or how many pounds you gained last month? What's better than ever-present, unwavering, unconditional love packaged in a snuggly body with a soft coat, endearing eyes, wagging tail, and bouncing prance? When I get to heaven, I won't be surprised if I find out that our pets were actually angels in disguise. After all, they perform the role of ministering spirits on earth.

With an emotional connection to dogs like this, it's easy to grasp that I was devastated by the malignant cancer diagnosis I received regarding the first dog I adopted on my own, a Boston terrier whom I named Macy. She was five years old when her cancer was discovered. A lumpectomy followed the initial diagnosis. Pathology results yielded excellent margins with only a five percent chance of recurrence. Six months later, the tumor returned in the same spot on her right rear leg where her calf muscle had been.

I desperately wanted her to survive, so I chose to amputate her leg. The doctor said that the genetics that caused the first tumor could cause another one even after the leg was removed. Following her amputation, I became the owner of a three-legged dog whose physical body reminded me that her genetics were against us. My perceived reality was that the death process had begun. She was the focus upon which I had poured out all of my ripened maternal instincts. If I lost Macy, I would cease to be a dog mommy, and I would lose part of my identity. There was so much at stake.

I begged God to allow her to reach ten years old. "Double digits, Lord," I would pray, "Please give me double digits, and I won't feel cheated." But I doubted He would grant my request, which left me feeling cheated already.

I tried to get emotionally ahead of losing her by saying my final goodbyes to her every single day for two and a half years. I could not get out from under the grief, but it eventually prompted me to adopt a second dog so that I might diversify my affections. My rescued Boston terrier, Pearl, needed me as much as I needed Macy. Pearl and I bonded over our common neediness.

When Macy's tenth birthday arrived, I threw her a birthday party. God granted my request! Not only did I still have Macy, but I also had a double portion of joy in Pearl. At the coveted ten-year mark, I began to grow grateful for Macy's cancer. Had Macy not been sick, I would never have adopted a second dog because I had not wanted to reduce the measure of love Macy received from me. It was better for me that Macy was healed than had she always been well.

Around this time, I caught an excerpt from *The Ellen DeGeneres Show* where Ellen asked Michael J. Fox how he stayed positive in light of the Parkinson's disease diagnosis he had lived with for over twenty years. Fox said,

"If you imagine your worst case scenario and it happens, you have lived it twice."

Michael's answer articulated a healthy way to handle extreme fears. I understood the gravity of what he said since my grandfather had Parkinson's disease and systemic staph infections which left him bedridden for seventeen years. Michael meant that he wouldn't surrender his enjoyment of the years he had control to a disease that he could not control. I finally got it. I should no longer forfeit the present by living in an alternate reality of projected catastrophe. This way, if the worst outcome were to come to pass, at least I would only suffer through it once: when it actually occurred. And I would avoid suffering entirely over things that never become reality at all.

I forfeited two-plus years with Macy to a cancer that never claimed her life. The cancer never returned. She turned thirteen years old, still beating Pearl at fetch and jumping up on the couch. In one month's time, Macy had a series of seizures, was diagnosed with Cushing's disease, and had a stroke, which left her vegetative, before I helped her to pass away. She was thirteen and a half years old.

The Lord was near me in my final days with Macy. He affirmed that it was time to own my feelings for Macy instead of letting my feelings own me. I had asked for ten years, was given thirteen, and should not respond greedily upon her death. He reminded me of Michael's message and that Macy had been adequately grieved in the past. After thirteen-plus years, it was appropriate to release her cooperatively. Her death was the appointed time to say "no" to grief and "yes" to gratitude.

God enabled me to say my final good-bye to her from a position of strength. He instructed me to protect my home as a healthy space, free from empty holes where it would be easy to imagine Macy's absence. He was insistent that I immediately implement self-talk that said, "Macy is welcome here but her ghost is not." "Ghost" in this regard meant my visualization of her being in spaces around my home where she would typically be. I wasn't allowed to indulge in such imaginations. Going there mentally would establish an atmosphere of emptiness that couldn't be undone. Speaking the self-talk I was given against the imaginations kept them at bay. God knew what I needed and let me know how to help myself, but I had to carry it out.

Today, I have a special Boston terrier/Jack Russell mix pup as my newest canine family member. Frankie, named after

Frank Sinatra, displays many of the spirited traits that Macy had. He's full of rambunctious energy, constantly moving, and can't be convinced that he's handicapped despite being born with a deformed, non-functional front leg, which was removed when he was five months old.

The mark of Macy's affliction—her three legs—now resonates with me as a dual triumph, both hers and mine. Her tenacity despite her handicap inspired me so much that I specifically sought to rescue a three-legged dog after she passed away. The Lord sent Frankie to a home where three-legged dogs are cherished, even preferred. Macy's affliction became my desire, and that desire brought Frankie home. Only the Lord can turn affliction into desire like that. What's so special about perfection, anyway?

Job 9:21 says, "Though I were **perfect**, yet **I would not know my soul**: **I would despise my life**" (KJV). A perfect person would never develop a relationship with God because he wouldn't perceive a need for it. Without imperfection, man won't comprehend that he has a soul, which is the breath of God within him keeping him alive (Gen. 2:7). A man, who has no awareness of his soul, will despise his life because it will be finite and ultimately meaningless. Our imperfection points us to God who sustains us. And knowing God is the path to enjoying life.

Adam and Eve were perfect before they sinned. They took their face-to-face relationship with God for granted. Their perfection kept them ignorant of what life would be like without Him. This bred a false sense of independence that lured them to sin. If you ever wondered what you would have done in their footprints, the answer is: exactly the same thing, because you, too, would have been perfectly miserable and looking for more. Once they sinned, they found out how desperately they needed God. It took imperfection to teach them.

"And He Himself [Jesus] **bore our sins in His body on the cross**, so that we might **die to sin** and **live to righteousness**; for **by His wounds you were healed**" (1 Pet. 2:24, NASB).

Jesus came to heal, so why do we resent our wounds, the very things that point us to His help? A disrespectable past is simply a place for Jesus to enter and establish new life. There is no place for shame in having once been dead in sin and now alive in Christ. It's the history that all believers share.

When taking inventory of your wounds and regrets, keep in mind that Jesus makes being healed better than being well. If you always were who you strive to become, then there would be no room in your heart for Jesus, and there are no happy endings without Him. Healing begins by first ceasing to despise our need for it. Becoming a new creation is guaranteed to all those who receive Christ.

What Does Walking by Faith Mean, and How Do I Do It?

The Word of God instructs us to "walk by faith, not by sight" (2 Cor. 5:7, NKJV), but we need to know the how-tos of the process if we're going to succeed. With this aim in mind, I'll try to explain the why, how, when, where, and who of "walking by faith."

Q) *Why* walk by faith?

A) Because you have a Lord who owns all rights to you. Walking by faith is the default setting of a Christian. It isn't optional.

"Do you not know that **your body is a temple of the Holy Spirit**, who is in you, whom you have received from God? **You are not your own**; **you were bought at a price**. Therefore honor God with your body" (1 Cor. 6:19–20, NIV).

What a hefty price it was, the perfect blood of God's only son. You have a savior who departed the sanctuary of heaven to endure all persecution, mockery, pain, and death for no benefit of His own. He has earned the right to your obedience.

"And **you are Christ's**, and **Christ is God's**" (1 Cor. 3:23, NKJV).

He formed you in your mother's womb (Ps. 139:13–14). There isn't one moment of your existence that doesn't belong to the Creator of heaven and earth. It is His generosity that keeps you alive. Job 34:14–15 states, "**If** it were his [God's] intention and **he withdrew his spirit** and **breath**, **all mankind would perish together** and **man would return to the dust**" (NIV). We owe Him our breath, our sanity, our salvation, our eternity.

The silver lining within this tough truth is that His love surpasses our understanding. God sent His only son to die (John 3:16) to spare us from permanent death, darkness, demonic possession, and eternal torment. You are safe in His hands and in His will, safe, that is, from damnation. He does not, however, promise a painless life on earth.

Before being captured by Nazi authorities for smuggling Jews out of occupied Holland, Betsie Ten Boom told her sister Corrie, "There are no 'ifs' in God's world. And no places that are safer than other places. The center of His will is our only safety—O, Corrie, let us pray that we may always know it!" (Ten Boom, *The Hiding Place*).

Although Betsie had faith that the center of God's will was their best possibility for protection, this didn't prohibit her and her family from being captured by the Nazis. To devout believers, safety is relative and worth risking to stay faithful to God. As Betsie's testimony further goes on to show, she could have rephrased her statement to say, "*There are no 'ifs' in God's world. And no places that are safer than other places. The center of God's will is the only place we should ever desire to be. Even if His will leads to unsafe situations, it is always best. Let us pray that God always upholds our faith in it!*"

Upon arriving at Ravensbruck concentration camp, Betsie urged her sister to give thanks for each detail of their surroundings, right down to the flea infestation in their barracks. Betsie said, "Give thanks in all circumstances. It [the Bible] doesn't say in pleasant circumstances. Fleas are part of this place where God has put us."

The sisters prayed and thanked God for His perfect will at work even in the midst of horror. They thanked Him specifically for the fleas. A short time later, they discovered that the flea infestation prohibited the guards from entering the barracks, which allowed them freedom to evangelize to hundreds of fellow prisoners before their executions. The fleas were instrumental in God's plan for the Ten Boom sisters to share the gospel with those destined to die.

I wonder if their prayer of thanksgiving actually *infused* the fleas with a power to intimidate, which didn't exist before their praying. Could their thanks have distributed positive power to the fleas? Can I do that, too? Can I infuse negative circumstances with positive power just by thanking God when it appears that there's nothing to thank Him for? If thanksgiving prompts God to infuse our circumstances with power, then let us by all means give thanks.

We're more inclined to ask questions than to give thanks, such as: "How long will this last?", or "Why are things so bad?" Yet God always desires that we give thanks, regardless of the answers to our circumstantial questions. Don't make God wait for praise or invite doubt by asking questions. Just give thanks.

Betsie Ten Boom referred to 1 Thessalonians 5:17–18, which says, "Pray without ceasing. **In every thing give thanks**: for **this is the will of God** in Christ Jesus concerning you" (KJV).

In everything, we should thank Him because He is at work in everything. It says that thanksgiving is the will of God "concerning you"—not your neighbor, not Christians who are more devout than you, not the most recent lottery winner, but *you* and me!

The reality you find yourself in today is God's will, and your thanking Him for that reality is also His will. You are in it because He put you there. He is watching and listening for expressions of gratitude.

What are you expecting God's perfect will to look like?

Have you thanked Him for the fleas?

I was still in the self-help phase of my battle with depression when my mother suggested that I inundate my negative thoughts with praise. She said, "Every time a negative thought enters your mind, give God thanks for something else. Can you find it in yourself to praise Him?"

I practiced the strategy. It played out like this:

My natural thought, "I am so broken."

Intentional reply, "Thank you, God, that the sun is shining."

My natural thought, "This is such a miserable job, but I can't quit. It's hopeless."

Intentional reply, "Thank you, God, that I don't have the flu."

My natural thought, "I am such a disgusting slob."

Intentional reply, "Thank you, God, that my car started this morning."

As I carried out this exercise, I had to insert praise approximately every four minutes to squelch the wave of despair swallowing my conscious thoughts. This depression detox continued for approximately thirty-six hours as I went about my normal workday. In the midst of this experiment, I had been preparing tax returns for several hours, when I stopped to take a bathroom break. The momentary release of my concentration triggered an inner monologue, which muttered, "Gosh, I hurt." Realizing I had just been focusing exclusively on numbers for the past three hours, I responded defiantly, "NO, YOU DON'T!" I almost said it out loud!

The depressive thoughts were actually intrusions into my normal stream of consciousness. They were outside messages invading my inner world; they weren't generated from within at all. Praise generated just enough light for me to discern what was going on inside me. Praise is the most powerful thing you can have on your mind at any given time. The devil has no argument against it.

Q) *How* do I walk by faith?

A) One conversation, one smile, one life lesson at a time.

Faith isn't accomplished in a quantum leap. Walking is the act of putting one foot in front of the other. This is true spiritually, as well. Like a scavenger hunt, God gives us one instruction, and when we complete that task, a new one is given. Each message requires obedience for the subsequent message to follow. In order to be in the right place at the right time for each intended message, we must drink of the Living Water and feast on the Bread of Life.

"But He [Jesus] answered and said, 'It is written, "Man shall not live by bread alone, but **by every word** that proceeds from the mouth of God"'" (Matt. 4:4, NKJV). By digesting God's Word through Bible study, you feed on the Bread of Life.

"**He who believes in Me** [Jesus], as the Scripture has said, **out of his heart** will flow rivers of **living water**" (John 7:38, NKJV). By believing in Jesus and engaging Him through prayer, living waters flow out of you.

Can you see the cyclical flow produced by an intake of God's Word and an outpouring of prayer? These are the gears that turn behind a life of faith.

When I first noticed 1 Timothy 6:6, conviction hit me like a billboard written in capital letters. It proclaims,

"But godliness **with contentment** is great gain" (KJV).

I had been a Christian a long time and studied God's Word for years, applying it as best I could. I considered myself "godly" but was discontented more than the average person. Before noticing this scripture, I had never realized that godliness without contentment is something short of godliness because its influence is impaired. Discontentment is a drought on godliness. It shreds the merits of godliness like a metal file reduces substance to nothingness. Contentment is the result of overwhelming gratitude and confidence in a greater good.

In my opinion, one of the saddest conversations in the Bible took place between Jesus and Peter. I can hear Jesus's heartache in it. John 6:66–69 recounts the scene: "From that time **many** of His disciples **went back** and **walked with Him no more**. Then Jesus said to the twelve, '**Do you also want to go away?**' But Simon Peter answered Him, '**Lord, to whom shall we go**? **You have the words of eternal life**. Also we have come to **believe** and **know** that **You are the Christ**, the **Son of the living God**'" (NKJV).

To paraphrase, Peter told Jesus, "*Now that I know the truth, what other option do I have but to stay by the side of the Living God?*"

We not only become content by taking more pleasure in the blessings we already have but in knowing, beyond a shadow of a doubt, that there's no greater gain anywhere other than right where we are: as close to Jesus as possible. Contentment doesn't mean settling for less or becoming indifferent. It's satisfaction in its purest form. Contentment perceives the goodness and blessings that God has bestowed as so immense that all hardships and burdens, even tragedies, become bearable. To be without anything is not a state of loss because awareness of one's past and present blessings fills in the gap. Contentment accurately distinguishes wants from needs and considers one's relationship with God during the process of goal attainment more valuable than the end result. The journey itself is an adventure, and reward is merely a bonus. We develop contentment by praising God as often as we can for as many things as we can.

Q) *Where* am I supposed to walk?

A) Anywhere God leads.

You are to walk anywhere God wants you to go. This may be toward church, away from certain people, into a new job, or to a new town, but it will certainly be only one step at a time, specialized just for you, and revealed by the Holy Spirit. Since building your faith is part of God's agenda, He doesn't have to give advance notice of what those steps will be. Just as He fed the Israelites manna in the desert one day at a time, likewise He will provide instruction as you need it.

Modern-day predators are well disguised along our journey. We need all the wisdom we can get to awaken our senses to the culprits lying in wait. We have that revelation available in the Bible. It's poised to form supernatural guardrails around our lives.

Psalm 119:105 says, "**Your word is a lamp** to my feet and a **light** for my path" (NIV).

The Bible also says, "The **path of the righteous** is like the first gleam of dawn, **shining ever brighter till the full light of day**. But the **way of the wicked** is like **deep darkness**; they **do not know what makes them stumble**" (Prov. 4:18–19, NIV).

When you "hide God's Word in your heart" (Ps. 119:11), it operates like a natural GPS system directing you through uncharted territory as if in full daylight. If there's poison ivy on your left, you can see it. If there's a briar patch to your right, you won't fall into it. If there's a rattlesnake up ahead, you know to avoid it. All of your enemies are exposed, and each day your discernment improves. With pitfalls like infectious diseases, heartache, regret, and the fires of hell, I prefer to live under strict yet merciful guidelines. Guardrails are good things.

Within God's protective orders, you'll discover that an ideal life is found "free in the box." This reference originated from a scene in my father's childhood.

Picture a five-year-old boy seated on a hard, oak pew in East Sanford Baptist Church in Sanford, North Carolina, in 1953. He's adorable with smooth, black hair parted on the right, smoldering brown eyes, and freckles. Dressed in a tweed coat and a miniature necktie, he's the portrait of a mannerly upbringing. It's a sticky, June Sunday and the windows are open in the sanctuary because there's no air-conditioning. The boy's mother pauses from fanning herself to join the congregation in prayer. The boy's father bows his head, as well. The whole church mellows to a reverent silence when something outside captures the boy's attention. He lifts his chin toward the window so that he can see out of it, and he notices children playing on the playground across the street. They're not in church, it's hot inside the sanctuary, and his suit is itchy. The little boy can't contain his interest, so he shouts, "WHAT ARE Y'ALL DOIN' OUT THERE?" The disruption gets him hurriedly escorted out of the church for a spanking.

My dad pulled off the charade that he was his parents' little angel until his heart showed through. He was in the right place at the right time to learn and grow, but there was no freedom in the box for him. He was just a child in a hot church on a sticky Sunday who wanted out of the box. Similarly, adults go through the motions of presenting themselves as Christians, too, but if their hearts aren't free in the box, they may as well be outside on the playground.

I can remember going from watching the kids on the playground to bowing my head during prayer with sincerity in my heart. The box is a lot more appealing from the inside than it is from the outside. Surrendering to it is the hardest part, but inside, there's the sweetest freedom. Self-confidence grows knowing you are pleasing the Lord. There are no wretched memories playing on repeat in your mind. There's honesty, growth, and grace. There's love from God and from His children. You are accepted, just as you are. Within it, you discover your whole identity. Freedom inside the box is the only true liberty available to mankind.

Adam and Eve weren't free in the box. The garden was a paradise: no trouble, no work, every need provided. But the box was framed by one guideline, and even one was one too many for them. They wanted life without a box, and so, they got it. In marched age, disease, heat, thorns, labor, pain, and death. Adam and Eve were created inside the freedom of the box but chose to exit it. We're born outside the freedom of the box but are offered entry into it.

Q) *When* do I stop, start, or change direction along the walk of faith?

A) Walk as long it takes to remain faithful.

Hebrews 12:13 says, "And **make <u>straight paths</u> for your feet**, lest that which is lame be turned out of the way; but **let it rather <u>be healed</u>**" (KJV).

My responsibility is my feet. I am to cautiously control *where* I put myself because I can't control *what* happens there. It's simple to put my feet where they belong: at home, at church, at work, outdoors, with friends who edify, in forums for ministry, and with family. I must deny my feet from running to sin, toward people who tear me down, or into dens of temptation. God will replace my fatigue with strength and power. He will compensate for my weaknesses. He will achieve what I can't. He will fight my temptations. He will reveal Himself to those I meet. He will speak through me, and He will do the work, if only I will be faithful with my feet.

You are to keep walking as long it takes to remain faithful. Jesus Christ is the same yesterday, today, and forever (Heb. 13:8). He will not tell you one thing today and contradict Himself tomorrow. The consistency of His guidance is reliable, and His timing is perfect. Although we don't know when the timer will stop on a certain episode of our lives, everything passes in time. We are to run the race focused on the goal of holiness and faithfulness, come what may. The Lord will end each season appropriately. He can be trusted to guide our steps to the north, south, east, or west. Until He pivots your step in a new direction, continue straight where He last set your feet.

Q) And finally, *who* am I to follow?

A) Follow the one who has gone before us: the Lord Jesus Christ!

Walking by faith is simply following the footsteps of the known Lord into the unknown. To strengthen your sense of security, get to know Jesus better. There is a Good Shepherd leading the way. His footprints are well marked. We only need to know *who* we are following and *how much* He loves us. Faith is a beautiful blend of the concrete with the mysterious. To dwell on the unknown fosters anxiety, but focusing on the known Lord and trusting Him is what the Bible calls walking by faith. What more do we need to know when our loving guide knows all? With the Word of God as our manual and our constant companion, Jesus, no further road map is needed.

Are You a Living Martyr?

What is the agenda of a dead man? Does he feel pain? Can he be wronged, and if he can, does he care? Where are his complaints? Or is he free—freer than any of us, free to be and abide where God puts him? This isn't a conversation about life after death; this is a conversation about living a surrendered life to the point of death and the earthly experience of those who practice it.

Many of us have considered, "Would I be willing to die for my faith?" For many years, the fear of martyrdom was my biggest fear. I didn't trust myself to endure torture without recanting. I accomplished the victory once in a dream.

I dreamt I was in a crowd of people where mass genocide of Christians was occurring. Falling behind in the crowd fleeing the scene, knowing the enemy was hot on my heels, I fell to the ground faking dead. Through closed eyelids, I saw an attacker straddle my limp body and lower his face near mine, studying it for signs of life. I was not sure if I had deceived him but soon felt the warm pressure of blood loss as a dagger penetrated my skull through my eye. There was no pain, just numbness, which started in my feet and inched its way up my body until I slipped out of consciousness. As darkness unfolded, full knowledge of my departure from this world arose. My distinct thought was, "I did it! I was successfully martyred! I did not recant!" and I was overjoyed that I had died faithfully, only to wake from the dream.

If you have also feared martyrdom because you aren't quite sure how you would react, take a moment to exchange the hypothetical for the practical. Examine your life for evidence that you're presently living out your faith. If not, then what makes you think you would die for a faith that you are not willing to live for? Dying is momentary, but living is laced with opportunities to display faithfulness in this hour, tomorrow, and next year. Proof of the kind of devotion that endures martyrdom is apparent right now.

What does that kind of devotion look like?

"The Spirit himself testifies with our spirit that we are God's children. Now **if** we are children, then we are heirs—heirs of God and **co-heirs with Christ**, **if** indeed **we share in his sufferings** in order that we may also **share in his glory**" (Rom. 8:16–17, NIV).

A living martyr looks like Christ. Jesus is the Son of God and God's heir. He was a resident of heaven before coming to earth (John 6:38), but none of this exempted Him from suffering. He fasted, prayed, and was tempted (Matt. 4). He served the ungrateful (Luke 17:12–17). He was abandoned by His followers, and He doubted the loyalty of His closest friends (John 6:66–67). He was humiliated, betrayed, falsely accused, imprisoned, beaten, and killed (Heb. 12:2). He persevered in holiness, dignity, and composure, no matter the offense (Matt. 27:13–14).

Jesus wasn't our perfect sacrifice without first suffering; obedience in the midst of suffering made Him perfect. Why do we hope for a different portion and grieve a similar refinement? If we share in His sufferings, we will share in His glory. If we bear His banner, we will inherit His kingdom. We come closer to reflecting the image of Christ as we endure our own version of the cross.

Taking up your cross is voluntary but should not be self-generated. There's such passion to please God that we consider forfeiting our blessings just to prove our devotion. Don't do that! Jesus didn't approach the chief priests and the Pharisees and ask to be arrested; He *allowed* them to arrest Him. He didn't chop down the tree that would become His cross; He *permitted* the cross to be placed upon Him. If you don't allow

God to define *what* your cross will be, then you'll generate your own suffering in vain.

There are two types of sacrifices we can make: those we select and those we do not select. You may think you have determined the maximum sacrifice God *should* ask from you, and so you chase it down, but when the price has been paid, you'll discover it wasn't the sacrifice the Lord wanted at all, and you must retrace your steps to where you took the decision away from Him. When you initiate sacrifices without the Lord leading, as I have done, then you consume resources that God intends for other purposes. Initiative is not the key to glorifying God; surrender is. Allow Him to be God even over your sacrifices.

In the foreword to Thomas Merton's book *Contemplative Prayer*, Douglas V. Steere says, "Self-chosen sacrifices are nearly always inferior to those unasked for ones, which the situation throws our way." The cross Jesus asks you to take up will come to you, it will be unasked for, and superior in transformative properties beyond anything you could contrive. Ready yourself to say, "Yes, Lord," to that which is presently a mystery to you. In the interim, your willingness to undergo the wait for it serves as a sacrifice of its own. Conditioning counts as a sacrifice.

"...**Burnt offering** and **sin offering** **<u>You did not require</u>**. Then I said, 'Behold I come; in the scroll of the book it is written of me. **<u>I delight to do Your will</u>**, O my God. And **Your law is within my heart**'" (Ps. 40:6–8, NKJV).

In the book titled, *The Kingdom of God Is Like...*, Thomas Keating writes, "The kingdom is present not in grandiose accomplishments, but in showing practical love in humble ways, day after day, and in refusing to allow our failures and disappointments to hide God's love from us. God invites us to share the divine emptiness. The divine emptiness might also be described as total vulnerability: the willingness to be hurt over and over again without loving less but more."

Living out a faith that you're willing to die for is outwardly visible. Check your life for these signs: "The fruit of the

Spirit is love, joy, peace, long-suffering, gentleness, goodness, faith, meekness, temperance: against such there is no law" (Gal. 5:22–23, KJV). These fruits are by-products of the Holy Spirit active within a person. They can't be falsely manufactured.

George Whitefield wrote:

> Very few Christians are willing to endure the suffering through which complete gentleness is obtained. We must die to ourselves before we are turned into gentleness, and our crucifixion involves suffering. It will mean experiencing genuine brokenness and crushing of self, which will be used to afflict the heart and conquer the mind. Today many people are attempting to use their mental capacity and logical thinking to obtain sanctification, yet this is nothing but a religious fabrication... Yet the heart-strings of their old nature have not been broken, and their unyielding character, which they inherited from Adam, has not been ground to powder. Their soul has not throbbed with the lonely, gushing groans of Gethsemane. Having no scars from their death on Calvary, they will exhibit nothing of the soft, sweet, gentle, restful, victorious, overflowing, and triumphant life that flows like a spring morning from an empty tomb. (*Streams in the Desert* by L.B. Cowman, June 11 entry)

Triumph is the empty tomb. We celebrate the victory of resurrection after we endure the sting of death. Does your life story include death to all your demands? If we are to share in His glory, we must taste our share of the pain of obedience. Jesus learned obedience through suffering, and it made Him perfect. It shall be the same for us. There is no other path to glory.

Matthew 10:24–25 says, "**The disciple is not above his master**, nor the servant above his lord. **<u>It is enough</u>** for the disciple **that he <u>be as his master</u>**, and the servant as his lord" (KJV).

It is *enough* to be like Jesus.

It is enough.

Letter to a Friend

Since I was diagnosed with major recurrent depression disorder and properly medicated, I've had a lot to learn about this thorn in the flesh, how it behaves, and how I can maximize its impact on my life for good. After all, when God designs us with a thorn in the flesh, He has a reason. I am not displeased with this thorn. On the contrary, I want to embrace it, so I have been searching myself for the roots of my depression, how my brain perpetuates it, and what lifestyle I should structure to stay at my emotional best on a consistent basis. Unfortunately, the result at the present looks a lot like isolation. There are two reasons for this.

In years past, most of my depression was sustained for long periods of time because I regularly forced myself through activities when I wasn't emotionally in a place to do them. Social encounters became emotional obstacle courses, and I spent more time recuperating from them than benefiting from them. I hated myself when I skipped church because I had failed to do the right thing, and I hated myself when I was there because I had taken myself there but felt trapped.

Before medication, I never gave myself grace. There was never an allowance to do anything other than the optimal choice in any circumstance. This doesn't mean I always did the best thing, but it does mean that I spent a lot of time blaming myself for what I wasn't doing. My self-talk barked at me that I was the reason I wasn't living the life I dreamed of.

Once I was adequately medicated, I realized I needed to do some things differently to stop the cycle of pain. These were: (1) Be honest with myself about my limitations, and (2) be okay with them.

I have spent these last few years trying to find a new, downgraded version of myself. Less Type A. Slower. Simpler.

Less demanding. Okay with quiet. A person who centers herself constantly and keeps a close watch on her emotional well-being. Honestly, I know I've gone overboard in this direction. I'm not balanced, but I am more peaceful like this. I'm more stable. I like life more. I have tried to erase a lot of my insistences—all of the things I insisted on from myself and from God. I don't want to drive myself to a place of chronic discontentment, which is all I've known since becoming an adult.

What if I just love what I already have? What if I spend my hours enjoying what's been given to me, being grateful, feeling blessed, praying without ceasing? If I embrace the single, living-alone life that God has apparently ordained for me to the fullest, then can't I just thrive right here in this? It has been my personal truth since 2013. I'm not chasing anything anymore, not a relationship, not a dream, not a hope, not an alternate life, nor attention, personal significance, or emotional support from others. I just want to be me. And I want to be okay with that.

Maybe this desire is too simple. Maybe it's not what God wants me to do with all this independence and freedom. But I'm sure of one thing: whatever the answer is, it won't look like the to-do list of life performances I forced on myself that kept me sinking deeper and deeper in depression all those years. I'm resistant to retracing those steps. I don't want to give flawed thinking any more ground, so I'm kind of stuck in this small, safe place. I realize I need to work on balance. God didn't say, "Go and be isolated until I come again." He said, "Go and make disciples" (Matt. 28:19, NIV). Being an example for others can't be carried out in isolation.

I ask God every day to make me a blessing to someone, and usually by the end of the day, I can look back and identify that day's recipient. Is that enough? Is that walking in the Spirit? I feel like it is, but it surely isn't very grand. It isn't newsworthy or pride-inducing. It's quiet and subtle, often secretive. But it glorifies God, I think. Could I be doing more? Oh, yes. I have always done more, much more, but it was always on my own initiative, in my pursuit of significance. If I'm satisfied with my own significance now, then my engine rides along slowly in first gear instead of fifth.

I've turned forty and weighed my satisfaction with the life I've lived thus far. I spent the majority of forty years being compelled by my Type A, high-achieving, life-maximizing personality. In my mind's eye, God and I rode aboard a horse-drawn carriage side by side, both sitting up front, but the reigns were firmly gripped in my hands. I stopped where I wanted to stop, I moved past what looked uninteresting to me, and I accumulated a pile of disappointments higher than I thought I would ever experience in the entirety of my whole life. Heartbreak to the point of despair—deep, utter despair and pain. Emptiness. Fruitlessness. Aloneness.

I want the second half of my life to be different. When I look back forty years from now, I want to see myself handing over the reins to Him. I want Him to drive us in unforeseen directions. I want Him to introduce me to hand-selected people. I want to see the sights only He knows about. I want my personal will to be discovering His personal will. That's all I want. I've had forty years to do things my way, and I'm disheartened by the fruit of it. Take me, Lord. Lead me. Thy will be done.

You wrote to me, "I want immediate deliverance, instant peace, joy. How come God does that for some people? He's never done it for me. My heart was sincere in my prayer requests."

Ah yes, all that you say is true. And since this too has been my perspective, I respond by saying that God reserves a special experience for exceptional cases. I believe, in fact, I know, that we have special relationships with God. Though our purging has been intense and the journey exceptionally long, there's a deeper relationship gained walking with Him through the jungle than others have the privilege of experiencing.

We have very strong personalities. First of all, recognize that God created us with these strong personalities for a reason.

To break a strong personality takes an inordinate amount of attention and patience. Now, don't we have *a lot* to be grateful for? Oh, how He should have walked out on our stiff-neckedness! But He has proven, and is proving, the true essence of grace and patience and faithfulness by keeping His Word to never leave or forsake us. Why? Because we are just so darn precious that we're a pleasure in His sight? No! Because He is faithful. The first time I truly noticed Revelation 19:11, it changed me. His first name is Faithful and True in capital letters! He cannot forsake us and still be true to Himself.

With this new initiative of mine, the most important things are humbling myself before God daily, praying almost constantly, and giving thanks for everything, even the slightest detail. I have already tried living a godly lifestyle in my own power. Guess how that worked out? I only succeeded at "christianizing my own autonomy" (Tripp, *A Quest for More*). I got frustrated and increasingly disillusioned. I grew angry at God. Why? Because I still had demands. "God, why won't you show me where to donate my extra money? Why won't you open up a mission trip for me? Why won't you answer me?" God doesn't respond to demands. It's the principle of the thing.

I had a conversation coming to me like the one He had with Job. In chapters 1 and 2, God brags to Satan about Job, "Have you seen **my servant Job**, a **blameless** and **upright** man?" Then, from chapters 3 through 37, Job grieves, pouts, questions, and laments before God for all of his misfortune. Were Job's arguments valid? Of course! He was one of God's most obedient children. Yet God holds His tongue for thirty-five chapters, letting Job fully express his narrow mind. Then God replies, in chapter 38, "**Who is this** who darkens counsel by words without knowledge? Now prepare yourself like a man; **I will question you**, and **you shall answer Me**" (Job 38:2–3, NKJV). I love that, "Who is this?" God didn't have amnesia. He knew exactly who Job was; He had pointed Job out to Satan, in chapter 1! But God says to us, like He said to Job, "*Who do you* *think you are?*" The rest of chapter 38 contains the speech we need to hear to grasp who we are before God and His agenda.

Then God proceeds to bless Job immensely. He wasn't unjust regarding Job's suffering. But God doesn't tolerate any challenge to His control, even if it's passive, subconscious, or disguised in good intentions. He sees right through it. Only He can show us how and where we are likewise guilty.

Daybreak

After walking through many valleys with the Lord, I came to the end of my strength. The challenges ceased and the ground leveled out. I paused—weary, aged, and exhausted—to review where we had been. The idealism that fueled the optimism of my youth was lost. I grieved for it. I longed for the positivity I once possessed when I was the person I was most proud to be, when loving the Lord was easy. But she was gone. Not only had the journey been painful, but recognition of this permanent change was an additional pain.

Before I could continue, I had to come to terms with God being the one who allowed life to steal my joy and convert me into a brutally realistic creature. I missed the old me. Why didn't He? Why would He prefer this me to the one I once was? He had been at the helm all along and could have preserved her. As usual, He helped me to understand.

Give a mural painter one color—red ochre, for example—to use on a solid white wall, and he will paint a portrait that the whole city can observe with just one color. All who pass by will look at it and murmur, "How lovely. What beauty. What talent!" But add to the artist's resources the color black and with it, he will go back over his painting, adding depth and shadow, sharpening edges, and developing contrast, enabling the subject to project from the background.

Should the image shout to the artist, *"BLACK? You have smudged me! You have ruined me!"*?

Only the image would be displeased by the added darkness placed upon it. To all the world, and to the wonderworker, the masterpiece has been infinitely heightened.

And so it is with us. Those who are weathered by tragedy now have edges. Those with regrettable sins now have shadow. Those with an inescapable thorn in the flesh have graduated to the realms of depth. All the elements of our lives are useful to the artist. What color will He add next?

REFERENCES

in order of appearance

Chapter 2 – Why Am I Unable to Help Myself?

Smith, Hannah Whitall. *The Christian's Secret to a Happy Life.* Westwood, NJ: Barbour Books, 1985.

Platt, David. *Radical: Taking Back Your Faith from the American Dream.* Colorado Springs, CO: Multnomah Books, 2010.

Brown, Stephen W. *Approaching God: How to Pray.* TN: Ballantine Publishers, 1996.

Chapter 4 – Why Won't God Fix Me?

Cladel, Judith, comp. *Rodin: The Man and His Art.* Translated by S. K. Star. New York: Century, 1917.

Packer, J. I. *Knowing God.* Downers Grove, IL: InterVarsity Press, 1993.

Chapter 8 – Where Do I Start?

Lewis, C. S., and Pauline Baynes. *The Voyage of the Dawn Treader.* New York: Collier Books/Macmillan Pub., 1952.

Nee, Watchman. *The Spiritual Man (Vol. 1).* New York: Christian Fellowship Publisher, 1968.

Elliot, James. *The Journals of Jim Elliot.* Edited by Elisabeth Elliot. Grand Rapids, MI: Revell, 1978.

Band of Brothers. Directed by Mikael Salomon. Performed by Matthew Settle and Marc Warren. YouTube.

December 26, 2011. https://www.youtube.com/watch?v=O5YpUsDsHmk.

Chapter 10 – What Have I Lost?

Packer, J. I. *Knowing God.* Downers Grove, IL: InterVarsity Press, 1993.

Chambers, Oswald. *Devotions for Morning and Evening with Oswald Chambers: The Complete Daily Devotions of My Utmost for His Highest and Daily Thoughts for Disciples.* New York, NY: Inspirational Press, 1994.

Chapter 16 – Why Wait on God?

Smith, Hannah Whitall. *The Christian's Secret to a Happy Life.* Westwood, NJ: Barbour Books, 1985.

Chapter 20 – Could I Be the Problem?

Krofft, Sid, and Marty Krofft, prods. *Sigmund and the Sea Monsters.* NBC. September 8, 1973.

Chapter 21 – What Does God Desire from His Creations?

Lawrence. *The Practice of the Presence of God: With Spiritual Maxims.* Grand Rapids, MI: Spire Books, 2003.

Chapter 22 – What Will I Gain?

Palms, Roger C. *Enjoying the Closeness of God: Knowing the Pleasure of Being His Friend.* Minneapolis, MN: World Wide Publications, 1989.

Chapter 23 – To My Eternal Valentine

Content is based on the following scriptures:
Paragraph 1 - Job 10:9; Job 34:14-15; Ecclesiastes 3:20, 12:7
Paragraph 2 - Isaiah 44:24; Jeremiah 1:5; Psalm 139:13-15; Job 10:8, 10:11-12, 33:4
Paragraph 3 - Philippians 1:6; Hebrews 12:2; Psalm 56:8
Paragraph 4 - Matthew 6:34; Revelation 21:3; Jeremiah 10:10; John 6:69
Paragraph 5 - 1 Peter 3:12; Psalm 33:18, 34:17; John 14:13-14; 2 Chronicles 16:9
Paragraph 6 - Isaiah 30:21; John 16:13; Proverbs 4:18
Paragraph 7 - Hebrews 13:5; John 17:21-24; Matthew 18:20; Revelation 3:20
Paragraph 8 - Matthew 28:20; Hebrews 2:17-18
Paragraph 9 - Hebrews 11:3; Psalm 33:6-9
Paragraph 10 - Job 14:5; Hebrews 9:27; Genesis 2:7; Job 12:9-10
Paragraph 12 - Colossians 1:16-19; Acts 17:28
Paragraph 13 - Ephesians 3:20; James 1:17; 1 Peter 5:6-7
Paragraph 14 - Isaiah 42:8; 48:10-11; Matthew 14:36
Paragraph 15 - Mathew 5:14-16; Ephesians 2:10

Chapter 24 – What Is God Up To?

Taylor, Howard, Geraldine Taylor, and Gregg Lewis. *Hudson Taylor's Spiritual Secret.* Grand Rapids, MI: Discovery House Publishers, 1990.

Elliot, Elisabeth. *Secure in the Everlasting Arms.* Grand Rapids, MI: Revell, 2004.

Chapter 26 – How Can I Go On?

Piper, John. *God Is the Gospel.* Wheaton, IL: Crossway Books, 2005.

Chapter 27 – Why So Much Pain?

Boom, Corrie Ten. *Not Good If Detached.* Fort Washington, PA: CLC Pub., 2009.

Chapter 30 – What Is This Going to Cost Me?

Sockman, Ralph W. *The Paradoxes of Jesus.* Nashville, TN: Abingdon Press, 1936.

Lewis, C. S. *Beyond Personality: The Christian Idea of God.* London: The Centenary Press, 1947.

Chapter 32 – What If You Never Heard the Name of Jesus?

Crafton, Barbara C. "Phillips Brooks and Helen Keller." *Outlook*, March 1992, 3-5. Accessed December 25, 2017. http://www.rci.rutgers.edu/~lcrew/joyanyway/joy232.html.

Chapter 34 – What Should I Do Differently?

Chambers, Oswald. *Devotions for Morning and Evening with Oswald Chambers: The Complete Daily Devotions of My Utmost for His Highest and Daily Thoughts for Disciples.* New York, NY: Inspirational Press, 1994.

Chapter 36 – How Should I Handle Difficult People?

Baillie, John. *The Sense of the Presence of God: The Gifford Lectures.* London: Oxford University Press, 1962.

Chapter 42 – How Can I Recognize God's Voice?

Blackaby, Henry T., and Claude V. King. *Experiencing God: How to Live the Full Adventure of Knowing and Doing the Will of God.* Nashville, TN: Broadman & Holman Publishers, 1998.

Chapter 43 – Does God Care About My Pain?

Smith, Hannah Whitall. *The Christian's Secret to a Happy Life.* Westwood, NJ: Barbour Books, 1985.

Chapter 47 – Is It Better to Be Healed or to Be Well?

Michael J. Fox on Staying Positive Through Parkinson's. Performed by Michael J. Fox and Ellen Degeneres. YouTube. September 18, 2012. https://www.youtube.com/watch?v=v8JCzz0tCds.

Chapter 48 – What Does Walking by Faith Mean, and How Do I Do It?

Boom, Corrie Ten, John L. Sherrill, and Elizabeth Sherrill. *The Hiding Place: The Triumphant True Story of Corrie Ten Boom.* New York: Bantam, 1974.

Chapter 49 – Are You a Living Martyr?

Merton, Thomas. *Contemplative Prayer.* New York: Image, 1989.

Keating, Thomas. *The Kingdom of God Is Like--.* New York: Crossroad, 1994.

Cowman, L. B., comp. *Streams in the Desert: 366 Daily Devotional Readings*. Edited by James Reimann. Grand Rapids, MI: Zondervan Publishing House, 1997.

Chapter 50 – Letter to a Friend

Tripp, Paul David. *Quest for More: Living for Something Bigger than You*. Greensboro, NC: New Growth Press, 2013.

BIBLIOGRAPHY

Baillie, John. *The Sense of the Presence of God: The Gifford Lectures*. London: Oxford University Press, 1962.

Band of Brothers. Directed by Mikael Salomon. Performed by Matthew Settle and Marc Warren. YouTube. December 26, 2011. https://www.youtube.com/watch?v=O5YpUsDsHmk.

Biblia Bilingu̇e: NVI, Nueva Versión Internacional Bilingual Bible: NIV, New International Version. Miami, FL: Editorial Vida, 2000.

Blackaby, Henry T., and Claude V. King. *Experiencing God: How to Live the Full Adventure of Knowing and Doing the Will of God*. Nashville, TN: Broadman & Holman Publishers, 1998.

Boom, Corrie Ten, John L. Sherrill, and Elizabeth Sherrill. *The Hiding Place: The Triumphant True Story of Corrie Ten Boom*. New York: Bantam, 1974.

Boom, Corrie Ten. *Not Good If Detached*. Fort Washington, PA: CLC Pub., 2009.

Brown, Stephen W. *Approaching God: How to Pray*. TN: Ballantine Publishers, 1996.

Chambers, Oswald. *Devotions for Morning and Evening with Oswald Chambers: The Complete Daily Devotions of My Utmost for His Highest and Daily Thoughts for Disciples*. New York, NY: Inspirational Press, 1994.

Cladel, Judith, comp. *Rodin: The Man and His Art*. Translated by S. K. Star. New York: Century, 1917.

Cowman, L. B., comp. *Streams in the Desert: 366 Daily Devotional Readings*. Edited by James Reimann. Grand Rapids, MI: Zondervan Publishing House, 1997.

Crafton, Barbara C. "Phillips Brooks and Helen Keller." *Outlook*, March 1992, 3-5. Accessed December 25, 2017. http://www.rci.rutgers.edu/~lcrew/joyanyway/joy232.html.

Elliot, Elisabeth. *Secure in the Everlasting Arms*. Grand Rapids, MI: Revell, 2004.

Elliot, James. *The Journals of Jim Elliot*. Edited by Elisabeth Elliot. Grand Rapids, MI: Revell, 1978.

Keating, Thomas. *The Kingdom of God Is Like--*. New York: Crossroad, 1994.

Krofft, Sid, and Marty Krofft, prods. *Sigmund and the Sea Monsters*. NBC. September 8, 1973.

Lawrence. *The Practice of the Presence of God: With Spiritual Maxims*. Grand Rapids, MI: Spire Books, 2003.

Lewis, C. S. *Beyond Personality: The Christian Idea of God*. London: The Centenary Press, 1947.

Lewis, C. S., and Pauline Baynes. *The Voyage of the Dawn Treader*. New York: Collier Books/Macmillan Pub., 1952.

Merton, Thomas. *Contemplative Prayer*. New York: Image, 1989.

Michael J. Fox on Staying Positive Through Parkinson's. Performed by Michael J. Fox and Ellen Degeneres. YouTube. September 18, 2012. https://www.youtube.com/watch?v=v8JCzz0tCds.

Nee, Watchman. *The Spiritual Man (Vol. 1)*. New York: Christian Fellowship Publisher, 1968.

Packer, J. I. *Knowing God*. Downers Grove, IL: InterVarsity Press, 1993.

Palms, Roger C. *Enjoying the Closeness of God: Knowing the Pleasure of Being His Friend*. Minneapolis, MN: World Wide Publications, 1989.

Piper, John. *God Is the Gospel*. Wheaton, IL: Crossway Books, 2005.

Platt, David. *Radical: Taking Back Your Faith from the American Dream*. Colorado Springs, CO: Multnomah Books, 2010.

Smith, Hannah Whitall. *The Christian's Secret to a Happy Life.* Westwood, NJ: Barbour Books, 1985.

Sockman, Ralph W. *The Paradoxes of Jesus.* Nashville, TN: Abingdon Press, 1936.

Stott, John R.W. *New American Standard Gift and Award Bible/economy Edition/burgundy/461453.* Nashville, TN: Holman Bible Pub, 1990.

Taylor, Howard, Geraldine Taylor, and Gregg Lewis. *Hudson Taylor's Spiritual Secret.* Grand Rapids, MI: Discovery House Publishers, 1990.

Tripp, Paul David. *Quest for More: Living for Something Bigger than You.* Greensboro, NC: New Growth Press, 2013.

CPSIA information can be obtained
at www.ICGtesting.com
Printed in the USA
FFHW020913140519
52454260-57857FF